The Reminiscences of
Captain Frederick A. Edwards, Sr.
U.S. Navy (Retired)

Interviewed by
Paul Stillwell

U.S. Naval Institute
Annapolis, Maryland
Copyright ©1992

Preface

Most of the Naval Institute's oral histories deal with the careers of line officers. Captain Edwards was officially a line officer for more than half of his career, but in fact he was a naval engineer for 30 of his 31 years of commissioned service. He graduated from the Naval Academy in 1923 and was designated officially for engineering duty in 1941. As a result, recollections of shipboard engineering plants predominate in this account, because Edwards preferred being an engineer to a deck officer, and the engineering memories have stuck much more firmly in his memory.

Captain Edwards has a splendid memory, as the reader of these recollections will discover. His recall, at age 90, is remarkable, and history is the beneficiary. With few of his contemporaries still alive to testify, his story is useful not only for the substantive information it contains but also as a reflection of the attitudes of naval officers of his generation. In a number of regards, Captain Edwards believes that the Navy--and, in some cases, society in general--is no longer what it once was. As he recalls the past, he does so fondly, especially when comparing it with the present, because he sees conditions as having gone downhill since the time he served. As he tells of such things as women at the Naval Academy, wider roles for blacks in the service, working mothers, and commanding officers who have lost the standards of old, it is clear that he preferred the era in which he served. His recollections help us understand that era better.

As he discusses means of ship propulsion during his time of active service, Captain Edwards reminds readers through his account that he truly lived through an evolutionary period. When he first went to sea in 1920 it was in a coal-burning battleship with reciprocating engines. As time passed, he served in four new-construction ships so he could be with state-of-the-art machinery: the battleship West Virginia, heavy cruiser Augusta, destroyer Mahan, and battleship North Carolina. By the end of that period, he was serving in a battleship with a steam plant that produced 600 pounds of pressure per square inch and a speed of 27.5 knots, figures unheard of when he entered the service.

Among his other tours of duty, Captain Edwards served in the battleship Nevada, four-stack destroyer Henshaw, the battleship New Mexico, in the Puget Sound Navy Yard and New York Naval Shipyard, twice in the Bureau of Ships, and on the staff of Admiral Marc Mitscher, and the Admiral William H. P. Blandy, when those two served consecutively as Commander in Chief Atlantic Fleet. Throughout that time, Edwards was interested in the material condition of ships individually and collectively as part of the fleet.

An intriguing sidelight to the memoir is the off-and-on relationship Captain Edwards had with Admiral Hyman G. Rickover, former director of the Navy's nuclear power program. Edwards relieved Rickover as senior assistant engineer officer of the New Mexico in 1937 and found that it took him a year to unfreeze the enlisted personnel who had been intimidated by Rickover. During World War II, the two served together in the Bureau of Ships, where Edwards frequently had difficulty dealing with Rickover. Finally, they were together again in the Bureau of ships in the early 1950s when the Secretary of the Navy directed the selection of Rickover for rear admiral. A member of the flag selection board later told Edwards that Rickover's selection deprived Edwards of the opportunity to become a rear admiral. Edwards is understandably bitter.

My thanks go to Captain Edwards for the considerable degree of cooperation he extended in the compilation of this memoir. In addition to giving the interviews themselves, he supplemented my own editing and proofreading of the resulting transcript. Historians should note that considerable editing has been done to go from the original verbatim interview transcript to this final result. In talking of a given topic, Captain Edwards often was reminded of something related and went on to discuss it as well, even if it was not in chronological sequence. During the editing process, various elements were rearranged--including being moved to interviews on other dates--so that the material could be presented in chronological order and with all discussion of a given topic in the same place. For intance, he talked about his time at the Naval Academy in nearly every interview. Now all of his midshipman experiences have been consolidated in the first interview. Captain Edwards has approved this rearrangement for the benefit of readers. Historians who want to know the precise date on which Captain Edwards discussed a particular topic may consult the verbatim transcripts on file at the Naval Institute.

In addition to the checking done by Captain Edwards himself, Linda O'Doughda of the Naval Institute staff has provided invaluable help also through her proofreading and her coordination of the duplicating and binding process.

          Paul Stillwell
          Director of Oral History
          U. S. Naval Institute
          April 1992

CAPTAIN FREDERICK ANDREWS EDWARDS, SR.
U.S. NAVY (RETIRED)

Personal Data

- **Born:** 19 July 1901, Troy, Ohio

- **Parents:** Ogden Edwards and Kate King Edwards

- **Married:** 25 August 1923 to Bessie McKichan, who died in November 1975
  February 1976 to Lydia Durel Whitgrove

- **Children:** Frederick Andrews Edwards Jr., born 27 July 1926
  Suzanne Elizabeth Edwards, born 26 October 1933 (now the widow of Donald Alecxih)

- **Education:** U.S. Naval Academy, Annapolis, Maryland, 1919-1923, Bachelor of Science
  U.S. Naval Postgraduate School, Annapolis, Maryland, 1928-1929
  Columbia University, New York, New York, 1929-1930, Master of Science

Dates of Rank

Ensign:	8 June 1923
Lieutenant (junior grade):	8 June 1926
Lieutenant:	1 February 1931
Lieutenant Commander:	23 June 1938
Commander:	30 June 1942
Captain:	1 May 1943

Decorations and Medals

World War II Citation Ribbon
American Area Medal
World War II Victory Medal
European Area Medal

Chronological Transcript of Service

June 1923-November 1923:	Bureau of Ordnance Instruction Courses
December 1933-March 1924:	USS West Virginia (BB-48) Communications
June 1924-October 1925:	USS Henshaw (DD-278) Assistant Engineer Officer
October 1925-June 1928:	USS Henshaw (DD-278) Engineer Officer
July 1928-September 1930:	Postgraduate Education Naval Postgraduate School Columbia University
October 1930-June 1932: (Including fitting out)	USS Augusta (CA-31) Electrical Officer
June 1932-July 1933:	USS Augusta (CA-31) Assistant Engineer Officer
July 1933-August 1935:	Naval Academy Engineering Instructor
August 1935-August 1937: (Including fitting out)	USS Mahan (DD-364) Engineer Officer
August 1937-June 1939:	USS New Mexico (BB-40) Assistant Engineer Officer
June 1939-December 1940:	Puget Sound Navy Yard Assistant to Design Superintendent
January 1941-March 1942: (Including fitting out)	USS North Carolina (BB-55) Engineer Officer
March 1942-October 1945:	Bureau of Ships Head, Destroyer Type Desk
October 1945-October 1946:	Bureau of Ships Head, Special Materials Desk
October 1946-May 1948:	Atlantic Fleet Staff Material Officer
May 1948-August 1950:	New York Naval Shipyard Planning Officer

August 1950-June 1954:   Bureau of Ships
                               Assistant for Ships,
                               Ships Divisions

Retired: 1 July 1954

Civilian Employment

1954-1959   Consultant and technical
                               writer, J. J. Henry Company
                               Naval Architects and Marine
                               Engineers

1954-1959   Consultant to the Maryland
                               Shipbuilding & Drydock
                               Company, Baltimore, Maryland,
                               and to an electronics
                               manufacturer

Authorization

The U.S. Naval Institute is hereby authorized to make available to individuals, libraries, and other repositories of its choosing the transcripts of five oral history interviews concerning the life and career of the undersigned. The interviews were recorded on 4 February 1992, 11 February 1992, 18 February 1992, 25 February 1992, and 3 March 1992 in collaboration with Paul Stillwell for the U.S. Naval Institute.

The undersigned does hereby release and assign to the U.S. Naval Institute all right, title, restrictions, and interest in the interviews. The copyright in both the oral and transcribed versions shall be the sole property of the U.S. Naval Institute. The tape recordings of the interviews are and will remain the property of the U.S. Naval Institute.

Signed and sealed this 18th day of March 1992.

Captain Frederick A. Edwards, USN (Ret.)

F. A. Edwards #1 - 1

Interview Number 1 with Captain Frederick A. Edwards,
U.S. Navy (Retired)

Place: Captain Edwards's Apartment, Annapolis, Maryland

Date: Tuesday, 4 February 1992

Interviewer: Paul Stillwell

Q: Just to start at the beginning, Captain Edwards, if you could tell when and where you were born and something of your childhood, please.

Captain Edwards: I was born the 19th of July, 1901, at Troy, Ohio. Troy is a satellite of Dayton. In those days, Dayton was *the* big town of that Ohio area. I spent my entire youth there, except for two years when my father was in business temporarily in Charleston, South Carolina. He was the treasurer of a company building an electric line there, so we went down there for those two years only. The rest of the time I lived in Troy.

I had a very happy childhood in that I lived in an enclave of perhaps three acres on a millpond and had the advantage of a country life, except for schooling. I went into town every day with my father and went to city schools, so I had the best of both situations.

Q: What sort of work did your father do?

Captain Edwards: My father was a grain dealer. He bought up grain from the surrounding area and either shipped it in carload lots or made flour or animal feed out of it. The flour mill was right near where we lived, about a mile from town. It had a capacity of 100 barrels of flour a day. He traveled quite a bit by train in going to various annual meetings of the grain dealers' association. He was also a racehorse fan; he had his own racehorse. Also, he was a pioneer in the development and installation of acetylene-gas lighting sets for rural homes.

To get off my father, when I was in high school I read an article about the Naval Academy in Boys' Life magazine, written by then-Commander Ralph Earle.* It so happened that my first commanding officer after graduation from the Naval Academy was Captain Ralph Earle of the U.S. Naval Torpedo Station at Newport, Rhode Island. After that I saw him off and on during the years. The last time, in the mid-Thirties, he was retired and the president of Worcester Polytech in Massachusetts. As such, he was a member of the Board of Visitors to the Naval Academy. I was then an instructor of engineering, and he happened to walk through. Without hesitation he said, "Hello, Edwards." That took me completely aback; after ten years he remembered my name!

---

*Commander Ralph Earle, USN, was in the Naval Academy class of 1896. He was an expert in ordnance and thus was promoted to rear admiral and made Chief of the Bureau of Ordnance soon after the United States entered World War I. The destroyer Earle (DD-635) was named in his honor.

Q: What was it about his article that captivated you?

Captain Edwards: It made me want to be a naval officer. The best way to a commission in those days was via the Naval Academy. I didn't know anything about the pay or much about the type of life, but I wanted to be a naval officer. So that was the urge, the bug that bit me!

Q: In what way did the article make being a naval officer so appealing?

Captain Edwards: Well, it was the travel, adventure, and meeting, I'll say, some important people in life. I lived in rural Ohio, where it was not a very interesting life. It was all right but nothing glamorous about it, so I wanted to get out of that situation. I wasn't unhappy, but I was looking for greener fields.

Q: What sort of course were you pursuing in high school?

Captain Edwards: It was a general course. In order to pass the academy's entrance examinations, I quit Latin and took up a special tutoring course with one of my teachers. Then I got an appointment to the Naval Academy, but it was only a first alternate, so I went to a prep school in

Annapolis, run by Bobby Werntz.* We called it "Bobby's War College."

Q: Where was the school?

Captain Edwards: The school itself was on the third floor of the old opera house, built perhaps 100 years ago. The building is still there, at the corner of Maryland Avenue and Prince George Street. Since that time it's been various things. There used to be a grocery down there, and now I think it's a portrait gallery and antique store. It has a long history of various activities. Bobby Werntz's office was downstairs at the street level. There was one large schoolroom, which was a recitation room and study room, and then two or three smaller rooms, including a toilet.

Q: Where did you live?

Captain Edwards: Well, he had a dormitory for candidates at the corner of Prince George Street and Randall Street, two blocks from the school building. This was a boarding house for the students, and we had perhaps 25 or 30 in that

---

*Robert Lincoln Werntz graduated from the Naval Academy in the class of 1884 and subsequently resigned his commission in June 1890. He then set up his preparatory school in Annapolis for prospective midshipmen and operated it for many years prior to his death in 1931.

building, plus the ones in the adjacent annex on Randall Street. We ate there and slept there and recreated there. That was our home--in my case until the following April.

Q: How did the school work?

Captain Edwards: He had about 40 to 50 pupils each year preparing for the Naval Academy's annual examinations in February and April. I elected to take the April ones, because I wanted to be sure I didn't fail. He had a very high reputation as to the number of candidates who passed exams, because perhaps a month or so before the exams, he looked over the people and decided which ones would probably fail. He dismissed them and sent them home. So of the pupils he kept, he had perhaps a 98 or 99% success record in getting them accepted.

Q: What was the basis for his predictions?

Captain Edwards: He made a general estimate of people's performance, attitudes, and how well we did on the quizzes as we went along. So he would get a good idea of who would pass and who wouldn't.

Q: What was the teaching method in the classes?

F. A. Edwards #1 - 6

Captain Edwards: Werntz used the Naval Academy entrance examinations since the Spanish-American War. He went over them and had tests and explanations. It was a very good way to cram. That's what it was, a cram school.

Q: Did he essentially read the questions and answers out loud?

Captain Edwards: Yes, and he also had blackboards. It depended on the subject.

Q: What are your recollections of the flu epidemic of 1918? That took place during the winter you were in this prep school.

Captain Edwards: It was severe, to say the least. It was the first major flu epidemic that this country has had. I'd say that maybe 25 of us had the flu in various degrees, but none of us died. It was so bad that the Naval Academy stopped classes and sent the midshipmen walking around outside, just to keep them away from each other. I believe 31 or 32 midshipmen died of the flu at that time. There was no known cure. It was just simply a matter of taking aspirin, I guess, and hoping for the best.

Q: Did your classes cease in the prep school during the

epidemic?

Captain Edwards: Yes, we did not go to school for perhaps a week or ten days. I was out of touch for several days myself. When I recovered, I asked the nurse for an apple. She replied that she didn't have any, so I told her, "Make one." That was how far gone I was from flu.

Q: How did you do after taking this course?

Captain Edwards: The exams were administered by the civil service. I took them back in Dayton, Ohio, and passed. Meanwhile, the Congress authorized an additional principal appointment per congressman to the Naval Academy, and I got one of them.

After the exams that April, I had about a month or so to go before I was due to report to the Naval Academy, so I worked for a while in western Nebraska, near Sidney. I went to help my brother, who was breaking in a 1,000-acre plot of ground out there. I rode out there by train and stayed with him during this period. My job was merely that of a handyman and helping him get organized.

One of the big jobs was to fence in this one plot of 640 acres, which was one mile by one mile square. We put in the fence posts every 50 feet and then tensioned the barbed wire by paying it out from a coil on the back of a truck. Actually, we put on three wires--top, bottom, and center. The fence was to keep outside cattle or horses from coming in, because my brother had no animals. Everything on his farm was mechanical.

Among the things still visible out on the plains then were ruts made by covered wagons during the Oregon Trail days. They were going diagonally northwestward, up to Oregon. Back in those days the wagons just cut right across the terrain, because there were no fences or restrictions. When one set of ruts got too deep, the settlers moved over a few feet and started another trail, so there were several sets of parallel tracks. They were still there as exhibits of the problems that these people had in taking the prairie schooners to the West.

After that time in Nebraska, I came east to enter the Naval Academy in June 1919.

Q: Were your parents supportive of your ambitions?

Captain Edwards: They weren't at first; my mother wanted me to be a lawyer. She wanted me to go to Princeton. One of my direct ancestors, Jonathan Edwards, had been president of Princeton, and colonial America's leading theologian. I had a bad time at first. My father used to bring me home articles about the bad life of the Navy-- hardtack and all that sort of thing from the sailing-ship

F. A. Edwards #1 - 9

days. But I pursued it. I took exams for Princeton and was accepted, but I said it would depend on the results of my exams for the Naval Academy. Well, I passed the exams to the academy, so I selected it, much to my mother's disgust. But, later on, she came around.

Q: Well, they supported you to the extent of sending you to that preparatory school.

Captain Edwards: Oh, yes, that's right. There was no problem about that. But mentally she wanted me to become a Philadelphia lawyer. In those days the Philadelphia lawyers were supposed to be the best. Of course, later on I realized, in engineering, I probably should have become a lawyer also--not to practice law but more or less to defend myself. [Laughter]

Q: How long did it take before your parents really accepted this choice?

Captain Edwards: When I graduated from the academy in '23. My father had died in the meantime, but my mother came up with my two brothers and one brother's wife and child. So it was a big event in our family's life. They always felt they were going to have to support me financially. Navy pay was and is relatively low, but I survived somehow.

Q: There was a lot of prestige associated with being a midshipman then, wasn't there?

Captain Edwards: That's right, but in those days they had about 2,500 or 3,000 midshipmen. Now they've got 4,500, and that's too many. They cannot give them the amount of personal attention that they would get with a fewer number.

Things were up and down. When the class of '22 graduated, the Navy allowed them to resign if they wished, and a number of them did.* When my class graduated a year later, they held us in till December of 1923, and then we were allowed to resign. Of course, I stayed in, because I loved the Navy. I had no objections, but I sometimes wonder, could I or would I do it again, because it's a hard deal.

Q: Speaking of hard deals, what do you remember about plebe summer?

Captain Edwards: It was physically about all we could take. Reveille, as I recall, was at 6:00 o'clock, and at 6:30 we had to fall in on the terraces and do physical

---

*In the wake of World War I, the "war to end all wars," the Washington Naval Treaty of 1922 decreed a much smaller Navy in the future. Newly commissioned officers were thus encouraged to resign because of poor prospects for careers.

exercises, ending up with a mile run.* We ran over to where the naval hospital is, all around there, and back. Altogether, it was approximately a mile, and the route was strewn with casualties. The leader was a fellow named Skinner, class of '20, who graduated early; he had run the mile on the track team.** So he ran at his pace, and we all ran with our tongues hanging out, trying to keep up with him.

Q: Well, you worked up a good appetite for breakfast.

Captain Edwards: That's right. And then it seemed like every hour on the hour we had to have a new kind of test. Every once in a while one of us fell out.

Well, anyhow, it was interesting getting acquainted, and they gave us quite a bit of naval information. They really worked us out. I think it was a good idea; we learned a lot.

Q: Did they have hazing during that period?

Captain Edwards: When we were plebes we were alone, except for a dozen or more newly graduated ensigns who were

---

*Midshipmen mustered on terraces of Bancroft Hall, the large Naval Academy dormitory that is still used today.
**Ensign Charles R. Skinner, USN. The class of 1920 graduated in the spring of 1919 because the academy's course was compressed to three years during World War I.

F. A. Edwards #1 - 12

assigned as company officers There was no hazing then. It all began when the upper classes returned from September leave. That was very difficult. In fact, I used to think that if So-and-so ahead of me could take it, I could take it. So I just steeled myself to accept it.

Q: What were some of the examples you remember?

Captain Edwards: Well, there were two kinds of hazing. One was called running. Running was more or less allowed. It was forced education. For example, I had to learn the main and secondary batteries of all the battleships between lunch and dinner one day. I went to the library and had a quick course on that sort of thing.

Q: Just memory work.

Captain Edwards: Memory work and all sorts of things which were good for us, but we didn't appreciate it at that time.

The second type of hazing was physical, which took various forms. For example, we had to do what we called stoop-falls; they now call them push-ups. And we all had to brace up, pushing our chins back into our necks, and sometimes the upper classmen would come and punch you in the belly. But as I look back, those things were probably the making of the man--the hard way.

Q: Were they trying to weed out people, do you think?

Captain Edwards: Not necessarily, but that was one idea. The idea was to satisfy their egos, I guess. We had to endure all sorts of what I would call insulting and excessive physical requirements.

Q: Any others that you remember especially?

Captain Edwards: Well, I remember what happened at the dinner table. There were 22 people at the table, the plebes at the center. If we didn't know the right answer to a question, we were forced to get under the table. For example, we had to know the dessert ahead of time. They published a list of desserts for the week up at the main office. We memorized those, because if someone said the wrong dessert, he didn't get one. If you said it was pumpkin pie, you ate "pumpkin pie," even though the real dessert was something else. You went through the motions of eating pumpkin pie!

Q: So you got an imaginary dessert instead of a real one.

Captain Edwards: That's right. And at the table we sat up on the edge of our chairs and braced up. On Sundays we were allowed to "carry on," or relax, if we won, say, the football game that week. Also we prepared what was known as a "bumwad," a so-called weekly newspaper. It contained clippings of interesting things that might have happened and also jokes. The worse the joke, the better the upper classmen liked it. If the bumwad received acceptance, we carried on. If not, we braced up.

Q: Were some upper classmen worse than others in dishing out this treatment?

Captain Edwards: There were certain "sour balls," whatever you want to call them. In every class there was a certain percentage. Maybe it's 5% or some percent like that of bastards who would punch you in the belly and punch you in the back and that sort of thing, brace you up and make you do various things.

They had certain reserved stairways in Bancroft Hall: first-class stairs and third-class stairs and so forth. Well, one morning I was ordered to find an upper classman's laundry. I began running up and down the various decks trying to find it, because it had apparently been delivered to the wrong deck. I was going to be late, so I cut down the first-class stairs. An upper classman was down there waiting for me, and I caught hell for it.

A plebe always had to be braced up and walk under rows

of lights in the centers of the hallways. If he failed to comply, he was hauled into a nearby room and worked over with brooms or paddles. These days an upper classman would be expelled or jailed for that. In those days that was normal procedure. I accepted it as such. I wanted to get through there, so I took whatever I had to take to get through.

Q: Could you describe the unpleasantness that the plebes experienced in the spring of 1920 when part of the class of '21 found out it wouldn't be graduating that year?*

Captain Edwards: The class of "1921B" took it out on the plebe class, which was my class. And some of it was beyond the pale, plain nasty.

Q: What sorts of things did they do?

Captain Edwards: Oh, a punch in the belly or a punch in the back or put you on report for being in unmilitary uniform or out of uniform--whether it was true or false. All sorts of nasty things. Not all of them, but some of them were that way.

---

*During World War I the Naval Academy course was shortened to three years in order to get officers out into the fleet more quickly. To return to normal after the war, half of the class of 1921 was graduated in 1920 and half in 1921.

F. A. Edwards #1 - 16

Q: Well, the punch in the belly and the back sound like the things you've already described as routine, so what was beyond the pale?

Captain Edwards: Well, that was it. That sort of thing, and bracing up. One of these upper classmen would say, "Brace up, Mister," and put the edge of his hand in your back and pull your shoulders back.

Q: So I guess what you're suggesting is that a lot of that had tapered off during the plebe year, and then in the spring of 1920 they brought it back.

Captain Edwards: Yes. There were a few jewels in the class, but they were not too apparent to me.

Q: Any that you would identify specifically as jewels?

Captain Edwards: Well, I'd rather not. Just offhand I can't put a finger on them, but some of them were very fine fellows.

Q: What kind of uniforms did you wear as plebes?

Captain Edwards: We had the so-called white works.* We

---

*White works was the name for the uniform that was essentially like the one worn by junior enlisted men--white jumper and trousers. Midshipmen wore sailor-type hats with a blue band to distinguish it from enlisted men's hats.

F. A. Edwards #1 - 17

also wore soldier-type khakis for infantry drill as midshipmen, but khakis for officers didn't come in until World War II or thereabouts. Our blue service uniforms were not provided until the beginning of the academic year in early September.

Q: What do you recall about dancing lessons?

Captain Edwards: In plebe year we were forced to take dancing lessons, and the academy hired a Professor Bell from Baltimore. He was quite a character. We had no girls at that time, so we had to dance with each other. He would first demonstrate the step, whatever it was, and he would keep time by using the expression, "Boom, drip, drip; boom, drip, drip." The midshipmen, of course, would all clap and throw pennies at him and so forth.

Q: How eagerly did the plebes take to this?

Captain Edwards: Well, it was hilarious, really hilarious, because it was a time to laugh and shout. Bell said, "I'm going to report you to the commandant," but he never did. So I think any man of my time could remember Professor Bell with a laugh.

Q: Something you mentioned when the recorder wasn't

F. A. Edwards #1 - 18

running was about rating the dates at dances.

Captain Edwards: Plebes could not go to dances, so they sat in the balcony overlooking the dance floor. We had to rate the upper classmen's dates at meals thereafter. And we'd use flowery language, of course, if we could. For example, "She had teeth like pearls. She had eyes like diamonds, and she had ears like shells." That sort of thing. And that was a routine description. Well, God help you if you didn't have some kind of a satisfactory description of this man's date the night before. One time I was extolling the virtues of one date, and this upper classman said, "You're a damn liar. I didn't even go to the dance."

Q: Was that one that you had missed?

Captain Edwards: Yes. I was rating this girl, but I never saw her. It turned out to be that this fellow didn't go to the dance. So I caught hell for it and went under the table.

Q: Did the plebes ever give honest evaluations of these dates?

Captain Edwards: No. They were 4.0 or a 3.99 at different

times. It was all a farce.

Q: What do you remember about some of the duty officers?

Captain Edwards: Well, I can't complain about them, but I do remember that one of them was J. J. Brown, class of '12.* He ferreted out any wrongdoing. One day some mids were playing bridge in a fellow's room, and Brown was around inspecting unexpectedly. He caught them, and he had them all show him the cards in their hands. Then he said, "You all have poor hands. You're on report." So they were all on what we called the "pap" for playing cards. Brown was also good at detecting upper classmen out of uniform.

Q: I think some of those duty officers took a sadistic pleasure in putting people on the report.

Captain Edwards: Well, some did and some didn't. I remember J. J. was one of the worst ones. Fifteen years later he was my executive officer in the New Mexico, and I was surprised at his memory. He still remembered most of our names, which really was impressive.

Q: That summer of 1919 was only a few months after the armistice at the end of World War I. Did you see any

---
*Lieutenant Commander John J. Brown, USN.

vestiges of the war at the academy?

Captain Edwards: At that time they had some tennis courts where the science and mathematics buildings are now. They had been used during the war for the reserve ensign program. During the summer I came there, they were just finishing one school of ensigns. We called them the "reverse ensigns" instead of reserve ensigns. We were friends and we were happy. Nevertheless, that was the joke.

Q: Did they have temporary barracks in place of the tennis courts?

Captain Edwards: Yes, they added some barracks. That wasn't the only place they had them, but this was one of the many training schools they had for young officers. These men were primarily being trained for the submarine chaser program--wooden 110-foot hulls, diesel or gasoline drive. Some of the boats got overseas during World War I, but most of them didn't. They were used for patrols of entrances to harbors, looking for submarines.

Q: Did you get any training in those boats?

Captain Edwards: Yes, we used them for practical work, so-called lab work. We took them out for ship-handling drills primarily.

Q: Well, and probably a little tactical maneuvering.

Captain Edwards: That's right, and that was a lot of fun. Later on, during the school year itself, destroyers were assigned temporarily to take upper classmen out into Chesapeake Bay.

Q: Did you take part in sports at the Naval Academy?

Captain Edwards: I tried basketball first, because I played basketball in high school. But in those days, we had to jump center after every basket and whenever the ball went outside the court. Nowadays, as you know, they throw the ball in. I had to jump 100 times or more every game. My arches gave way; I couldn't take it. I also tried football, which I played in high school. I was a tall, skinny kid; I weighed only 150-some pounds and was the same height I am now, six feet. The varsity used us as tackling dummies. After about one week I was so sore I couldn't get out of bed. So I turned in my suit, and that was the extent of my athletic experiences at the academy. I just wasn't physically ready to engage some of these people.

F. A. Edwards #1 - 22

Q: Did you play any intramural sports at the Naval Academy?

Captain Edwards: No, as I said, I had these physical problems and I didn't play intramural sports. I probably should have started there, rather than going into the big sports.

Q: What do you remember about some of the Army-Navy football games? They were played up in New York, weren't they?

Captain Edwards: Well, the first three were played in New York at the Polo Grounds, and the fourth one was played at Franklin Field in Philadelphia. I especially remember the first one, which was in 1919. Before the game Jack Dempsey, the world heavyweight boxing champion, was introduced to the crowd. He was obviously a reserve who joined up purely to get out of the war.* When they introduced him, there was a tremendous "boo." He was very unpopular, because everybody knew why he joined.

It rained slightly that day.** We all wore our bridge coats, not raincoats. These were warm coats, knee

---

*William Harrison "Jack" Dempsey was world heavyweight boxing champion from 4 July 1919 to 23 September 1926.
**The game was played on 29 November 1919; the Naval Academy yearbook described the weather as a "slow, steady rain throughout the game." It was the Naval Academy's first football victory over the Military Academy since 1912.

length or longer, and they got thoroughly soaked. We also wore overshoes. Before we got into the stands, half our overshoes were embedded in the muck as we walked around the Polo Grounds. Then we stood in the stands for three hours with these heavy, soggy coats and no overshoes. A lot of the upper classmen had flasks in their inside coat pockets. When the excitement died down for a minute, they'd take a swig of whiskey through a straw. Being plebes, we had to take the chill without any such help. The thing I remember most is that we beat the Army, 6 to 0!

Q: That was a real highlight of the year, wasn't it?

Captain Edwards: Yes, but one of the New York newspapers headlined, "Army Loses." It wasn't, "Navy Won, Army Loses."

That night I was supposed to go to a show. My parents came up, so I took off my coat and hung it over a radiator in their hotel room to dry it out. The middies stayed overnight after the game, and then at 8:00 o'clock the next morning we had to fall in, hangovers and all.

I don't remember much about the other two Army-Navy games at New York. We shifted down to Philadelphia for the game in the first-class year.*

---

*The senior year at the Naval Academy is referred to as the first-class year and members of that class as first classmen. Juniors are second classmen and so forth.

Q: Did you take the train up to New York for these games?

Captain Edwards: Yes, and there had to be, of course, equal treatment. So B&O and Pennsylvania each ran a train.* One of them went up through the town of Odenton. We ran up to Odenton and there got on the main line and went north. The other train went across the bridge over the Severn River and up through Baltimore. Half of us went via one route and half went the other--to keep the railroads happy. And we always pulled the shades down going through Baltimore, because the "word" was that we'd lose if Baltimore looked at us as we went through.

Q: I've heard that custom, but why was that? I mean, just a superstition?

Captain Edwards: It was before my time; I have no explanation, except it was superstition. And in those days the middies were really pepped up. We had bonfires, Indian powwows, and all that sort of thing. It was really something. Nowadays the Army-Navy game is more or less just another game.

---

*B&O--Baltimore and Ohio Railroad, now defunct but then one of the most noted railroads in the nation. It had a terminal in Jersey City, New Jersey, but not in New York City itself.

Q: I don't know about that. I think that's still a special game.

Captain Edwards: In my time the plebes all had to attend every game, or else. Because we had to describe the game in detail at the table that night--who did what and when. God help you if you didn't, because most of the upper classmen had attended.

Q: Where did the trains go in New York?

Captain Edwards: One went to Penn Station downtown, and the other one to Jersey City. That first year, I recall, my train went to Jersey City, and then they put us on a ferry that went up to some street in New York City. Then we marched from there over to the Polo Grounds.

During that ferryboat ride I saw for the first time--and only time--one of the ships-of-the-line. She was then called the Granite State.* She had been laid down as the New Hampshire, and then was on the stocks for 30 or 40 years. When the Civil War came along, they completed her. She served then not as a combat ship but a depot ship. She went down to Port Royal, South Carolina. The ship remained

---

*Her keel was laid in 1819, but she was not completed and commissioned until 1864. She was decommissioned in 1892, then renamed Granite State in 1904 so a battleship could be the New Hampshire. She served the New York State Militia until she caught fire at her Hudson River pier in 1921.

there for a couple of years, then came back up to Norfolk and finally to New York. She eventually became a station ship for the Naval Reserve of New York State and tied up alongside a pier in the Hudson River, or North River, as it was also known. That morning, as our ferry proceeded upstream in the fog, there loomed the tremendous hull of the <u>Granite State</u>.

Q: What a memory. That's neat.

Captain Edwards: Well, it really was overawing with its three gun decks. We were down at water level, and this hull stood up there, 50 feet or more to the main deck.

The <u>Granite State</u> was there for many years as a reserve training ship. Men went down there for drills. The Navy later sold her for junk. They towed her to somewhere in New England, where they burned the hull to recover the copper. All the metal in those ships was copper, which was very valuable at that time. That's the only one of those ships-of-the-line I ever saw. It truly inspired me, although I had read a lot about them already. I learned still more later on.

Q: What do you remember about the academics at the Naval Academy?

Captain Edwards: After I was graduated from high school, I went to prep school for a year--"Bobby's War College" in Annapolis. Then at the academy I found out I didn't know a thing. The first four months of plebe year I had a review of high school mathematics. We called it "book-of-the-month club." One month would be plane geometry; the next month, algebra; the third month, trigonometry; and so on. In geometry, for example, there'd be ten theorems a day instead of just one. The review was done so everybody would have basically the same background.

Now, of course, certain things I liked. In school at home I liked geography and history and that sort of thing. But at the academy, of course, the emphasis was on engineering--mathematics, science, and so forth. In the second year, I remember, we were taking calculus, which I hadn't had before. Some of my classmates had already taken it, because they had had anywhere from one to two years in college. Well, one month I starred; the next month I was on the "tree," which was the unsatisfactory list. So my progress depended on what the subject was.

Q: How helpful were the instructors?

Captain Edwards: Oh, I guess 50-50. I can't complain too much. The system was such that they didn't have to do too much. They had the written questions, maybe ten questions for that particular day, and they called them "slips." They cut them and put them face down on the instructor's table. You drew slips, and then you either recited verbally, or you went to the blackboard and wrote the answers. Then there was a very short discussion period available.

I know when I was an instructor ten years later I made sure that a person who asked me a question had spent some time on it himself and wasn't just trying to kill time or seeing what I knew. Unless they could show me some work of their own, I didn't bite when they suggested I work the problem for them.

Q: Probably the review process was able to help you overcome this lack of background you had as a new midshipman.

Captain Edwards: We had advanced work, as I recall it, three months of the term. Then we had a month's review. Then we had semiannual examinations. At the end of the year we had final examinations. I think the examinations counted 40% and daily marks counted 60%; that's my recollection. I have to say that everything I know I learned at the Naval Academy. It was very good, really. But I never went to class feeling I had been fully prepared for recitation. The idea was to stretch one's capacity to absorb.

Now, once in a while, you could get ahead of the instructors. I remember once in electricity we were required to sketch and describe streetcar controllers. They had two types of controllers in the book, and they had just two slips in class: number one and number two. Well, I'd spent all my time on number one, but I drew slip number two. Boldly I worked right ahead with number one, however, and the instructor didn't notice. He said, "Fine, 4.0." That's one time I fooled the system.

Q: Well, it was a lot of memory work overall.

Captain Edwards: Yes, a lot of memory. We had a lot of practical work, laboratory work. I remember one time in electricity a midshipman had burned out an ammeter by having the wrong connection. Slipstick Willie, the instructor, said, "You know, in the Navy you just reach for a survey slip if you burn out an instrument, but in civilian life you reach for your hat."*

Q: What else do you remember about him?

---

*"Slipstick Willie" was the nickname given Professor Earl W. Thomson because of his prowess with a slide rule. He taught at the Naval Academy from 1919 to 1959. For details see Shipmate magazine, published by the Naval Academy Alumni Association, June 1982, page 13.

F. A. Edwards #1 - 30

Captain Edwards: Well, he had a good sense of humor, but he kept right on the line. He didn't give you any favors, but he was fair. I got to know him better later in life when we both belonged to the local branch of the Retired Officers Association here in Annapolis.

Q: How competitive were the midshipmen among themselves?

Captain Edwards: Very competitive. I wanted to do the best I could, and I did. I stood 119 out of 412 graduates.

Q: That's certainly respectable.

Captain Edwards: Well, I know, but I had to completely revamp my mental processes to adapt to the Naval Academy's pressure on science and mathematics. I was in math class with one mid who had been two years at the University of Kansas. He stood number four or five in his class for the year. Up against a man like that, it's tough. When we were in class he would work, we'll say, ten problems in perhaps 15-20 minutes. Then he would do an about-face and stand at parade rest. The rest of us were sweating and struggling and maybe getting three or four in a half hour. This "brain" would sort of stand there and leer at us while we stupid oafs were sweating and trying to work these problems.

W. N. Landers, class of '25, entered the academy when he was 19 years of age.* He had already graduated from Harvard in three years. Following graduation from the academy he became a naval constructor. He was later secretary of the Naval Architects and Marine Engineers Society for quite a few years.

Q: Did you have much contact with the superintendents?

Captain Edwards: The superintendent I reported to was Admiral Archibald H. Scales.** He was more or less a fuddy-duddy. His relief was Henry B. Wilson, whom we thought of as an up-and-coming guy.*** He inspired us.

Q: Wilson was very popular with the midshipmen, I think.

Captain Edwards: Very popular. He had the highest standards of service. One time I saw him walking--and he always used a cane. A midshipman was holding hands with this girl he was walking with. Wilson walked up behind them, took his cane, and went WHOP--right on their hands. He didn't say a word, just WHOP.

---
*Midshipman Wilbur Nelson Landers, USN, stood fourth among the 448 graduates in the Naval Academy class of 1925.
**Rear Admiral Archibald H. Scales, USN, was superintendent of the Naval Academy from February 1919 to July 1921.
***Rear Admiral Henry B. Wilson, USN, was superintendent of the Naval Academy from July 1921 to February 1925.

Much later I was on duty at the New York Navy Yard, '48 to '50. Admiral Wilson was then retired and living in the city. He used to come over to the yard and have lunch there at the officers' club, because he wanted to see Navy people. Here he was, a retired admiral, carrying his tray around, serving himself. We had a round table that seated about ten people. He used to sit at the round table. I, being a captain, sat at the round table too. So here he was, this great man, carrying his tray and fraternizing with us. He had our respect; there's no question about it.*

Q: Well, and I'm sure he enjoyed still being associated with the Navy.

Captain Edwards: That's right, yes. That was the reason. He used to come over there maybe once a week and have lunch at this club.

When I was a first classman, I was a three-striper.** The superintendent would invite maybe eight or ten of us each Sunday to have lunch with him. He had a big long

---
*Wilson, who was born 23 February 1861, retired by law on his 64th birthday in 1925. He was advanced to four-star rank on the retired list in 1930. He lived in New York until his death on 30 January 1954 at the age of 92.
**"Striper" was the term for an individual designated as a midshipman officer by the number of stripes on his sleeves. During the year a class had two sets of midshipman officers in order to give more men an opportunity for the duty.

F. A. Edwards #1 - 33

table, must have handled 20-24 people. Admiral Wilson would have a sprinkling of officers or civilian guests. Well, I entered through the lower door to his quarters. There was a cloakroom down there, and in it was posted a seating arrangement for this long table. But I did not see it and didn't even know about it. So I went upstairs happily and met all the guests and so forth.

When it came time to eat, Henry B. Wilson got up, took the leading lady by the arm, and started marching in. People fell in behind him, two by two, see, like the animals in Noah's Ark. At that point a cold sweat came over my head. I thought, "My God, where do I sit?" Well, I just fell in accidentally and marched in. When we got to a certain stop, I turned around and looked, and there was my place card! God help me, there was my name. Otherwise, I thought I'd have been thrown out of the Navy.

Q: I'll bet you felt a big sense of relief.

Captain Edwards: Oh, boy.

Q: There was a story you mentioned at lunch that is worth putting on the record. It had to do with your experience when the Assistant Secretary of the Navy, Franklin D. Roosevelt, visited the Naval Academy.*

---
*Franklin D. Roosevelt was Assistant Secretary of the Navy from 1913 to 1920, during the administration of President Woodrow Wilson. Roosevelt was President from 1933 to 1945.

Captain Edwards: One Sunday evening when I was a plebe I attended what was called the YMCA meeting, which was held in Memorial Hall. Most plebes were there, because it was required--one of those unofficial requirements. Roosevelt gave a very inspiring address. I was so impressed that I wrote my parents at that time and told them that I had heard him, and he obviously would be more in the news as time went on. I envisioned he'd be a senator or governor or some such. He turned out to be much more than that.

Q: What was it about him that impressed you?

Captain Edwards: His voice and manner. He developed a very personalized manner of speaking. He made you feel that he was talking to you only, and his voice had a very nice ring to it. He was a polished speaker. He would be listened to on any subject.

Many years later my wife and I took a motor trip up through New England. We made a stop at his Hyde Park home, where I saw the big marble slab over his grave. His widow has since been buried up there too. It's a very wonderful location, but the house furnishing was not good. My wife agreed with that too. It was very casual, not becoming to a President of the United States, I felt. He should have had an interior decorator in the home there.

We saw his car there also. You know, he had a Ford car with hand-operated controls. Of course, he couldn't use his legs.

Q: Did you enjoy your time at the Naval Academy?

Captain Edwards: Yes, in a spartan sort of way. You don't expect it to be beer and skittles. It isn't that kind of a course. I'm very happy I went there, but I always felt uneasy academically. As I said, I never felt I was prepared for a class, and I was always hoping to God I got the right slip or the right question.

Q: So you couldn't really relax and enjoy it.

Captain Edwards: No. It wasn't that kind of thing. And I was not a "ladies' man." I was what they called a "Red Mike." I did not drag girls on the weekends, except once or twice.

Q: Why not?

Captain Edwards: Well, I decided it would detract from my capacity to get through the academy. I went there with one purpose in life only: that was to get through the Naval Academy, come hell or high water. So I put everything I had into getting through. And anything that detracted from that, I avoided. Some of the guys were moonstruck, and their grades went right downhill.

Oh, a couple of times, girls from my home town would be visiting Washington. They'd come down, and I'd show them around, but there was no regular social life. Some mids were in town with girls all the time; we called them "lounge lizards." A "Red Mike" avoided girls. Well, I avoided girls--not because they were girls, but because I wanted to get through the academy.

Q: Did you go to the hops?

Captain Edwards: Oh, only as an extra. I went stag. I wasn't interested in anybody, but it was just another way to pass the time.

Q: Did the midshipmen violate Prohibition?

Captain Edwards: Some, yes but not too much. I told you about the one Army-Navy football game when quite a few of them had flasks in their inside coat pockets. But that was an exception; that was not the rule at all. I can't recall anyone being drunk.

Q: Did some of the men get sent to the Reina Mercedes for

offenses?*

Captain Edwards: A Class A offender went to the ship. A Class B offense was only so many demerits. Fortunately, I was a good boy, more or less. I had only 20-some demerits in four years, which is not a record, but it points out I was regulation. That is, I played the game as it was supposed to be played. I didn't try to get away with anything. So many people always think they're smarter than the boss is, in and out of the naval service.

Q: Who were some of the classmates that you were closest to and made friends with?

Captain Edwards: Well, a fellow named Scruggs as a midshipman.** He later was an LST squadron commander in the far Pacific. Also, a fellow named Downs, who had tuberculosis and finally went to Fitzsimmons General Hospital in Denver.*** I'm just thinking of some of my immediate associates. Of course, I knew a couple hundred of them fairly well; another couple hundred, not so well.

---

*USS Reina Mercedes (IX-25), captured during the Spanish-American War, served as a station ship at the Naval Academy from 1912 to 1957. Until 1940, midshipmen being punished for various disciplinary infractions slept and took meals on board the ship but continued to go to classes ashore.
**Midshipman Richard M. Scruggs, USN.
***Midshipman Harry A. Downs, USN, who resigned his commission in April 1924, less than a year after becoming an officer.

I recall something that happened when I was in the New Mexico, 14 years out of the academy. One day they had a gunnery exercise and brought observers over from another ship. When one officer introduced himself, I asked, "What class are you?"

He said, "Twenty-three." I almost fell off my chair.

Another classmate on board was Will D. Wright, who had never seen or heard of this fellow.* Hard to believe it, but we two had never even heard of him before. But that's the only example. You generally knew of your classmates even if you didn't know them personally.

In those days they had French and Spanish battalions. You either took French or Spanish. If you were in a Spanish battalion, and some classmate was in a French battalion, you seldom had a chance to meet him. But on summer cruises they assigned us alphabetically. That's how I got to know quite a few other midshipmen whom I had not met back at the academy.

Q: Did you know Arleigh Burke when he was a midshipman?

Captain Edwards: No, I didn't, just as a classmate. The first time and only time I had duty with him was on the Atlantic Fleet staff. That was after the war. He'd had

---

*Lieutenant Commander William Dudley Wright, Jr., USN.

quite a war record, as you know.*

Q: One of your classmates who earned the Medal of Honor was Sam Fuqua in the Arizona.** What do you remember about him?

Captain Edwards: I read an article about him, and it was very interesting.*** I didn't know the details of the event. I knew he escaped being killed by a bomb that fell not too far from him. I met him during plebe year. In fact, we sat at the same table for meals. He got the nickname "Ben" at that time because he had one eye that was off center. He later had that corrected. He was nicknamed after Ben Turpin, a famous or infamous cross-eyed movie actor of that period.

Q: What do you remember of Fuqua as a midshipman? What kind of a guy was he?

Captain Edwards: Very friendly but nothing special. I never served with him on active duty, but his wife and my

---

*Arleigh A. Burke served during World War II as Commander Destroyer Squadron 23 and later as chief of staff to Vice Admiral Marc A. Mitscher. As an admiral he served as Chief of Naval Operations from 1955 to 1961. His oral history is in the Naval Institute collection.
**Lieutenant Commander Samuel G. Fuqua, USN.
***See Paul Stillwell, "Sam Fuqua and the Death of the Arizona," U.S. Naval Institute Proceedings, December 1991, pages 41-43.

F. A. Edwards #1 - 40

wife were very good friends. In fact, our first babies were delivered at the San Diego hospital at the same time back in 1926.* That's how our wives met. Ben and I were in destroyers at the time. After that we just saw each other occasionally. In fact, I lost track of him, duty-wise, before the war.

Q: Another midshipman during your time was Cat Brown.**

Captain Edwards: Cat was what we called rather "non-reg." He was frequently on the report for various things: out of uniform, unmilitary conduct. He went into aviation later on, and I was so surprised when he made vice admiral. He must have completely changed his way of life.

Q: Your point is that you can't always tell about somebody from his midshipman characteristics.

Captain Edwards: That's right. He was in command of the Mediterranean fleet when the British and French were approaching the canal to retake it from the Egyptians.*** He got orders from Washington about what to do to the

---
*Frederick A. Edwards, Jr., was born 27 July 1926.
**Midshipman Charles R. Brown, USN, class of 1921.
***This was the Suez crisis in late 1956 when Vice Admiral Brown was Commander Sixth Fleet.

enemy. He wired back, "Who is the enemy?" At a cocktail party later I asked Cat, "Was that a true story?"

He said, "Yeah, that's true." It's hard to believe.

Q: Where did you go on your various summer cruises?

Captain Edwards: The first was in 1920 in the USS Michigan, and we sailed from Annapolis.* The first stop was Guantanamo Bay, Cuba, and then we went to Panama and through the canal. We coaled in Panama. Then the next stops were Hawaii, Seattle, and San Francisco. The next two stops we split, three ships to San Diego and three to San Pedro. Then back to Panama, Guantanamo Bay, and to Annapolis. That was a three months' cruise.

Q: That was a full summer.

Captain Edwards: A full summer. And I got my sea legs then.

The second cruise was in the South Carolina in 1921.** That year we went to Europe. We first sighted

---
*USS Michigan (BB-27) was commissioned 4 January 1910. She had a standard displacement of 16,000 tons, was 453 feet long, and 80 feet in the beam. She had a top speed of 18.5 knots and a main battery of eight 12-inch guns. She was decommissioned in February 1922 and scrapped under the provisions of the Washington Treaty of that year.
**USS South Carolina (BB-26) was a sister ship of the Michigan. She was commissioned 1 March 1910. The ship was decommissioned 15 December 1921, only a few months after Edwards's cruise on board. In 1924 she was sold for scrap, in keeping with the 1922 Washington Naval Treaty.

the Azores, then went up to Christiana, now Oslo, Norway. We were there two weeks, and then we went down to Lisbon, Portugal, and to Gibraltar. We finished up by operating briefly off Cuba, then going to Hampton Roads and back to Annapolis.

The third cruise, in 1922, was in the Florida.* That was Annapolis, Panama, Trinidad, St. Kitts, Culebra Island, Halifax, and Hampton Roads. We fired guns off Hampton Roads, then returned to Annapolis.

Those were the three cruises. They were all three-month cruises.

Q: You were a long way from Troy, Ohio.

Captain Edwards: Right. I used to ask myself a question: "Why in God's name did I ever join the Navy?" I never had a good answer, except that I wanted to.

Q: Did it live up to the expectations you'd had when you read that Boys' Life article?

Captain Edwards: Well, yes and no. My opinions as a kid

---

*USS Florida (BB-30) was commissioned 15 September 1911. She had a standard displacement of 21,825 tons, was 522 feet long, and 88 feet in the beam. She had a top speed of 21 knots and a main battery of ten 12-inch guns. She was decommissioned in 16 February 1931 and scrapped under the provisions of the London Naval Treaty of 1930.

were glamorous, but the realities fell short. Still, I'm glad I did it.

Q: What do you recall specifically about that 1920 cruise in the *Michigan*?

Captain Edwards: She was a coal-burner, and about every ten days or so we coaled ship. That's the most god-awful experience a man can have.

Q: Please describe it.

Captain Edwards: You got up at dawn, and either a collier came alongside your ship, or your ship went alongside her. The crew broke out wheelbarrows, which they called "buggies." They put scores of them on deck. Then the collier rigged large cranes with clamshell buckets. They'd go down into the collier via large opened hatches, get a big bite of coal, and whip it over to the battleship's deck. Then we in the crew filled the buggies and wheeled half of the coal to each side of the ship. We then struck it down coal chutes into the bunkers. When the bunkers were full, some of the mids had to level off the bunkers by shoveling coal to the corners. The coal dust was so dense that overhead lights just glowed dimly.

We coaled ship anywhere from 24 hours on up, depending

on how much coal we had to take aboard. I've coaled 36 hours, stopping only for coffee and sandwiches and going to the head; that's all.

Q: So in addition to being dirty, you'd be really fatigued.

Captain Edwards: That's right.

Q: You'd lose a lot of your effectiveness after so many hours.

Captain Edwards: Well, I know, but the job had to be done. We worked till it was done.

Another thing about the job was that there was always a bunch of what we called "soldiers," men who would become musicians for the coaling-ship period. They'd play a tune while all the rest of us were taking on the coal. Then as soon as the coaling was over, they went back to their regular jobs. We called them "soldiers," because they were soldiering on the job.

Q: Still, I think that would help relieve some of the tedium for the other men.

Captain Edwards: That was the idea, but there was still a

certain amount of bad feeling, that here were these bastards up there tootling a whistle or horn while we were down there shoveling coal.

Of course, once we were done with all the shoveling, then we had problems getting the coal dust off ourselves with salt water. The coal dust permeated throughout the ship. Our lockers were closed and sealed with papers to keep out the coal dust, but when you got your clothes out for inspection, the "whites" were stained with black streaks. You hosed the ship down and scrubbed it the best you could. It was never 100%. It required a big scrub down with brushes and what they called "squeegees." It took even longer to clean up than it did to coal ship. Then, depending upon the schedule, we did it all over again!

I remember one time when I was in a hospital in Ohio on one of my leave periods. I asked my mother to bring me some pictures from home and mentioned one of me in particular taken after coaling ship. She said she couldn't find it. When I got home, I found it in a pile of pictures. I said, "Here it is."

She said, "I thought that was a black man." There was no difference in color between the face, the shirt, and the shoes.

They always said that after you coaled ship, you had to watch it; you might be shaving somebody else's face by mistake. With those mirrors, you had to be careful. You might be shaving the man right next to you. [Laughter]

After a cruise I'd go to a barber shop and have a shampoo and everything, complete. I'd have coal dust in my ears that I couldn't get out. Those coal-burners were man-killers, absolutely man-killers.

Q: How did you clean your uniforms when they got that coal dust on them?

Captain Edwards: We had a laundry then, and we wore them the way the ship did them--laundry clean. It wasn't 100%, but that was all we could do about it.

A funny thing--we said there were two kinds of midshipmen. One half of them went aboard ship with a full bag of clothing and with no laundry-marking kit. The other half went aboard ship with no clothing and with a marking set. And when they returned, the people with the marking sets had the clothing.

Q: They took somebody else's.

Captain Edwards: That's right.

Eventually during each cruise, we were assigned to the firerooms--the "Black Gang." Our job was to feed the fire

doors on a coal-burning boiler each time a bell rang.*
Then every hour or so you pushed a steel slice bar, 10 or
12 feet long, under the fire bed to break up the clinkers.

Q: You were exposing more coal to the air.

Captain Edwards: That's right. In the morning, at daylight, we got rid of the clinkers. We'd haul them out with a big, long-handled hoe. Each man had a handkerchief over his eyes and nose. A fireman stood alongside of you with a hose. As these clinkers came out on the floor plates, he put the hose on the clinkers, resulting in a cloud of steam. Someone then broke up the stuff and shoveled it into the ash chute. The chaplain said he never before appreciated Kipling's line, "Dawn came up like thunder from China [Indo-china] across the bay."**

Q: Were there doors in the sides of the ship that opened up to let out these clinkers?

Captain Edwards: No, those chutes went right up to the weather deck. When the covers were unclamped, the water and clinkers discharged overboard. That was an early-morning routine at sea.

---

*The Michigan had 12 water-tube boilers manufactured by Babcock and Wilcox.
**Rudyard Kipling was a noted British poet and author who specialized in stories about the exotic Far East.

Q: What lifted the clinkers up from the fireroom to the weather deck?

Captain Edwards: Water from the fire main.

Q: I see, so it was kind of like a garbage disposal.

Captain Edwards: That's right; the same idea, only heavier garbage.

Q: How hot was it down there?

Captain Edwards: The humidity and the temperature together were god-awful. About 25% of the midshipmen passed out.

Q: How long was a watch, four hours?

Captain Edwards: Four hours, and you stood a watch in four.* During the idle time between watches you were supposed to sleep, have drills, and God knows what else to recover. So it was a continuous occupation.

---

*A watch in four meant that there were four different sections standing these watches in rotation.

Q: What were the messing arrangements in the Michigan?

Captain Edwards: We ate at eight-man tables, which were brought down from the overhead for each meal. After we ate and the tables were cleaned, they were re-stowed on the overhead, along with the benches we sat on. In rotation midshipmen were assigned as mess attendants for ten days each. Those who had been on prior cruises bought a lot of jellies and cookies ashore. They would chip in $10.00 or $15.00 apiece to guy a lot of goodies to supplement the rations of plain food.

When they had a good meal, the enlisted men would say that the paymaster had provided "shipping-over chow" to get them to reenlist.*

Q: Did you have any trouble sleeping in a hammock?

Captain Edwards: Yes, you had to learn how. You had to have a very taut connection to the overhead. I remember coming back from liberty once in a foreign port. One mid swung his hammock in the upper level. During the night he had an upset stomach and heaved on the lower level of hammocks. The recipient below pulled him to the deck and gave him a first-class beating. They had nettings, as they

---

*Shipping over is a Navy expression for reenlistment. The idea was that cooks would sometimes serve better-than-usual meals in order to get enlisted men to stay in the Navy.

were called, where hammocks were stowed when not in use. Once a week or so the hammocks were aired in the sunlight. It often rained during that time, so you got your bedding wet while you were airing it.

Q: Did some of the crew members leave the ship to make room for you?

Captain Edwards: Yes, they cut down the size of their crews for the midshipmen's cruises, in order to make room for the mids. Perhaps 40% or 50% were ashore on leave while we occupied those spaces. The senior petty officers stayed to help, like running the firerooms. You had to have an experienced man to keep the water level in the boiler steam drum at midpoint. Otherwise, in a fireman's language, you would "haul fires and haul ass."

A vertical glass tube, known as a "glass," indicated the water level in the steam drum. The water tender's job was to keep the water level at the approximate center of the glass. If it was too low, the boiler would "melt down." If it was too high, water would carry over into the main engines. In case of low water, the procedure was to haul the burning clinkers out of the boilers onto the deck plates in order to reduce combustion.

F. A. Edwards #1 - 51

Q: Did you spend any time with the engines in the Michigan?

Captain Edwards: Yes, they rotated us. We'd have ten days in one division and ten days in another division.

Q: Was that the triple-expansion plant?

Captain Edwards: Yes, four-cylinder triple-expansion engines. Together the two engines developed 16,500 shaft horsepower. They were two decks high and required a lot of space compared to a turbine engine of comparable horsepower--perhaps four times the space.

Q: How big was the largest cylinder?

Captain Edwards: Approximately 30 inches in diameter. There was a high-pressure cylinder, 150 pounds per square inch, and an intermediate-pressure cylinder in the center of the engine, flanked by a low-pressure cylinder at each end. In operation those engines were awe inspiring.

Q: How long was the piston rod?

Captain Edwards: Probably 10 to 15 feet.

Q: That's a good-size engine.

Captain Edwards: Yes. We had to oil the main bearings and piston slides, which contaminated the feed water. To get rid of the oil, the water was then passed through loofa sponges, which had to be replaced on a regular basis.

Q: Did you have any topside duties in the <u>Michigan</u>?

Captain Edwards: Oh, yes. I went to the gun divisions, rotated ten days in a turret, ten days in a broadside division, then ten days on the bridge. We had 80-some days afloat, and we had about eight different assignments during that time.

Q: What are your specific memories of each of those stations--the bridge, the turrets, and the broadsides?

Captain Edwards: The most interesting to me was engineering. The other departments were interesting, but I had no desire to serve in them.

Q: What were your duties in the turret?

Captain Edwards: We'd load and fire dummy rounds. We had target practice at the end of each cruise. All the guns would fire low-capacity charges at targets only a mile or two away. I was amazed at the turrets. The turrets were beautiful pieces of machinery; they really were. And the same way now, a turret on the _Iowa_ class is also a magnificent piece of machinery.

Q: Did you ever stand watches up on the foretop or maintop?

Captain Edwards: Yes. If you were in the maintop, you either got some combustion smoke in your face or you got a gun blast. It was a dirty place.

Q: What do you recall about the radio communications when you were in the _Michigan_?

Captain Edwards: During that cruise in 1920 there were six ships, two divisions of old battleships in the squadron. The radio shack of the _Michigan_ was manned all night, and they were trying to talk by voice over to the other ships. Even though they were only 1,000 or so yards away, they had difficulty. All night long we would hear, "_Michigan_, _Michigan_, _Minnesota_, _Minnesota_, _Minnesota_," etc. I remember this because I was trying to sleep near there. That shows the progress of voice communication by radio since 1920.

F. A. Edwards #1 - 54

Q: The <u>Michigan</u> and the <u>South Carolina</u> were the first U.S. dreadnought-type battleships.* What do you remember about the characteristics of those ships?

Captain Edwards: Well, they were my first big ships as a midshipman. I was, of course, awed in a way. But the fact that they were coal-burners took some of the pleasure away. Now, on my first cruise, on the <u>Michigan</u>, we went from Panama to Hawaii without stopping. We were not coaled en route. At Panama we took on a regular load, plus a deckload. That was the longest cruise ever made by a U.S. battleship without coaling at sea. I checked the mileage, and it even surpassed the longest leg steamed by the Great White Fleet, when it went from Hawaii to New Zealand.** So we were burning, let's say, 115 tons a day, and we were under way for 15 days anyhow.

Q: Did you sleep topside in the warm weather when you were on board the <u>Michigan</u>?

Captain Edwards: Yes, because there was no adequate ventilation below decks. It got so hot when we were off

---

*Named generically for HMS <u>Dreadnought</u>, which went into service in 1906, all subsequent battleships emulated her pattern of a relatively small number of large guns, rather than having a mixture of gun sizes. The <u>Michigan</u> and her sister <u>South Carolina</u>, although designed before the <u>Dreadnought</u>, did not go into service until after she did.
**The Great White Fleet, comprised of 16 U.S. battleships, steamed around the world between 1907 and 1909. The leg from Honolulu to Auckland, New Zealand, was 3,850 miles, quite a chore for the older pre-dreadnought ships.

the west coast of Mexico that most of us came up to the topside with our hammocks. We'd lay them on the deck and sleep up there. If you were aft, you were liable to get coal soot on you, so most of us went forward and slept on the forecastle. One night, however, I put mine under an onion locker in order to get out of the way of other people, and during the night we had a rain squall. The onion juice trickled down onto me, so the next morning I was really something to smell.

Q: I guess the ships sort of played leapfrog with those rain squalls.

Captain Edwards: That's right. We normally steamed in two columns of three ships each. The battleships themselves were 1,000 yards from the one ahead or astern, and the columns were perhaps 2,000 yards apart. You could watch these rain squalls come along and leapfrog over and around the ships. You could almost predict to the minute when you were going to get hit by a rain squall.

Q: Any other recollections of those topside berthing arrangements in the *Michigan*?

Captain Edwards: I remember one night when a bunch of us were spread out on the forecastle. It so happened that the timing of the waves and the ship's speed coincided about every seventh or eighth wave. One particular wave brought green water right over the bow. You could hear the screaming and yelling of all these people that had to jump up sopping wet from this wave.

Q: What specific memories do you have from some of those liberty ports that the ships visited?

Captain Edwards: I have a lot of memories, mostly good. However, at St. Kitts I went ashore in a motor launch, walked several blocks to a statue of Queen Victoria, and walked back to the dock. Years later, as a tourist on a cruise ship, I received the full treatment. Among other things, I saw a very famous 18th-century fort, high on a bluff there, which I didn't know existed.

Q: Why didn't you look for more when you were a midshipman?

Captain Edwards: There were no tours, no taxis, and no buses. We just walked around town. As I said, I went to the Queen Vic statue, came back, and waited for the next boat.

I had many good liberties, but that was a bad one.

Q: What kinds of things did you typically do on liberty?

Captain Edwards: Oh, take a tour. Usually several of us would rent a car and drive around. We would go into small shops to buy souvenirs and postcards. We also went into restaurants. Later I prepared scrapbooks, using snapshots and postcards from the cruises. I wrote home to my parents about those experiences, and the letters were published in a local newspaper. Excerpts from those newspapers also wound up in the scrapbooks. My observations were boyish--the impressions of a 19- and 20-year-old.

Q: What was Panama like in those years?

Captain Edwards: Very glamorous, in a way. I was glad to go there because of the canal's reputation. Three or four of us hired a car to go out to old Panama. And just to go through the canal itself was quite a thing; I was really impressed.

The Panama Canal Zone had big commissaries in those days, and we were able to buy things at very good, reduced prices. Perfume for women was one of them; we bought Chanel number five for one-fourth or one-fifth of what it cost out in town.

I bought my father a so-called Panama hat. They're made, actually, in Ecuador, and they're woven underwater. They're very finely woven. But they're sold in Panama, and therefore called Panama hats. Well, I bought my father one for $15.00 or $20.00, and he had it blocked at Dayton, Ohio. The owner of the shop said, "Mr. James Cox wanted to buy your hat. He offered $100.00 for it." Well, James Cox ran for President back in 1920, with Franklin D. Roosevelt as his Vice President. I bought that hat in 1920, and my father died a year and a half or two years later, so I inherited the hat again. I finally gave it to the Smithsonian. They were happy to get it, said they didn't have a hat of that type in their collection.

That black elephant up there in the middle [on a shelf in Edwards's office], I bought that and gave it to my mother. After her death, I inherited it. That's the sort of thing that you got at greatly reduced prices. Everybody bought Panama things. Every kid bought a pillow with Panama on it at one of these tourist traps.

But to go through the canal, that was a very impressive experience.

Q: What do you recall about Hawaii?

Captain Edwards: Back then Hawaii was still a place to go to. Now it's a tourist trap. I was there two weeks, and we went around the island, of course, and did all kinds of things. I was very, very taken by Hawaii. In fact, I said if I ever got married I was going on a honeymoon there. But now it's overrun with tourists.

Q: It's still a pleasant place to go.

Captain Edwards: Yes. There are five islands that are inhabited, open to the public: Kauai, Oahu, Molokai, Maui, and Hawaii. The Lanai Pineapple Island and Nihau are closed to the general public. I was very, very delighted to go to Hawaii, because I had heard a lot about it, and it was up to form in those days. In those days the only hotel of any note was the old Moana, on Waikiki Beach.

The Outrigger Canoe Club was there, next to it. Right now the Royal Hawaiian, built in 1926, is where the beach club used to be. And the beach club then moved out toward Diamond Head. I had my first wristwatch then. I bought it before I came out, and I forgot about it when I went swimming. I dived in, wristwatch and all, so that ended my wristwatch. But it was a very glamorous place to go.

Q: There was a bar at the entrance to the harbor. Had that been cleared out by then?

Captain Edwards: Yes. We went into Pearl Harbor itself

and tied up at Ten-Ten Dock, which was to starboard after you entered the harbor. We took the narrow-gauge train downtown. It was quite a thing.

Those were really glamorous ports. That was my first big trip away from home. And Seattle and Frisco, in turn, were very delightful. Next my ship went to San Diego. San Diego then had 150,000 people and was a delightful town. Now it's the second-largest city in California, over a million. It's just beyond belief. That's taken the glamour out of it. Then, on the way home, we coaled ship again at Guantanamo Bay.

Q: How did the sailors in the crews of these ships react to the midshipmen?

Captain Edwards: Most of them were semi-hostile. And some of the warrant officers and the lieutenants who had been sailors were unfriendly. There was a chasm there between the two groups, unfortunately. The midshipmen didn't start it, but the former enlisted men were resentful of our presence. But the older petty officers, most of them first class, were understanding. And the academy officers, the regulars, were also understanding. But we had a lot of ex-enlisted men who became lieutenants overnight during World War I. They were sort of unfriendly. Once, when we lined up to go ashore, the officer of the deck culled out all the sailors and sent them ashore in the first boat. So we stood in the sun and waited for our turn. You know, just harassment.

Q: Which ship was that, do you recall?

Captain Edwards: Oh, it was the <u>Michigan</u>, I think. But all of them were more or less like that--not friendly. We didn't come to blows or anything like that. It was just mental harassment.

Q: Well, your life probably got easier later, say, during the first-class cruise, didn't it?

Captain Edwards: Yes, because we stood junior-officer-of-the-deck watches then.

Q: So they treated you with more respect.

Captain Edwards: That's right. We were standing watches as the assistant navigator or the junior officer of the deck. Or if we were at sea alone, one of us would be the officer of the deck. And in engineering we'd stand engineering officer of the watch. But the junior midshipmen were still on a par with the enlisted men, and there was some friction there.

Q: What do you remember about standing bridge watches as a first classman in the Florida?

Captain Edwards: Well, we were the flagship. Our usual jobs were running a stadimeter, taking bearings with the pelorus, relaying the leadsman's readings, and whatever else we were ordered to do. I remember the skipper, Captain George E. Gelm. He wasn't too friendly. I recall his bawling out the officer of the deck in the presence of the bridge watch, which wasn't too good.

They were instructive cruises. I'm glad I took them, but they weren't a bowl of cherries.

Q: Did you get any experience in ship handling?

Captain Edwards: No, except during the final ten days of the first-class cruise. They had midshipman officers who stood the watches of the ship's officers. Some of my classmates were midshipman admiral, midshipman captain, or midshipman department head, and so on. Somehow I got to be a midshipman chief machinist's mate, down in the control engine room. I was on the main throttle. Maybe that forewarned me of what I was going to do the rest of my life, more or less.

Q: Are there any midshipman officers you remember specifically from those cruises?

Captain Edwards: A man named Higgins was chosen as the midshipman admiral.* He resigned early in the game. He became a reserve officer who came back on duty in World War II. Later he shifted over to the regulars again after being out of the Navy for almost 20 years. Somehow, he knew the right people at the right time. He got to be a captain, USN. And then he got to be a rear admiral.** That made me sore as hell, because the rest of us had been in the regular Navy for all this time. He was a nice guy and all that, but he didn't merit that kind of recognition. After all, he didn't think enough of the Navy to stay in it. He got out and worked for an elevator company or something.

We had six ships in this midshipman squadron. I don't recall any of the so-called midshipman captains who distinguished themselves later in life.

Q: Do you remember anything about senior officers from the training squadron?

---
*Midshipman Ronald D. Higgins, USN.
**Higgins resigned in 1924, then was a reserve officer from 1925 to 1946. In 1946, as a captain, he was returned to the regular Navy. He received a tombstone promotion to rear admiral when he retired in 1957.

F. A. Edwards #1 - 64

Captain Edwards: Yes, they tell a funny story about Captain Craven, who was skipper of the South Carolina in 1921; it's just a story.* He later commanded the Yangtze patrol boats in China. He was invited by his British counterpart to a certain cocktail party. The invitation was addressed to himself and his wife. Craven had a grown daughter with him in his household, but the British admiral didn't know that. So Craven sent back a note: "We have a daughter."

The Brit came back and said, "Congratulations." He thought Craven was announcing the birth of a daughter.

Another one I remember was the flag officer in the Florida, Rear Admiral Newton McCully.** He had been in Russia for a long time before the war, quite a character. The funny thing about him was that every morning when we were at anchor, before breakfast he'd go out on the boat boom, dive in, and take a swim around the ship. Here he was in his 50s. Later on, after he retired, he bought himself a subchaser and converted it into a personal yacht. He had several Russian children he had adopted.

The ships' officers were, I'll say, average of that period. As I said, we resented this partial treatment by some of these mustangs who had chips on their shoulders.***

---
*Captain Thomas T. Craven, USN.
**Rear Admiral Newton A. McCully, USN, was embarked in the Florida as Commander Control Force Atlantic Fleet.
***"Mustang" is a term for an enlisted man who becomes an officer without going through college or the Naval Academy.

Now, that had all disappeared, as far as I know, by the time World War II came along. In the North Carolina we received approximately 15 graduates of the Naval Academy. The same day of the same week we got 15 reserve officers. Everything went along fine. They got along splendidly. However, in the older times there was a feeling between the reserve officers and the regulars. Fortunately, that has long since disappeared, to my knowledge.

Q: The Florida was a somewhat newer ship than those other two. In what ways could you tell that she was more modern?

Captain Edwards: For one thing, she was a turbine drive. The other two ships had reciprocating, up-and-down engine drives. All three were coal-burners. And the Florida had five turrets--five two-gun turrets. The Michigan class only had four two-gun turrets. Then they went on to the New York and Texas; each of them had six two-gun turrets. They were adding up as they went along, 12-inch guns to 14-inch guns and eventually to 16-inch guns. The North Carolina, for example, had nine 16-inch/45-caliber guns.

Q: Were you topside in any of these three ships when they fired their main batteries?

Captain Edwards: Not topside, no. I was down below, and the ships jumped sideways, it seemed, a couple of feet. Whether that was true, that was the impression we had--that it jumped sideways.

Q: How much emphasis was there on spit and polish in those ships?

Captain Edwards: A lot. I was glad of it in a way, because we kept the ships clean, and people were proud of those ships. Nowadays, I think, in general they're not as clean, and perhaps they're not as proud of their ships as they were in those days. That's my impression only. We had a Friday below-decks inspection, where everybody had a chance to see the spaces. Nowadays the ships are so damn big and things are so busy that the senior officers don't get a chance to get down below or see people. In my day they had a routine Saturday morning inspection topside. And we had to appear like we were clean and proud of our ship. But nowadays the skipper might see two or three divisions; that's all, if he sees any of them. The exec takes over the job. So, I say, the Navy's gotten too big to be clean and be proud. I'm not trying to downgrade the Navy, but, I mean, it's gotten too big for its britches.

And the same way at the Naval Academy--the Naval Academy is too big. We should be at 3,000 instead of

4,500. We've lost the personal touch in many cases. I'm not against women as such, but I'm against women at the Naval Academy or in any military academy. Why in God's world a woman would want to go to a military academy is beyond me. I just can't understand it. It compromises the function of the academy; it really does.

Many congressmen voted for that change only because they felt that if they did not vote for it they wouldn't get reelected, due to the womenfolks. That's a terrible thing. These women can become officers like they used to--go to college and then have one year of a breaking-in period, and they do fine in certain jobs. In fact, in certain jobs they do better than men do, but they shouldn't be taking men's military billets. For example, if you have 80 or 100 women in a class of 1,000, they are taking billets for which 80 or 100 other men might be taking combat billets. I wouldn't want to be in a combat ship with a bunch of women.

Q: Well, I don't think the clock's going to turn back on that.

Captain Edwards: But they're compromising the function of the Naval Academy. I hate the thought. During the war I had a lot of enlisted women and officers who went their way and did a damn good job for me, but I didn't have them in combat billets. They were in administrative billets. I think it's utterly wrong that they be there, but this women's lib now runs affairs. Nobody asked me, but that's my opinion.

Q: Did you see much rivalry between these battleships when you were in these cruises?

Captain Edwards: Oh, yes, a lot of rivalry. We had race-boat crews and baseball teams. Every ship had a couple of racing cutters. They'd go out before breakfast in the morning in port and row all around. Those men were in excellent shape. Each ship's crew would bet their last dime on the race results. Now I don't think anybody gives a damn.

Q: Were you in leadership positions as an upper classman?

Captain Edwards: During first class year they had two sets of stripers. In the first set I was a three-striper; that meant I commanded a company. In those days a company was about 300 men; we had eight of them. In the second period I was a permanent two-striper. They had two groups of stripers each year to give more people a chance to operate as midshipman officers.

Q: Do you have any other recollections from your Naval Academy years?

Captain Edwards: I enjoyed being and was proud of being a midshipman. We had a handful of, we'll say, skunks. But 99% or 98% were very fine guys, and they proved themselves as time went on. My class had a very high percentage of high rank. For example, at one time Arleigh Burke was the Chief of Naval Operations. His Vice Chief, Don Felt, was another classmate.* The Commander in Chief Atlantic was Dennison.** And two of the bureau chiefs were also classmates. So we had a slightly higher than average rank structure in our class, and the usual percentage of captains and commanders and so forth.

Q: Just to wind up your Naval Academy recollections, what do you recall about your graduation?

Captain Edwards: One of the things that happened just before graduation was that we got our copies of the Lucky Bag.*** We went to Memorial Hall and laid out the books,

---

*Admiral Harry Donald Felt, USN, served as Vice Chief of Naval Operations, 1956-58, and Commander in Chief Pacific, 1958-64. His oral history is in the Naval Institute collection.
**Admiral Robert E. Dennison, USN, was Commander in Chief Atlantic and Commander in Chief Atlantic Fleet, 1960-63. His oral history is in the Naval Institute collection.
***Lucky Bag is the name of the Naval Academy yearbook put out by each class.

open at the pages showing our individual photographs and biographies. Then we walked around the tables, autographing each one. Thereby, I got a couple of hundred signatures a day or so prior to graduation. In that book are a lot of names that are precious to me. Secretary of the Navy Denby was the guest speaker for the graduation ceremony.* (Incidentally, his son, Edwin Denby, Jr., was in the class of '35, and I taught him in engineering classes.)

After having worked very hard for those four years, this was it. My family came up and attended. I was very proud to be a graduate of the academy. It isn't the best school in the world probably, but it's one of the best--I hope.

Q: Well, it was very highly respected back then, certainly.

Captain Edwards: The college boys didn't like the academy. Among other things they called it a trade school and the "Boat and Barge Club," but one year four graduates received Rhodes scholarships. Anyhow, it was 70 years ago. There was a certain animosity between the general colleges and the Naval Academy and the Military Academy. I think it was

---

*Edwin Denby was Secretary of the Navy from 6 March 1921 to 19 March 1924. He resigned in the wake of allegations that he was not sufficiently vigilant during the Teapot Dome scandal involving leases of Navy oil reserves.

terrible, but there was. I think there's less of that now. I hope there is, because, after all, we're all in the same boat. You may get there by a separate route, but you're all in the same boat. It was a grueling experience, and yet a very satisfying experience, if I may use those terms.

Q: The more grueling it is, probably the more satisfying.

Captain Edwards: Well, I used to say to myself, "If So-and-so ahead of me can make it, I can make it."

Q: You mentioned earlier that you were skinny as a plebe. Had you filled out over the course of the four years at Annapolis?

Captain Edwards: No, when I graduated I weighed 155 pounds. All our uniforms were sized to that, leaving no spare cloth. So after a year and a half or two years as officers, we all had to get new trousers and sometimes new outfits entirely. That was done intentionally by the tailors so they'd have more business two years down the line.

When we started out as ensigns, we had the full outfit of dress and work and everyday uniforms. In fact, they took about 20 bucks out of our amount available each month.

In four years' time we had accumulated over $1,000. In those days that was quite a bit of money, so we could buy a complete outfit. Now, that John Paul Jones hat up there [on the wall of his office in the apartment] and those two dress epaulets and that dress buckle were part of that outfit.* Those and the sword are all I have left.

When World War II came along, that old-fashioned full-dress uniform went by the board, and we just had normal work or service uniforms. But until then we had the "works," including what we called railroad trousers with big, wide stripes down the trouser legs. We had evening dress; full dress day, which was a long frock coat that came down knee length; and we had that cocked hat. We were something to behold. I've got some snapshots somewhere showing me in that outfit.

I graduated in June 1923 and then married that following August to a young lady that I met under, I'll say, interesting circumstances. A high school classmate of mine had left school in his junior year, in 1917, and joined the Marines.** When I next ran into him, I was a midshipman, and he was in Washington, D.C., going to an officers' training school. He knew I couldn't come out and see him, so he asked if he could come down and see me at

---

*The hat to which he refers was phased out with the coming of World War II. It was a throwback to the sailing-ship Navy, dark blue decorated with gold.
**After the United States declared war in April 1917, many Americans rushed to enlist in the armed forces

the academy. Then he added, "P.S. May I bring a girlfriend?"

I said, "Sure." Well, we had a very interesting, very pleasant day. He later got his commission and went out to Guam on duty. He wrote me a letter after a while and gave me the address and name of this girl he had brought with him to the academy. He said she was a nice girl and wrote, "Look her up sometime."

So I wrote back and said, "Thanks, pal, but I already married her."

Her name was Bessie McKichan; that's a Scottish name. She had a good sense of humor. She said she'd have to, to have married me. She still, at that time, had a slight Scottish burr, which she lost as the years went along.

Q: Was she born in Scotland?

Captain Edwards: No, she was born in Michigan, after her parents came over to Canada and then went to the United States. So she had a lot of Scottish characteristics--good ones, by the way. We were married 52 years.

Interview Number 2 with Captain Frederick A. Edwards,
U.S. Navy (Retired)

Place: Captain Edwards's Apartment, Annapolis, Maryland

Date: Tuesday, 11 February 1992

Interviewer: Paul Stillwell

Q: Captain, in our previous interview you said that your first commanding officer after graduation from the academy was Captain Ralph Earle. He was the same man who wrote the magazine article that inspired you to go into the Navy. How did you happen to report to him?

Captain Edwards: Actually, I had orders to the <u>West Virginia</u>, which was then our newest battleship. However, the ship was still several months away from being commissioned. That would have meant sitting around in the Navy yard, so the Bureau of Navigation farmed out perhaps 15 or 20 of us ensigns to various activities on the East Coast. This gave us some useful familiarization with things we would encounter on board ship.

The only extended temporary duty of that tour was at the Naval Torpedo Station at Newport, Rhode Island, and Captain Earle was in command. So it was a real pleasure for my new wife and me to call on the Earles. We knew their daughter for the rest of our naval careers. Calling on seniors was a good custom.

Q: What are some of the details that you learned up there in Newport?

Captain Edwards: The *West Virginia* was the last of the battleships to have torpedo tubes. They were for the Mark 7, Mod 4, which was a special long-range torpedo. However, within a period of five years, or probably less, the Navy decided it didn't need torpedoes on battleships anymore. But that was still in the future, so six of us junior officers had to go through this torpedo school, and it was useful. The submarine torpedo was a smaller, faster torpedo, but we didn't spend any time with that. We just spent time on this long-range Mark 7, Mod 4, which had a pistol-type exploder.

Q: What do you recall about the town of Newport from being up there in 1923?

Captain Edwards: It was a most interesting town. It was once the playground of the wealthy people of New York City. The rich people had what they called cottages. Well, the "cottages" were mansions by any other description. And there was a walkway all the way around front. The only way you could see them really was to take this walkway, which they call the Cliff Walk.

Q: Yes, I've been on that.

Captain Edwards: It's at least four or five miles long. I took that several times and saw these beautiful big homes. Later I went through the Vanderbilt home, called the Breakers. I've been through that two or three times. It was really very interesting, and in those days they still had tennis matches there at the Casino. I attended some of them.

It was a very historic town too. Back in pre-Revolutionary War days an Englishman wrote a letter to a friend of his in New York City. On the envelope he put in parentheses, "Near Newport." Newport is very proud of that letter. I think it was in a museum up there. So that showed the importance of Newport in those days. It was bigger and more important than New York.

Q: What was the relationship between the young naval officers such as yourself and some of these Newporters?

Captain Edwards: Well, we were, you might say, ignored.

Q: You were in your own world.

Captain Edwards: Two worlds entirely.

Q: Did you have any association with the war college people in 1923?

Captain Edwards: I went up there to hear a few lectures. Years later, when I was material officer on the Atlantic Fleet staff, I gave a lecture to the war college on material maintenance of the fleet. I gave this lecture up there for an hour, and I expected that would be it, but, believe it or not, I had an extra hour answering questions. That was my only contact.

Q: Where else did you go besides Newport?

Captain Edwards: Another place we visited before we reported to the ship was the Naval Proving Ground down at Dahlgren, Virginia. The skipper there was Captain Bloch, who later became commander in chief.* Well, we 15 or 20 ensigns reported in. About a day and a half later, Captain Bloch sent for the senior man in our group and said, "Young man, are you familiar with article number so-and-so of the Navy Regulations?" This fellow Daisley, who stood number two in our class, said, "Well, sir, not by number, but I'm probably familiar with its contents."**

---
*Captain Claude C. Bloch, USN. As a four-star admiral, Bloch was Commander in Chief U.S. Fleet, 1938-40.
**Ensign Gordon W. Daisley, USN.

Bloch said, "Well, go out and refresh your memory."

Daisley went out and read the regulation, which directed that you were to call on the commanding officer within 24 hours after reporting. At 4:30 that afternoon all 15 or 20 of us were lined up to call on Captain and Mrs. Bloch.

Q: Bloch couldn't just come out straight and tell you to do it.

Captain Edwards: No, no. It was, "Are you familiar with article number so-and-so of Navy Regulations?" That business of calling went on until World War II. It died with World War II.

Q: Did you think that was a useful practice?

Captain Edwards: With a smaller Navy, yes, it was good. You got to meet the wife, as well as any children.

Q: Any specifics you remember from the proving ground, beyond the calls on Captain Bloch?

Captain Edwards: We saw them shooting 16-inch guns downrange 25 miles. Separately they were firing 5-inch/25s for antiaircraft. They were being proven for installation later on, of course, aboard ship. That was interesting, really.

Q: That testing must have been sort of theoretical by 1923 because they knew they weren't going to finish that next generation of battleships.

Captain Edwards: They had the 16-inch guns well along. In fact, many of those guns later were turned over to the Army coast artillery. During that time I also spent a week at the gun factory in Washington, and people there were then converting many of those guns for Army use. So the guns themselves were already built.

Q: Did you see any tests of those guns against armor plate?

Captain Edwards: No, I did not witness it. I saw pictures of them and descriptions, but I personally did not witness those tests.

Q: What else do you remember about that stop in Washington?

Captain Edwards: I spent a week at the optical school at the Washington Navy Yard, and that was interesting. They

F. A. Edwards #2 - 80

were German range-finder optics primarily, Bausch & Lomb. The company had a U.S. factory, but they were basically German optics. So I was very glad to spend a week there.

Q: Was that the stereoscopic thing that you had a split image and tried to bring it together?

Captain Edwards: Yes.

Q: And when it was in focus, that indicated the range.

Captain Edwards: That's right. Actually, there were two different types of range finders at that time. One type was the split image; the other involved changing lens angles. One lens was trained straight at the target, and the other lens was varied at an angle to determine the range. Each turret had its own range finder; then there was a special one up on top of the conning tower for the convenience of the skipper.

Q: But that would be a shorter base.

Captain Edwards: That's right, but the captain had full control. On the long-base range finders on the turrets he didn't have control. He had to ask for the range, and then they had to train the turret and report the range. Here he

F. A. Edwards #2 - 81

had an immediate answer--maybe not as good an answer but an immediate answer as to what the range was.

Q: It's always satisfying to be able to see for yourself.

Captain Edwards: That's right.

Q: It sounds as if the Navy, with this sort of training, was trying to give you a well-rounded background before you got into your ship.

Captain Edwards: That's right, and which I appreciated very much.

Q: Well, after all this you finally got to the West Virginia.

Captain Edwards: Yes, the West Virginia was then just being completed.* We were fitted out first at the Norfolk Navy Yard. Then we went to New York Navy Yard to get our fire control equipment, which was being built at the Ford Instrument Company on Long Island.

---

*USS West Virginia (BB-48) was commissioned 1 December 1923. She had a displacement of 33,590 tons, was 624 feet long, and 97 feet in the beam. She had a top speed of 21 knots and a main battery of eight 16-inch guns. She was the last battleship completed by the U.S. Navy until 1941.

Q: What sorts of things did you do during that month in Norfolk to get the ship ready?

Captain Edwards: The supply officer, of course, was probably the busiest one, getting the stores aboard. As far as I was concerned, there was very little for me to do, because I was in communications, and communications were few and far between, except via telegram. When we got up to New York, we were right near Governors Island on a foggy morning. We damn near had a collision there. A tug was towing a big barge, and he was almost out of control. We had to back down full, and we missed him by 50 feet or something like that.

Q: What was the nature of your duties on board ship?

Captain Edwards: I was in the communications division.

Q: Please tell me what you remember about communications in that era.

Captain Edwards: Most of my time, believe it or not, was spent teaching candidates for third class radioman. We went out into the New York Navy Yard, to a certain building, every day for five days a week, for half a day at a time. My job was to teach them the textbook requirements, and I had a first class radioman to teach them the nuts and bolts of being radiomen third class.

Q: What was included in that book learning?

Captain Edwards: Communication instructions. There was a regular manual that we used as a textbook.

Q: Radio was still pretty primitive in that era. What do you remember specifically about the equipment?

Captain Edwards: Well, actually, I didn't get to use the equipment on the ship because we were in a Navy yard all this time.

Q: They had a rotating-spark system.

Captain Edwards: I think it was a spark-gap type, which these days, of course, is obsolete. They removed it a couple of years later and installed vacuum-tube units.

Q: How reliable was the equipment back then?

Captain Edwards: It was reliable but short in range and noisy--a lot of static. Static reminds me of a story about Admiral Charles Badger, who was Commander in Chief of the

Atlantic Fleet several years earlier.* He was bedeviled by the constant alibi of messages being incomplete because of static. So he finally put out a tongue-in-cheek dispatch, which I saw a copy of many years later. It said, "Hereafter in the Atlantic Fleet there will be no more static."

Q: You described your torpedo instruction up at Newport. Did you ever get down into the torpedo room in the West Virginia?

Captain Edwards: Yes, just as a spectator. But I was not in gunnery.

Q: Well, what are your recollections of being in that space?

Captain Edwards: It was very large, and it was in the very toe of the ship. It was a triangular-shaped space that came down right in the bow of the ship, so it was forward of the armor belt. It was very clean and very well kept up. But, as I told you, that type of torpedo outlived its usefulness. A few years later, torpedoing by battleships became a no-no.

---

*Rear Admiral Charles J. Badger, USN, was Commander in Chief Atlantic Fleet from January 1913 to September 1914.

F. A. Edwards #2 - 85

Q: Well, it didn't make sense, because the guns had much longer range.

Captain Edwards: That's right.

Q: That torpedo room probably went from one side of the ship all the way to the other so torpedoes could be fired out both sides.

Captain Edwards: Yes.

Q: How were torpedoes stored in the torpedo room?

Captain Edwards: In racks, is all I can say. I don't recall the details, but they were king-size racks. They had chain falls to bring the torpedoes over into position. The torpedomen used big torpedo slides to get them into the tubes. They were fired by compressed air.

Q: They went out perpendicular to the axis of the ship, and then the gyros took over.

Captain Edwards: I don't think it was perpendicular. I think it was perhaps 45 degrees.

F. A. Edwards #2 - 86

Q: Oh, really?

Captain Edwards: I won't stand on that, but it's my recollection they were approximately 45 degrees, because otherwise they would get an awful side thrust when they were being launched if they were 90 degrees.

Q: There was a protective sleeve that went out to impede that water resistance.

Captain Edwards: That's right. They withdrew it, of course, as soon as the torpedo was fired.

Q: Were you involved in any of the shipyard work on the West Virginia?

Captain Edwards: No, not there. The work in New York was primarily the installation of the fire control gear. That involved all kinds of cables. My God, thousands of feet of cable were running all over the ship, besides the instruments.

Q: So she hadn't really been finished.

Captain Edwards: No. She was finished as a ship but not as a warship until she got that work in New York.

During our time in the New York Navy Yard, I saw the battleship Illinois being stripped down.* It really hurt to see that beautiful old ship with all her armor being taken off and put on the dock. I was then in the latest battleship afloat, and here was the Illinois, one of the oldest afloat, being dismantled.

Q: I know that the Illinois had a structure like a wooden house built on the hull. Did the Granite State have something like that too when you saw her in 1919?

Captain Edwards: Yes, they built a house over it that looked like a barn. It was essentially a barracks ship.

On the same pier with the Illinois were armor sections and turret sections from two ships of the new South Dakota class. They had been under construction there but were being scrapped under the terms of the Washington Naval Treaty of 1922.** Before that, when the West Virginia was still fitting out down in Norfolk, I saw the North

---

*The USS Illinois (BB-7), first commissioned in 1901, ended her active service in 1919 and was loaned by the Navy to the New York Naval Militia. Under the terms of the Washington Naval Treaty of 1922 she was demilitarized and fitted out as a training ship. She was renamed Prairie State in 1941 to free the name Illinois for a new ship.
**Because of the treaty, construction of the following ships was canceled in February 1922: South Dakota (BB-49) and Indiana (BB-50), being built at New York; Montana (BB-51) at Mare Island Navy Yard; North Carolina (BB-52) at Norfolk Navy Yard; Iowa (BB-53) at Newport News Shipbuilding; and Massachusetts (BB-54) at Bethlehem Steel, Quincy, Massachusetts.

Carolina, which was another one of those scrapped ships, up on the ways. I walked by her one day. I never realized that 18 years later I would be the chief engineer of her successor, the new North Carolina. It was really very saddening to see these beautiful hulls being scrapped in the name of peace.

Q: Do you recall any specifics from seeing the ships of the South Dakota class being dismantled?

Captain Edwards: I saw these big slabs of armor plate parked all around the yard. Some of it was 15-inch, 16-inch armor plate. The conning tower was 16-inch plate.

Q: Did you see the men with cutting torches cutting these hulks apart?

Captain Edwards: Yes, and they were dismembering a Navy, really. These were beautiful ships, but they were never completed.

Q: What do you remember about the commissioning of the West Virginia?

Captain Edwards: Well, it was at the Norfolk Navy Yard, Portsmouth, Virginia, and it was a very memorable occasion.

She was the last battleship of the World War I period. We had all kinds of rank there, of course. The executive officer of West Virginia was later CNO, Molly Stark.* We were at Portsmouth for a month or less. Then we moved up to the New York Navy Yard.

Q: Do you remember anything about Commander Stark as the exec?

Captain Edwards: No, because he was too far above me to get in personal contact. When the North Carolina was commissioned in 1941 Stark was then an admiral and CNO. He made the North Carolina's commissioning speech, so I saw him on that occasion.

Q: Well, in between that time, Stark commanded that ship too.**

Captain Edwards: I believe he did, later on.

Q: Captain Senn was the first skipper of the West Virginia.*** Did you know him?

---
*Commander Harold R. Stark, USN, was later Chief of Naval Operations from 1 August 1939 to 26 March 1942.
**As a captain, Stark commanded the West Virginia from 14 December 1933 to 17 October 1934.
***Captain Thomas J. Senn, USN.

Captain Edwards: Just, well, casually, because, after all, I was only an ensign and he was a four-stripe skipper.

Q: What impressions did you have?

Captain Edwards: He was a very nice gentleman. By the way, he had a son in the Navy, then a lieutenant. I just met him casually. He was a submarine officer at that time.* Well, there again, my wife and I went out and called on Captain and Mrs. Senn at their temporary home in New York.

Q: Did you view a call on Captain and Mrs. Senn, for example, as a duty or a pleasure?

Captain Edwards: Well, we had it as a duty, but it became a pleasure.

I'll tell you another funny experience. While the ship was there at the yard, the commandant was Cy Plunkett.** Oh, he was a very tough guy. He had commanded the naval railroad gun battery in France during World War I. Well, he had a daughter, Julia. One evening it so happened several ensigns of the West Virginia were up at her house. The admiral was somewhere else at the time.

---
*Lieutenant Elliott M. Senn, USN, was then commanding officer of the submarine S-18.
**Rear Admiral Charles P. Plunkett, USN, Commandant New York Navy Yard and Commandant Third Naval District.

These ensigns were playing the piano and singing, among other things. The admiral came back, oh, we'll say 11:00 o'clock, and this going on in the living room was against his desire. So he called Julia out in the hall, and he said, in a deep, booming voice, "Julia, tell those young fools to go home." [Laughter] They went home.

Q: Did you have the opportunity to go out on liberty any in the city of New York?

Captain Edwards: Oh, yes. I had duty in New York five different times, so I got to know it too well in some ways. It was dangerous in parts in those days.

Q: Was it dangerous around Brooklyn?

Captain Edwards: Yes, Brooklyn Navy Yard--it was really dangerous.

Q: Did you have to take security precautions?

Captain Edwards: We had shore patrols. In fact, every day we had a shore patrol in town, certain areas. And I, in my turn, used to have shore patrol there. That was to protect our people from being mugged, especially on paydays. In fact, the paymaster would never announce publicly when our payday was, because that would be inviting muggings and sluggings of sailors with their money. In fact, one of our JOs was mugged in a subway. He was thrown on the tracks, but he scrambled up off the tracks in time. Otherwise, he'd have been killed.

The Navy yard was in a tough neighborhood. I always took precautions. I never just blindly went into an area. I took a streetcar or taxicab to get through that area. It was surrounded then by hooks and crooks and all kinds of people like that. But then they built high-rises, public high-rises there, and got a better group of people. But many of the employees, the older men in particular, didn't live in that area. They lived out in the suburbs and commuted in.

I remember a funny story about a court-martial at that time. The prosecutor pointed to the defendant and asked a prostitute, "Do you recognize this man?"

And this old gal said, "I don't recognize him, but I recognize him, him, and him."

Q: Was she pointing at the members of the court?

Captain Edwards: Members of the court.

Q: Did you get over to Manhattan during that period?

Captain Edwards: Yes.

Q: What were the attractions there?

Captain Edwards: Well, I guess the same attractions they have now, the theater district and all kinds of nightclubs. I avoided the nightclubs for two reasons; I didn't have the money, and they were more or less dangerous for young people.

Q: What do you remember about the modern equipment in the West Virginia?

Captain Edwards: The West Virginia was electric drive, and in those days that was the thing to be--electric drive. But when the battleships were flooded at Pearl Harbor, they decided that they didn't want any more electric drive, because they had to rewind these motors and generators, which was a terrific job. A steam turbine plant could be just flushed out and dried out and within a matter of weeks could have been put back in commission. So that was the end of the era of electric drive.

Q: How long did this whole process last at New York?

Captain Edwards: The ship was in the yard for probably six months. We were only supposed to be there a couple of months, but it wound up taking much longer than expected to finish the installation of the fire-control equipment. With the class of '24 coming up over the horizon, they just took most of us from the class of '23 and shipped us to the active fleet. The only ones who stayed were four or five ensigns who were going to the school at the Ford Instrument Company school. They were to be in the West Virginia's fire control division. So while she was still in the New York yard, I was transferred over to the Nevada.*

Q: What do you remember about the operations of the Nevada while you were on board, where you went and so forth?

Captain Edwards: The first stop from New York was at Culebra Island, Puerto Rico, as I recall. Next we went to Guantanamo Bay, Panama, and through the Panama Canal. Then we went up to San Pedro and the Long Beach area. We were based there for about three months. We had gunfire exercises and so forth off there every couple of weeks. We were offshore there every other week or so, firing a practice.

---

*USS Nevada (BB-36) was commissioned 11 March 1916. She had a displacement of 27,590 tons, was 583 feet long, and 85 feet in the beam. She had a top speed of 20.5 knots and a main battery of ten 14-inch guns. After service in both World Wars, she was sunk in atomic bomb tests in 1946.

I remember one time I was invited to dinner by some ex-schoolmate up in L.A. My wife and I accepted. The ship was supposed to get in around 3:00 o'clock or 4:00 o'clock, so we'd have 6:00 o'clock or 7:00 o'clock dinner. But the fog came in, and we got in at 8:00 or 9:00 o'clock at night. No apology could be accepted. As far as I was concerned, yes, but for a civilian to miss dinner and not even call until midnight was pretty bad.

Q: What do you recall about formation steaming?

Captain Edwards: Well, steaming in those days was usually 500 yards apart, in column, and in order to avoid the underwater effects of the ship ahead we'd be off on the quarter. The number-two ship would be on the port quarter, we'll say, and number-three ship on the starboard. They were staggered back and forth, so you wouldn't have all this turbulence, which would affect steering and steaming. That was the normal interval, 500 yards, but, of course, that wasn't 500 yards between ships; that was 500 yards between masts--mainmasts or foremasts, whatever the case may be. So you were closer than that.

It was mostly uneventful, except for one time when we were coming into Long Beach to anchor in column. The _Pennsylvania_ was ahead of us; she was our division flag. The _Nevada_ was supposed to back down and anchor so many yards astern of the Pennsylvania. The main throttlemen had been having trouble. Up came the word from the engine room that the astern throttle was stuck, and we were headed for the stern of the Pennsylvania. Fortunately, a few seconds later the word came back that everything was all right. But in the meantime, the skipper, who was John Luby, was jumping up and down on the bridge, because here we were approaching collision with the Pennsylvania.* He didn't have room enough to shear out.

Q: That would get his attention, all right.

Captain Edwards: John Luby was a lieutenant at Veracruz in 1914. I have a book on the subject here. Luby was appointed postmaster at Veracruz during the limited time there until the Army arrived.**

Q: What were your living arrangements like on board those two battleships?

Captain Edwards: We had roommates, of course. They were double staterooms. And we had a JO mess. All those older ships had a JO mess.

---

*Captain John McL. Luby, USN, commanded the Nevada from December 1922 to September 1924
**See Jack Sweetman, The Landing at Veracruz 1914 (Annapolis: Naval Institute Press, 1968), page 151. Luby was a commander at the time.

Q: What was the camaraderie like in that JO mess?

Captain Edwards: It was pretty good, except obviously I was a newcomer in the Nevada. The rest of the boys on board had been on there for a while. You normally were two years in a JO mess in those days. The class of '22 had been there for a year and a half. My classmates had been there for eight months. So I was a fish out of water. Nothing personal, but the fact was that I was excluded from the innermost councils.

Q: Did that feeling gradually subside?

Captain Edwards: Oh, yes. There was nothing personal about it. But here I was, the fresh guy on board, and they were all old salts, in their opinions.

Q: I've heard that in some of those JO messes it was almost like a college fraternity house, a lot of pranks and informal living.

Captain Edwards: Yes, it was informal living. There was a lot of stuff that went on there which is not for the book.

Q: Well, you can put some of it on the record. The

statute of limitations has expired.

Captain Edwards: I was married, so I didn't socialize much with these bachelors, who were out on the town on every opportunity. Somewhere I have a picture of all of them. They were average, run of the mine. Well, Moosbrugger got himself in print later on.* Moosbrugger was a destroyer division commander who was under Arleigh Burke in some of those Guadalcanal actions. I think he was probably the most distinguished of our group--about 20 of us.

Q: What do you remember of him as a junior officer?

Captain Edwards: Uneventful, just another JO. Nice guy but nothing special.

Q: How well did the crew of the Nevada and the junior officers observe Prohibition?

Captain Edwards: Since the statute of limitations has expired, I can tell you about one occasion when we were anchored at Guantanamo Bay, Cuba, for a couple of weeks. Certain people would go ashore and order liquor to be delivered to the ship. The deliveries took place sometime

---

*Ensign Frederick Moosbrugger, USN, served in the Nevada and later was a decorated destroyer division commander in the Solomons in 1943. He retired as a tombstone vice admiral.

between midnight and 6:00 in the morning. We called them "hawsepipe deliveries." One of the recipients was Harley Cope of the class of '20.* He had a very large order. The staterooms had drawers under the bunks. His were completely full, and he had some hidden overhead as well. He was not a drunk, but he was conveying this stuff north for party use later on. That's the biggest delivery I ever recall. Like I say, it went on more or less often. I always played it safe. I never did that sort of thing.

Q: Well, I guess it was legal to buy it in Cuba but not to have it on board ship.

Captain Edwards: Oh, yes. The conveying and the distributing of it was the problem. Perhaps 25% of our officers bought liquor for use later, but I never risked that myself.

Of course, whenever the ship got up to San Pedro, or wherever she went, the feds came aboard and inspected the rooms. The smugglers had to get rid of that stuff or put it somewhere else between the time we anchored and the time the inspection group came aboard. It was a little ticklish.

---

*Lieutenant (junior grade) Harley F. Cope, USN. Cope was commanding officer of the USS Tennessee (BB-43) in 1945 and later a prolific author. He wrote three editions of Command at Sea (1943, 1951, and 1966); Battle Submerged (1951); and The Petty Officer's Guide (1953). He was coauthor of Our Navy, a Fighting Team (1943).

F. A. Edwards #2 - 100

Q: Did the senior officers more or less wink at this on board ship?

Captain Edwards: How senior, I can't say. I know at least one who had a good load himself. But whether the captain or the exec knew anything, I'm not in position to say.

Q: You mentioned previously that you served with Les Kniskern during your time in the Nevada.* What do you recall about him?

Captain Edwards: Well, Les was a very smart guy. In fact, he became a naval constructor later. He was then just about to go to MIT.** I was never personally fond of him, but there was nothing wrong with him. I was assigned to him, and I performed duties under him. We had nothing personal beyond that, nothing social, except for maybe cocktail parties. Later he commanded Naval Shipyard Philadelphia, and I think he was in charge of design in BuShips.***

---
*Ensign Leslie A. Kniskern, USN. He later achieved flag rank as an engineering duty officer.
**MIT--Massachusetts Institute of Technology.
***After World War II Rear Admiral Kniskern commanded the naval shipyards at Puget Sound, Philadelphia, and New York. Following his retirement from active duty in 1958 he became a vice president with Gibbs & Cox, naval architects and marine engineers.

Q: What was the fire control setup like in the Nevada back then?

Captain Edwards: Well, by modern standards, crude. I can't give you the marks and mods of the instruments, but they were state of the art at that time.

Q: Well, you had the optical range finders, for one thing.

Captain Edwards: Oh, yes, that's right. By the way, we were in port off and on at Long Beach, and we would take those occasions to calibrate our turret range finders. I once was in charge of calibrating them, and I went around to report to my gunnery officer, Lieutenant Commander Comerford, that we had finished the job.* He said, "If the first salvo of this long-range practice coming up is not a straddle, you'd better reach for your hat." Fortunately, it was a straddle.**

That year we had long-range target practice of about 20,000 or 25,000 yards. The first salvo, of course, was on range finders. After that we spotted and corrected as necessary. So, as I say, the gunnery officer put me on the spot with his warning.

---
*Lieutenant Commander Francis J. Comerford, USN.
**A straddle amounted to an initial salvo of projectiles in which some fell just short of the target and some just beyond. In other words, the shooting was almost on target and needed only slight additional corrections to hit.

Q: Were you working with air spotters then?

Captain Edwards: Certain practices, yes, we had air spotters. But this first long-range practice was only on range finders.

I want to mention a funny thing. We were out for one practice when we had some civilian engineers aboard to look at various systems. One man was a sanitation engineer from L.A. He was there to look at our sanitation arrangements. Also, he particularly wanted to see this firing, so where would the best place be? We told him to go up to a certain place about halfway up the foremast to get a good view. He did. Turret two, as I recall, was elevated almost at maximum angle. When the turret fired, a blast of hot air, smoke, and flame came right back. When he came down, his eyebrows were singed; his hair was singed; his coat was torn. That was a dirty trick, but he had a closeup view.

Q: What was your specific job down in the plotting room during these gunnery practices?

Captain Edwards: There were duplicate sets of plotting room instruments which could control the forward and after turrets, separately or combined. Kniskern had the forward set, and I had the after set. Ballistic corrections and "spots" were set in the plotting room instruments and transmitted automatically to the turrets. They were confirmed via headset telephones.

Q: I've heard about this business of matching pointers. Was that what they did?

Captain Edwards: Yes, they matched pointers. You turned your pointer to a certain position, and the men in the turret turned theirs. At the same time, you gave a telephone backup. It's so long ago--that was 1924--that I am unable to give you any intelligent comments on fire control gear at that time. Also, it was only a three-month deal.

Q: There was just one plotting room, wasn't there?

Captain Edwards: One plotting room, and you went down through a tube to get there. A ladder was inside of a tube, so if the ship were ever sinking, your only exit would be up this damn tube. You were way down below the waterline.

One gunnery practice I especially remember was a day we were out firing at long range. During that exercise I was observer in, I think, the Tennessee, and the Mississippi was also in the column. We were in a column of three ships, and they were firing in succession--BOOM, and maybe a couple of minutes later, BOOM, BOOM--one, two, and three. Then I noticed that one ship didn't fire. I was down in the plotting room. We wondered why, and the next time again it didn't fire. Then we got the word to secure; we were proceeding to port. When we got up on deck, we found out that the Mississippi had had a turret explosion.* She kept that turret headed to seaward because they still had a load in one of the guns, I believe. So we went in, and she finally fired offshore before we went in.

That was the most notable occasion of that period. We had a Navy public funeral there. Most of us went ashore in formation to attend the funeral at Trona Field. Admiral Pratt delivered the funeral address.** It was a masterful delivery. He later became CNO.

Q: Was there a renewed emphasis on safety after that?

Captain Edwards: Oh, yes. As I recall, they did not have full air pressure for blowing out the tube after the

---

*During practice on 12 June 1924, turret two of the USS Mississippi (BB-41) exploded, killing 48 and injuring 9.
**Rear Admiral William V. Pratt, USN, Commander Battleship Division Four, delivered the speech at a public funeral on the Navy athletic field at San Pedro on 17 June 1924. Pratt served as Chief of Naval Operations, 1930-33.

preceding firing.* Some burning embers from the preceding round ignited the next powder charge before the breech was closed. One of my classmates got his tail burned. He was down in one of the levels below. When that happened up there, he dived down to the next deck. He didn't wait for the ladder; he just dived down, and he got his tail singed as he went down. We lost one classmate, Marcus Erwin.** There were about three officers lost in that casualty. Well, again, the Mississippi had the same problem during World War II, and I believe due to the same reason. They either cut off the valve, or they didn't have enough air pressure to blow it clear.

Q: Well, one explanation I heard for the 1924 explosion was that there was a strong wind, and it blew back down the barrel.

Captain Edwards: I've heard that too. But they should have had enough air pressure to overcome that. Usually around 75 pounds per square inch was enough to clear it. You hear all sorts of stories, depending on whom you talk to.

---

*Turrets were equipped with a gas-ejection air system for just this purpose--to blow out the residue from the firing of the preceding round so there would be no burning embers remaining to ignite the next powder charge in the barrel.
**Ensign Marcus Erwin, Jr., USN.

Q: How well did the Nevada do in shooting?

Captain Edwards: She did very well. One time she cracked a gun slide in one of her main battery turrets.* The only place that could fix it was the Navy yard, so the ship was ordered to Bremerton. The yard at the same time regunned the whole turret and renewed the slide. In view of the fact that the ship was going to the yard ahead of schedule, they decided to have the admiral's quarterly inspection the morning we left.

Someone told me the night before that I would have the machine-gun squad, even though I knew nothing about machine guns. I went ashore that night to tell my wife that we were going to move in the morning. I took along a copy of The Bluejackets' Manual because it had a chapter on machine guns.** That night I boned up on machine guns. The next morning I got the assigned men dressed and outfitted with guns. I had time to teach them only two things: "action forward" and "action rear." That's all I knew. When the time came, the admiral and his minions came aboard, and the crew fell in on the big fantail there. When the admiral approached, I said, "Action forward."

---
*A slide was a heavy piece of metal that held the breech ends of the 14-inch guns. In battleships of the Nevada's vintage, the slide had all the guns of an individual turret in it, so they all elevated and depressed together.
**The Bluejackets' Manual, which has been published by the U.S. Naval Institute in various editions over the years, has long been considered the "bible" for Navy enlisted men. It is a basic textbook and reference volume on a wide variety of naval subjects.

He said, "Deploy your squad."

I said, "Action rear." And they all knew that.

Then he said, "Very well, very well," and marched on. Otherwise, I would have been kicked out of the Navy! I had several narrow escapes like that.

Q: Well, this was the whole idea of the Navy training, that you had the ability to look in the book and get the answers.

Captain Edwards: Well, as I said, I was not a gunner, but I did whatever the exec or another senior officer told me to do. That move was on the spur of the moment. I told my wife, "Pack up." And the next day the Nevada sailed for Bremerton. Bess, of course, caught a train and then joined me up there. That's when I was transferred to the Henshaw (DD-278), which had just arrived in the yard.*

Q: What kind of adjustments did you have to make in going from a battleship to a four-stack destroyer?

Captain Edwards: Well, you became more responsible. On a battleship I was only the junior officer of the deck. The

---

*USS Henshaw (DD-278) was commissioned 10 December 1919. She had a standard displacement of 1,200 tons, was 314 feet long, and 31 feet in the beam. She had a top speed of 35 knots and a main battery of four 4-inch guns.

lieutenants and senior jaygees were officers of the deck.* On a destroyer, you were it. When we were about to leave the yard at Bremerton, I asked the executive officer whom I would stand watch with. He said, "Stand watch with? Hell, you're _it_." I'd never stood a senior officer watch under way, and here I was, cold sweat on my brow. I was keeping the ship 250 yards from the ship ahead of me, mast to mast.

Q: You grow up in a hurry that way.

Captain Edwards: You grow up in a hurry. When you were making 25 knots and you had 250 yards between your mast and another mast, there wasn't too much leeway. You had to be on your toes. Many a time I stood there with a stadimeter in one hand and an eye on the ship ahead so there'd be no collision.**

Q: That short interval between ships helped account for how many destroyers piled up at Point Honda.***

---
*Jaygees--lieutenants (junior grade).
**A stadimeter is a device for calculating the range to another ship by measuring the distance between the mast top and horizon.
***On 8 September 1923 seven ships of Destroyer Squadron 11 were wrecked when they ran aground at Point Honda, near Santa Barbara, California, steaming in column in heavy fog. Among the ships lost was the USS Young (DD-312).

Captain Edwards: That's right, they were close and steaming at 20 knots, I believe. And they were inshore of what they thought they were. In fact, the reason I joined the Henshaw at that yard was that she replaced the Young, which was lost at Point Honda. We had quite a few survivors on board who transferred from the Young.

Q: What was your job in the Henshaw?

Captain Edwards: I was ordered as the assistant engineer officer to Virgie Korns, class of '20.* Virgie was a great guy, personally and also professionally. He later became a commodore. I always said that I learned nothing new, and I forgot nothing that I learned on the Henshaw under him. Slightly exaggerated but a good story.

Up to the time I went to the Henshaw and was assigned to engineering, I'd seen nothing or heard nothing that I particularly liked in the Navy. I was not impressed, so I just did my job. That changed when I met up with Virgie Korns, who was a good engineer. I followed him around like a dog, because he was such a great guy. That's why I stayed in engineering for the next 30 years. From 1924 to '54 I did nothing but engineering, because I had met Virgie Korns and worked with him. In fact, I had the longest continuous time in engineering of any member of my Naval Academy class.

---
*Lieutenant (junior grade) Virgil E. Korns, USN.

F. A. Edwards #2 - 110

Q: What was the skipper like?

Captain Edwards: The skipper was a very nice gentleman. He was Turner F. Caldwell, class of 1905.* We called him "Paddy," although not to his face. Paddy Caldwell was a fine guy. He was not a top-notch naval officer, but he was a good guy to live with. His son later became an aviator and a vice admiral.** I first met that son when we came back from the '25 cruise. He was 11 or 12 years old, and the captain had him aboard for lunch one day. Later on, I was an instructor in engineering at the academy, and young Caldwell was a midshipman.

Commander Caldwell was not demanding. He wanted you to perform the job, but he was not abrasive about it. We had a voice tube from the bridge down to the wardroom. One day a lieutenant, an ex-warrant officer, was standing watch up there. He nervously called down, "Ship bearing [so-and-so and so forth]."

The skipper yelled back, "Dodge her." But Caldwell eased up and took a look from the well deck. He wanted to make damn sure it was all right. But that was his reply, "Dodge her."

He was a nice guy; I got along with him fine.

---
*Commander Turner F. Caldwell, USN.
**Turner F. Caldwell, Jr., graduated in the Naval Academy class of 1935.

Wentworth, class of '12, was exec, and he fleeted up to skipper when Caldwell left.* Wentworth was an officer and a gentleman of the highest type. We got to know him socially. In fact, his wife was very helpful when our son was born. At that time the Henshaw was up at Bremerton, Washington, for overhaul. The captain's wife was a good friend of my wife's, so she came out, got Bess, took her home, and did all the chores that I would normally have done.** I say, slightly exaggerated, that I saw my son for the first time when I got back from that trip, and he opened the door and let me in. [Laughter]

Q: Did the naval hospitals provide care for dependents in that era?

Captain Edwards: They provided it if you paid the bill. It was not free. Afterwards I believe they had free deliveries at naval hospitals only.

Q: Was your son born in a naval hospital?

Captain Edwards: Yes, the Navy hospital at San Diego. They've since built a brand-new one. In fact, I was out there about three years ago, and it was just then being

---

*Lieutenant Commander Ralph S. Wentworth, USN.
**The captain's wife was Gladys Wentworth.

completed. It's quite a big hospital and a very nice one, because that area is very, very Navy.

San Diego almost reminds me of Newport, Rhode Island, before World War I. There was a saying that there were so many Navy people in town that you couldn't throw a rock and not hit a retired rear admiral. Since then Norfolk has, I believe, taken over that honor.

Q: Did the Navy just send you a bill after the baby was born?

Captain Edwards: No, you paid it when you checked out.

Q: I see. They weren't even going to trust you out the door.

Captain Edwards: I got along with Wentworth so well that several years later he asked me to be his exec when he was taking command of the Hull.* I told him I appreciated the request, but I'd had a 4.0 relationship with him as engineer officer, and I didn't want to go with him as exec and spoil it.

---

*Commander Wentworth was the first commanding officer of the USS Hull (DD-350) when she went into commission on 11 January 1935. The Hull was one of three destroyers sunk in a typhoon off the Philippines on 18 December 1944.

F. A. Edwards #2 - 113

Q: Why did you think you'd spoil it?

Captain Edwards: I was not cut out to be a deck officer. I stood scores of deck watches, but I had no love for the job. I was an engineer. I loved engineering. I didn't want to be on the bridge as navigator and spoil it. We remained very good friends with the Wentworths throughout the years. I used to visit them when they lived on Pendennis Mount, just across the river from Annapolis. Eventually, I went to their funerals.

Wentworth was the highest caliber of officer, and I often felt that he got a bum deal in a way. Shortly before World War II, he commanded the light cruiser Nashville. Then during the war he was shuttled over to London on Stark's staff, which killed him for any promotion.* He became a commodore, but that was just a face-saving device. He, in my opinion, should have been an admiral without any trouble at all, but he didn't have the right guys for him at the right time.

Q: What was the engineering plant like in the Henshaw?

Captain Edwards: She had four boilers, with saturated steam at a pressure of 250 pounds per square inch. They

---
*Shortly before the United States got into active combat in World War II, Captain Wentworth became a special naval observer in London, later a member of the staff of Admiral Harold R. Stark, Commander U.S. Naval Forces in Europe. In that role Wentworth was one of the principal planners for the Allied invasion of North Africa in 1942.

didn't have superheat then. Two engines, port and starboard. They had a high-pressure turbine, an intermediate-pressure turbine, and a low-pressure turbine. In one end of the low-pressure turbine was the astern turbine. It was an elementary plant, as plants go. We had a total of 26,000 shaft horsepower, and we had about 32 knots top speed. We could make 25-26 knots on two boilers, which we did many times. We used four boilers only for certain occasions. Once a year we had to make two full-power runs of four hours each. After an overhaul, I had the real pleasure of being on board the first time that ship had ever made her required full power.

Q: Anything you remember about the reduction gears or the shafts or the propellers?

Captain Edwards: Well, once in Gatun Lake the <u>Henshaw</u> hit a submerged timber. Apparently it had been there since they built the canal and flooded the lake. We had to hump until we got back to Bremerton some months later, and there we got a new propeller. Wentworth was the skipper then and he told me he thought, "There ends my naval career," when he hit that damn thing. It wasn't his fault at all. It was just one of those spots out of maybe 100 acres, and he was unlucky enough to hit it.

F. A. Edwards #2 - 115

Q: One of the great things about going through Gatun Lake was the opportunity for a fresh-water washdown.

Captain Edwards: We frequently would go up there and stay there for several days, simply to get a washdown and get the barnacles to fall off.

Q: What do you recall about the annual engineering competition?

Captain Edwards: At first, as I said, I was Virgie Korns's assistant. Later I became chief engineer myself. In both jobs I indoctrinated my crew, as well as the skipper and the officer of the deck, on using the least oil to do a given job. If we were in formation, we'd steam at whatever speed we had to steam, but you could make a difference in independent runs. For example, if we were going to make a run by ourselves from San Diego to Mare Island, I had two good spots in my turbine throttle settings with which I could make the best score. There was no logical reason for it, but in the high-pressure turbine were eight or nine valves to be opened up, one after the other, to get more speed. Well, I found out at 20 knots, when I had only number eight open, I made a score of 120%, based on the fuel allowance. So I told the skipper the speed should be 20 knots, and he concurred. Other ships didn't know that, so they'd go at maybe 105% score. Well, that was part of the game--nothing wrong with it. I didn't pass that word around, because things were very competitive. And your fitness report depended on it somewhat. The results of the engineering competition could either help or harm, as the case may be.

I had the engineering crew with me, and we got the red E for greatest improvement. And they were proud of themselves; they were proud of their ship. And when they had inspections, they looked like men. Their uniforms were tops; their haircuts and shaves were proper. Everything was fine. When they got a recruit on board, they worked on him. He was soon indoctrinated. So, I say, there was a spirit of competitiveness, which we've lost, I'm sorry to say.

Q: Well, it may not be as bad as you suspect.

Captain Edwards: I hope it isn't. But, I say, I compare what I went through with and what I think goes on now. I've been aboard some of the newer destroyers, and they were dirty. They didn't show any spirit which I'd been associated with. When I got out of the Navy and sat on the sidelines, I said, "Thank God I'm retired." Because I thought things were maybe going downhill. My son retired as a captain, a generation later.* When he retired, he said, "Thank God I'm retired." So maybe the curve is still going down. I don't know. I say that for a laugh only.

Q: Well, it's interesting you mention that, because your classmate Elliott Strauss, whom I interviewed, said essentially the same thing in almost the same words.** And he said he heard his father talking to one of his contemporaries and saying the same thing.

Captain Edwards: I knew Elliott, of course, and I knew his father too. I think that's true; our class has seen the best of the Navy. At least I think we have. I hope it gets better; it will get better as it gets smaller. I think we expanded beyond the limits of efficiency. I guess they can say that the Navy's gone to hell and all that, but there's some truth in it. I don't think it's all true. I think when we get a smaller Navy, as we will in the next five years or so, we'll have a better Navy, per ship and per man.

Q: Well, let's hope so.

---

*The son is Captain Frederick A. Edwards, Jr., USN (Ret.), who graduated from the Naval Academy in the class of 1950 and retired from active duty in 1977.
**Rear Admiral Elliott B. Strauss, USN (Ret.), expressed this thought in his own Naval Institute oral history. His father was Admiral Joseph Strauss.

Captain Edwards: It won't necessarily be good overall as a smaller Navy, but at least we'll have a better small-ship Navy.

Q: Sometimes I think the rivalry between ships back in those years became competition for the sake of competition, rather than toward a desired end.

Captain Edwards: Well, I think that was probably true in some cases. I knew one destroyer, a four-stacker, in my division that decided it wanted to beat the racket, and it did. The score was a combination of hits at the range and time to get those hits off. Well, this particular destroyer, the _Sinclair_, went out and fired a torpedo practice in a matter of seconds or something like that. And they had a couple of hits. They stood number one. Another ship had more hits but worse time, so to keep everybody happy they made them co-champs. That was wrong, but that was only one case in four years that I knew of.

I'll tell you a funny story about the _Henshaw_. I was the chief engineer when we were firing a night gunnery practice. For that practice the gunnery officer needed a gunfire spotter. I was not familiar with the practice, but he insisted. My eyes had not yet adjusted to the darkness when the first round was fired, so I said, "No change," meaning no adjustments in aiming were to be made before firing the next round. Later, on the reverse course, I was looking over the wrong side of the ship when another blast was fired. Again, I said, "No change." Fortunately, we were on target on both legs and had the best score in the division, which was pure luck. I didn't tell that story for some time.

During some of these battle problems they had circular formations. The main battle force was in the center, and then we had station circles. For example, if you were number 6.10, that meant you were on circle 6, and you were number 10 ship. The commander in chief who was running the critique asked one skipper, "Who were you?" And he answered up with "606," which was the same number as a sexual lotion that was sold before the war. It was to ensure that one would not get syphilis or "Old Joe." Everybody laughed like hell, because that ship's station number was the number of this lotion that was being sold all over the world as a cure-all for venereal diseases.

Q: How well did the Henshaw ride?

Captain Edwards: Well, for 1,200 tons she rode well. We wanted to be sure we were trimmed by the stern. Otherwise, the ship would dig in. So we'd make sure we were down by the stern, maybe a couple of feet. She was 310 feet long, so that wasn't very much. As she speeded up, she tended to rise. Otherwise, if you got in a heavy sea, you'd get a blizzard of spray.

Q: Well, it depends on which direction you're going relative to the waves too.

Captain Edwards: That's right.

Q: Did you have problems with seasickness at all?

Captain Edwards: I was only seasick once in my life. I was in the Henshaw. We were going up to Frisco from San Diego in a very stiff sea. The Omaha was our flag; she was riding along very nicely.* She was a 7,000-ton ship. I had the 8:00 to 12:00 watch, so I had a breakfast of eggs and bacon at 7:00-7:30. When I got up on the bridge, I knew something had slipped. I just turned around, and I painted the forward stack yellow. We were only a 1,200-ton ship, and we were plunging. Finally, the formation slowed down, and after I got rid of my eggs, I was all right. But that was the only time for me.

Q: Well, it's good to be blessed with that kind of a stomach when you're serving in a destroyer.

---
*The flagship for Destroyer Squadrons Battle Fleet, the type commander, was the light cruiser Omaha (CL-4), which bore a resemblance to the four-stack destroyers but had a much larger displacement.

Captain Edwards: Well, I'll tell you, when I went to a second destroyer, the Mahan, I didn't feel as comfortable as I did ten years before. Now, back to the Henshaw. I had a machinist's mate, throttleman, who had a lot of guts. He used to get deathly seasick, but he stood at the throttle and he did his job. He had a bucket in front of him, and he just heaved into a bucket of water. He insisted on standing his full four-hour watch. Now, you've got to have a lot of guts to do that. That's the sort of thing that made you love your shipmates, respect them. And if they're engineers, even more so.

We would be inspected by our admiral once in a while, and we always got 4.0 reports. These people would work half the night getting ready for an inspection the next morning. I didn't tell them to. They were down there cleaning, scrubbing, painting, and polishing to get that ship ready for inspection. They did it on their own.

Q: I would suspect, though, that there wasn't as high a degree of spit and polish in a destroyer as in a battleship.

Captain Edwards: No, but my engineering spaces were spotless. Now, you got a lot of salt water topside, and you had to hose down pretty often. Down below, of course, you didn't have that. You just had moisture and oil.

Q: What were some of the missions the Henshaw had?

Captain Edwards: Well, among many things we were carrier plane guards for the big ships, the Lexington and Saratoga.* I saw the Langley at sea many times, but I don't think we ever plane-guarded her.**

Q: What difference did it make in fleet operations when the big carriers came in and you got more aviation?

Captain Edwards: Well, more of us had to be plane guards in order to pick up some guy who got dunked. We had to be very careful when we operated with the carriers. They would change speed or course with no warning whatsoever, and you had to be alert all the time. We also went out on simulated attacks on other destroyers or on big ships. We'd lay smoke screens, and we'd fire guns and torpedoes. It was as realistic as it could be under those conditions.

Speaking of operations, I recall that one year when I

---

*The U.S. Navy's first two large aircraft carriers, the Lexington (CV-2) and Saratoga (CV-3), were commissioned in late 1927, a few months before Edwards left the Henshaw.
**The USS Langley (CV-1), commissioned in 1922, was the U.S. Navy's first aircraft carrier.

was in the Henshaw she was just out of overhaul at the Puget Sound Navy Yard. We joined a massive search group in the Eastern Pacific, looking for missing planes of the Dole flight from San Francisco to Hawaii. We spent a week or ten days there. We operated at high speeds during daylight, shifted zones at night, and then resumed searches on the following days. We found nothing. Planes made air searches, and ships made surface searches but to no avail. One of the missing planes ditched west of the islands and later sailed back to Hawaii.

Q: Those attacks sound pretty exciting.

Captain Edwards: Well, they were. I mainly supervised the engineering plant. I stood deck watch only when we were going to be under way more than 24 hours. It was interesting and all that sort of thing, but my heart wasn't in it.

Q: Why do you think that was?

Captain Edwards: I don't know. It wasn't until I reported aboard the Henshaw and was assigned to engineering that I had any type of duty that I was really enthusiastic about.

Q: But you just felt comfortable with it.

Captain Edwards: That's right. You could physically see and hear what was going on. If you were up on the bridge you were isolated, obviously, from the direct contact. I said many times that I would rather be the chief engineer of a ship than the skipper. I felt sorry for the poor old skipper. He was up there, stuck by himself and having to take his information from at least one voice, maybe two voices down. Well, I got mine directly. I lived with my people. As ships got bigger, I stood engineering watches. In a destroyer I didn't stand engineering watches. I had a chief machinist's mate or a chief water tender stand the watches, although I was available 24 hours a day.

Q: How capable were the enlisted men in that era?

Captain Edwards: Very capable, more capable than they are now.

Q: Why do you say that?

Captain Edwards: Because they were trained longer, and there were not so many of them. Now they are overmanned in many phases. I only had 35 to 40 engineers, and they all had to produce. Otherwise, we were in trouble. And we had engineering competitions in those days. The first year I got the red E for the greatest improvement out of 100 or so destroyers. The Henshaw stood number five. We had six ships in our division. There were three divisions of six each, plus a squadron flagship.* That's 19 ships to a squadron. At that time we had two squadrons in DesPac, Destroyers Pacific. There were approximately 125 destroyers in commission at that time.

Q: I suspect those sailors weren't as well educated as today's, but they had a lot of practical knowledge.

Captain Edwards: Yes, many of them were deficient in book learning, but they were excellent with their hands.

Q: One thing I've heard about those old engineering plants is that you could tell when something was wrong by the sound of it.

Captain Edwards: That's correct. My room was right next to the forward bulkhead of the forward fireroom. And I could feel certain vibrations and hear the noises. I knew what was going on more or less by vibrations. And we did things, I'll say, together. When we fueled ship, all my people got on the job. It was respect, up the hill and down the hill. If you get that, then you have something.

---
*The Henshaw was in Destroyer Division 30; Destroyer Squadron 11 also included Division 31 and Division 32.

Q: What was involved in fueling? Was that strictly in port?

Captain Edwards: No, we fueled under way. Seomtimes we'd be under way two weeks at a time. When you were out of fuel, you fueled.

Q: What method did you use for that?

Captain Edwards: We went alongside an oiler or a large combatant ship, and they had a long hose and a crane holding the hose up. We had fueling trunks. It took about two or three men to hold that hose down, and they held it into a trunk until it was full.

Q: So there wasn't any kind of a coupling to hold it?

Captain Edwards: No. We fueled forward or aft at the same time. And, I say, it took about three men to hold the hose down with 100 or more pounds pressure on it. Before we fueled we emptied certain tanks and filled other tanks so we could take the maximum amount of fuel from the oiler. That was perfected pre-World War II. That was routine, let me say.

Q: Well, I think they still had a spring line between the fueling ship and the destroyer, didn't they?

Captain Edwards: They used to lace the ships together, more or less. At first they had four lines. Then they got to two lines. Finally they got down to one line, and that's all you needed. The chief quartermaster had to be on the wheel and watch it very carefully. The skipper was up there too. We just had one line, and you eased out to a 45-degree angle, maybe 50 feet or so. But the fueling at sea was routine before World War II.

Q: Did you have any mishaps doing that?

Captain Edwards: Well, once in a while.

Q: What do you recall about maintenance, both in your destroyer base and at the shipyard?

Captain Edwards: Always something to do. When the four-stackers came into port in San Diego, our tender, the _Melville_, was there. We always took over one or more valves or pieces of pipe which were falling apart or leaking during our last week at sea. And I, being the engineer officer, had to stay aboard to fuel. The rest of the officers went ashore for liberty over the weekend. I stayed aboard often because I had to fuel the ship, and I never knew when the barge was coming alongside. It had to fuel maybe 15-20 ships, so I waited my turn. I felt like I was at sea although I was in port.

The shipyard at Bremerton did the big jobs. Since the destroyer base at San Diego serviced only the ships that were out of commission, we were supposed to do what they called the "fleet maintenance" between yard visits. That included things that were within our capacity, both manual and with cranes. You had to have chain falls to do certain things, of course, such as hoist pumps and turbine casings. We repaired all the small valves, say, 5-inch, 6-inch, and lower. The yard repaired the big valves. The tender did most of the brazing, welding, and pipe jobs--except for the new ships. The new ships got to the temperatures where the flanges were welded tight. There were no gaskets. Expansion was accommodated by the expansion of these piping loops. We had 950 degrees steam temperature.

Now they talk about all this asbestos. I'll call it crap. Because I lived with asbestos half of my life. We had varnished coverings over it, so there was no problem at all. These people ashore are making jobs for themselves, tearing out all this asbestos in schools and office buildings. It's a farce; it really is. If it's covered, there's no leakage.

Q: What else do you recall about the yard at Bremerton?

Captain Edwards: Once the Henshaw was under overhaul at Bremerton and was across the pier from the Arizona. The Arizona had ordered some long monel metal stock, which they aimed to use to make pump rods for reciprocating pumps. Well, during the night one of these big bars disappeared off the pier, and all hell broke loose. I was accused of stealing it, and I, of course, pleaded innocent and offered access to my ship. So the Arizona people came over and looked all over and couldn't find the missing bar. But still they knew that somehow, somewhere, I'd had something to do with it. Later on, I found out I had. Some of my people had stolen that bar and put it under a bunch of boiler tubes in a rack in a corner of one of the firerooms. It was not visible during the search. So I really had inherited these potential pump rods.

I had three chief machinist's mates, one of whom had studied for the priesthood. Somewhere along the line he decided he didn't want to become a priest. Instead he enlisted in the Navy and became a hell of a good machinist. In fact, he was the best one I ever saw, before and after. We had only a 12-inch lathe and a small drill press. For anything beyond his little machine shop's capacity he would go to a larger ship or a repair ship and make what he wanted. So he was my lifeblood, really, for repairs.

Q: What kinds of things did he make?

Captain Edwards: Mostly pump rods. In those days most of our auxiliaries were reciprocating, and after you installed these tight, leak-proof glands, in months or weeks, if not days, the rods would become worn. You'd have excessive leakage, so you'd have to renew the rod. To buy a rod was excessive because you had to go back to the factory. So he kept the ship going, really, with these reciprocating rods. He got stock, and he would cut it down, in length and also diameter, to suit the particular pump that needed a new rod.

He had a beautiful handwriting. In fact, I kept a machinery log in which I had him head all the pages.

Q: How important was that business of keeping machinery records?

Captain Edwards: As far as I was concerned, it was very important. Everybody had his own method, I'll call it. I kept a very nice book for my machinery, because I had to know what had gone before in order to be intelligent in going ahead.

Just as an aside, I remember another kind of record

keeping in the Henshaw. I'll tell you a funny story about the ship's chief commissary steward. He probably got through the fourth or fifth grade, but he was a hell of a good cook. He went up the line and got to be a chief commissary steward. Well, the mess records in his office consisted of daily and weekly entries and so forth. Finally, the next-to-last column was "Odds and Ends." And the last one was "More Odds and Ends." We didn't have an adding machine; he had to do all this adding by hand. So he would add up number one and two and put the sum of those two at the bottom of the second column. He progressively added the newly formed columns to the right until a final sum was reached. Before I left, the ship got an adding machine. But that was how crude the thing was previously.

Q: Did you do preventive maintenance in those years?

Captain Edwards: Oh, yes.

Q: What did that include?

Captain Edwards: Well, it depends on what you're talking about. If you're talking about a boiler, it meant cleaning the tubes of soot and also renewing brick work in the firebox. For the pumps it meant renewing the rods if necessary or valves or trimming the valves to restore their

100% contact. On piping we would renew gaskets which were leaking. We normally would have two weeks alongside the tender and four weeks operating. That was the peacetime norm. After about four weeks we began to need more than band-aids. Then we'd go alongside the tender for services.

Q: What was the tender able to provide that you couldn't?

Captain Edwards: Larger machinery and more materials.

Q: Did you carry a fairly adequate stock of repair parts?

Captain Edwards: Yes. One of the first things I did as assistant after I reported was to find out the authorized spare parts list for each piece of equipment and get them either from Navy stock or even factory stock. The ship had been bled white as a source of materials for other ships. She had been out of commission at the San Diego destroyer base before she rejoined the fleet as a replacement for the Young.

Q: So she was cannibalized.

Captain Edwards: She was cannibalized; that's right. And so my job right away was to get our spare parts on board. Now, a couple of times we had to officially lie. Somebody would have trouble, and they'd send out a dispatch, asking for anybody who had parts for this and that unit to let them know. I told the captain, "Sorry, I don't have any." I had them, but I knew damn well that if I gave up mine and needed them, I'd have an awful time getting them back. So I used to lie officially to preserve my own domain.

Q: Officially you didn't have them, but unofficially you did.

Captain Edwards: That's right. And I told you we also had to watch these midnight requisitions by other ships. We had to have a deck watch in port. Otherwise, we'd lose our deck valves and spanner wrenches. Even though the wrenches had chains on them, they would disappear overnight unless somebody was on deck.

Q: Sailors have a great deal of ingenuity.

Captain Edwards: That's right. Well, you had to have that to live.

Q: How hot did it get down in those spaces under way?

Captain Edwards: In the newer ships we had spot ventilation. We had a certain area where the watch stander

F. A. Edwards #2 - 134

stood normally. And there it was probably, oh, 100 degrees, more or less. But then if you got ready to do something, you went to places that got as high as 130 to 140 degrees. You didn't ventilate the whole space; you couldn't. There was spot ventilation, watch-stander ventilation. And there, I say, it was comfortable. We always took water and salt tablets. And I would sometimes be down in the control engine room for eight to ten hours and have meals sent down to me. I was at the watch station there, where you were reasonably cool.

Q: Did sailors in that era have problems with their hearing because of the noise of the machinery?

Captain Edwards: No, I don't recall that, but they had trouble with TB on certain ships.* The four-stack cruisers, the Omaha class, had a lot of people who were sent to Fitzsimmons General Hospital, Denver. They were overheated, because they didn't have enough ventilation. But in later years I don't recall too much noise. I don't recall a single man going to a hospital because of noise.

Q: Well, it's not the most pleasant kind of life. How did you get guys to reenlist in that situation?

---
*TB--Tuberculosis.

Captain Edwards: They liked it.

Q: Why did they like it?

Captain Edwards: They were stupid--like I was!

Q: It just appealed to them.

Captain Edwards: That's it. You get the bug. For example, if you get the railroad bug, you become a railroad engineer. I say that because I once had a friend who was a railroad division superintendent out in San Diego. He said, "Once the bug bites you, why, you're an engineer." There's no logical, reasonable explanation. I could see and hear and had a certain amount of control over this machinery, and I liked that.

Q: My experience serving in a small ship is there's much more sense of family than in a large one.

Captain Edwards: I loved ships, because I felt they were part of me. I felt the same on every ship. I was four years on the Henshaw, and I just hated to leave. Now, that's hard to explain to some outsider, but it's true. Even now I get letters from enlisted men who were on ships with me.

Q: What were your accommodations like in the _Henshaw_?

Captain Edwards: I had a single high bunk that took up a third of the stateroom. I had clothes lockers, of course. Then I had a locker for hanging clothes. We had to have a clothes press in it that you could push up against the clothes on the horizontal bar. Otherwise, these uniforms would wear themselves threadbare by moving back and forth due to the rolling of the ship. So when you put your jacket or whatnot in this locker, you always pushed the press tight.

Q: I'd be interested in what life was like for a young married couple in the San Diego area in the mid-Twenties.

Captain Edwards: It was very pleasant but limited. My wife and I lived on my salary and allowances, which--believe it or not--came to about $2,100. In those days, that bought quite a bit. And it was very pleasant. San Diego then was a city of 150,000.

I was based in San Diego for four years, but we did a lot of traveling. One year we were on the East Coast for four or five months and back again. In fact, one year I figured we were in our home port of San Diego, I think it was three or four days. The rest of the time we were either on the East Coast, overhauling at Bremerton, at sea, Hawaii, and so forth. So the term "home port" was not too meaningful.

Q: Why did you spend so much time on the East Coast?

Captain Edwards: We had fleet maneuvers. One year they'd be on the East Coast, and then they'd be on the West Coast. We all went through the Panama Canal, back and forth. In fact, I got to feel like I was more or less the mayor of Colon. [Laughter]

Panama was a wild place. Once I saw a line at least a block long, maybe a block and a half long, waiting to be serviced by the same woman or her relief. They had what they called cribs. These gals would get in these cribs, spread themselves open, and the next man up performed. She used a towel, and then she took on the next man. After five or six men, she'd get up and go away and another girl came. I heard that these gals came from the States on contract. They worked so many weeks at a time.

Q: How much privacy was there for that? Were these cribs in a building?

Captain Edwards: Oh, yes, but the doors were wide open. Anybody passing along the sidewalk could look in and know

F. A. Edwards #2 - 138

what was going on. That was par for the course for some people.

Q: It demeans what we think of as lovemaking.

Captain Edwards: That was not love. That was relief of passion.

Q: I gather that the shore patrol did not interfere in any way with this prostitution.

Captain Edwards: No, no, it was accepted practice.

Q: Was it legal in Panama?

Captain Edwards: Anything was legal in Panama at that time.

Q: Or if not legal, not enforced.

Captain Edwards: Right. I can almost say the same thing applies right now. Anything goes in Panama.

These sailors were country boys, most of them, away from the States for the first time. Many of them would get some beer in their bellies, and under the hot sun they would start staggering around and then pass out. The shore patrol brought them back in small trucks to a place we called the bullpen. It was maybe half an acre, something like that. They'd collect them in there until the ships' boats came in from, say, the Tennessee. These men had tags on them, so the shore patrol would pick up all the Tennessee men, throw them in the boat, and send them out to the ship. The people there would hoist the sailors up on deck by boat crane, put the hose on them, and bring them to. That was typical back in the Twenties.

Q: You probably didn't have to punish them, because they felt so bad afterward from the effects of all that.

Captain Edwards: We didn't punish them unless they got into fights. If they got into fights, then they would go to captain's mast.

Q: Did you go along on that fleet cruise in 1925 to Australia?

Captain Edwards: No, I went as far as Hawaii. My division was due for overhaul back at Bremerton in the middle of that, so we went out to Hawaii and then returned to the West Coast. The fleet went on down south on the first day of July, or thereabouts. We stayed out there about two months and then went on back to Bremerton for overhaul.

Before that we went down to Maui and fired practices. We'd get up at daybreak, go out and have a torpedo practice or a gun practice, and come back in around 1:00 o'clock in the afternoon. Then we'd go ashore or go swimming. It really was an ideal place and time. Very nice.

Q: The Navy held a fleet problem on the way out to Hawaii that year. What do you remember about the way the fleet problems went?

Captain Edwards: Well, it was a big fleet, it really was-- the East Coast plus the West Coast. And I remember it took two weeks to go out, because they ran all kinds of practices on the way. These were mostly tactical-- simulated torpedo attacks and that sort of thing. The weather was good, except we rolled a lot. The prevailing wind and sea were from the northeast, and we were going down to the southwest. It hit us on our quarters, so we did an awful lot of rolling. In fact, we put what they called fiddle boards on the tables to keep the cups and plates from moving. And there were several stanchions in the wardroom, so I'd hook my left arm around a stanchion and eat with the right hand. Day after day we did that.

Q: What about sleeping? Did you have to wedge yourself in?

Captain Edwards: Well, believe it or not, we'd use a pillow to keep from rolling. Otherwise, one's skin would get sore.

Q: I've heard some of the old four-stackers were infested with rats. Did you have that problem?

Captain Edwards: I'd say yes, but only briefly. Once we went into the public health station at Port Townsend, Washington, in Puget Sound. We tied up there in the Henshaw, got up steam on one boiler, and closed her up. Everybody got off the ship for a couple of hours, and the public health people put out poison for rats, cockroaches, and whatnot. And you'd be surprised how many they got.

They would come aboard in food, such as bags of potatoes. The rats might also run aboard on mooring lines. Unless the health people used a certain type of poison, the rats might die up between the sheeting and the siding of the ship. So they used this stuff that caused the rats to be thirsty, and they put pans of water on the decks. The rats would be thirsty, and when they came down to get a drink of water, they'd die right there. Otherwise, they'd die in out-of-the-way places and stink to high heaven. So that was quite an interesting day. We got a few pounds of rats and cockroaches that came out of the cracks and were killed.

Q: What would the crew do while this was going on?

Captain Edwards: Well, we sat on the dock or played baseball, just to kill time.

Q: What sorts of things did you and your wife and your son do there in San Diego on the evenings and weekends when you were home?

Captain Edwards: Saturday and Sunday afternoons we'd go out driving. We had a car then, only because my mother gave it to me; I didn't earn the car. And we'd travel around there and once in a while go to the zoo and places like that that families would go to.

And socially, why, we had cocktail parties and that sort of thing for adults only, of course. Those were the days of Prohibition, and we had what they called rotgut liquor and beer, which we manufactured. I remember one time I manufactured some beer, and I had it out in the hall to age. My mother was visiting, and pretty soon we heard "BANG!"

"What was that?"

"Well, I don't know what that was."

Pretty soon: "BANG!"

I was afraid to tell her this beer was exploding. She was in the WCTU.*

Q: Did you put too much in a bottle or what?

Captain Edwards: I don't know what it was now, but anyhow the recipe was too strong.

Q: Did they have commissaries and Navy exchanges then as they do now?

Captain Edwards: Yes, but much smaller than the ones now. We seldom went to the exchange, because it was too hard to get to.

Q: So you just went to regular grocery stores?

Captain Edwards: That's right.

Q: Were you involved in sports during your shipboard days?

Captain Edwards: Sometimes I went ashore and played tennis, golf, or whatnot--nothing organized.

Q: Did the destroyer force get involved in sports the way

---
*WCTU--Woman's Christian Temperance Union.

the bigger ships did?

Captain Edwards: They had a destroyer combined group. It would be destroyer squadron teams against battleships or maybe a cruiser division. Destroyer crews were too small for individual ships to have teams, so the men from several ships would form a group team.

Q: It would be harder to get the same kind of team spirit as when they're all shipmates.

Captain Edwards: That's right. They were just pickup teams.

Q: How was morale in the crew of the Henshaw?

Captain Edwards: Excellent. I only had one man I think I put on report in my whole life. He was the coxswain of one of our boats and a rather surly individual, and I put him on report once. That's the only man I had trouble with. He wasn't one of mine, but I put him on report because of his attitude toward officers in general. So we got rid of him.

Q: The ship was probably pretty stoutly built, wasn't it?

Captain Edwards: Well, yes and no. There were nearly 300 destroyers built during World War I, and they turned them out like peas in a pod. I had a Squantum-built boat.* Squantum had the worst reputation of all of them. The Bath boats were the best, built in Bath, Maine. Then three or four Navy yards built some. Also, the Newport News Shipbuilding and Dry Dock built some, and so did Fore River. Of them all, the boats that were the worst were the ones like the Henshaw built at Squantum. Even so, we stood number five one year out of 110 boats and got a red E for it. Of course, I was accused of being a crook. [Laughter] But it was merely attention to duty and getting the other people interested.

Q: You were telling me at lunch about the business of the Navy yard building ships to fill in gaps for the work force. Could you cover that please.

Captain Edwards: When I went to Bremerton with the Henshaw, I saw the Navy yard building this one auxiliary--I think it was the Medusa--over a period of time.** There was no time schedule for her completion. The idea was to absorb or give up manpower as the active ships required. A battleship would go out, and there would be several hundred

---
*The Henshaw was built by the Bethlehem Ship Building Company of Squantum, Massachusetts, near Boston.
**The USS Medusa (AR-1) was a repair ship that went into commission in September 1924.

men standing around looking at each other. So they would put them on this ship they were building. Then, when another ship came in for overhaul and they needed some men, they'd pull them off the new construction. So it was a topsy-turvy sort of thing, but it did smooth out the manpower curve, which everybody wanted.

Q: And you had an interesting description for the Medusa too.

Captain Edwards: The naval constructor in charge of her building ate his lunches with us, because it was handy and we knew him. He remarked one day, "I'm putting another henhouse on the Medusa." He had gotten a new plan, showing it needed an optical shop or some such shop, and so they had to add on another "henhouse" somewhere on topside. So she looked like the Santa Maria when they got through with her.

Q: How capable was the yard in dealing with the Henshaw and her overhauls?

Captain Edwards: We had very pleasant relations. One time I had a problem. I had a job order to overhaul 50 valves of miscellaneous sizes. Well, we took the 50 to the shop.

Then some of my men decided we could get some more done on the same job order, so they took up 15 or 20 more after dark. Finally, the master machinist got wind of it. He gave me hell, but we made up. His boys were really getting scammed on valve repairs.

Q: Well, you've heard that term cumshaw, where you give them little bribes. Did you do that?

Captain Edwards: Yes and no. It all depended on the man and the situation. We'd have them down for lunch maybe and things like that. Or if we knew of some financial break, we'd buy things in the commissary for him. Then he'd repay us, saving him about maybe 15% or 20%. Those were things they called cumshaw.

Q: Right. Coffee's always a very popular item for cumshaw.

Captain Edwards: Come down for coffee and talk over your troubles.

Q: Well, or they give somebody five pounds of coffee all at once.

Captain Edwards: Now, when I was on duty in the yard, much

F. A. Edwards #2 - 148

later, I used to go down and have coffee with some of the ships' officers. That way you'd get their feelings and desires. It was a good way to get along together. I was in design and planning, and I'd come down and talk to them. If they wanted something somewhere bad, we'd get it on to the plans somehow.

Q: Well, that's good to get it firsthand.

Captain Edwards: So our relationships were good; they were very excellent. I felt at that time it was the best Navy yard in the country, and it probably still is.

Q: Well, after the <u>Henshaw</u> you came ashore for the PG School.

Captain Edwards: I went to the PG course in '28. I spent a year and one summer at the PG School, which then was here in Annapolis. Then I went to Columbia University and spent a summer and a year there. Then the following summer I spent traveling around.

Q: What was involved in the course at Annapolis?

Captain Edwards: It was a review and advance of mathematics and science. We had courses in such things as calculus, mechanics, and higher math. And we covered the piping of fluid mechanics. It was a high-class course.

During that time I was in Annapolis, Ralph Root was the senior mathematics instructor--a very good one, by the way. He later went out to the West Coast when they moved the school out there, and they named Root Hall after him.* One day during our course he spread a series of calculus equations on the blackboard. Referring to a certain one, I said, "Professor, where did you get that equation?"

He gave me a withering look and said, "We all can't be bright." Thereafter, that was the watchword for a question.

But I got back at him. Mechanics is supposed to be the most difficult branch of mathematics, and one day we were studying the mathematics of current automobile crankshafts. We had half a dozen of them--Cadillac, Ford, and so forth. Essex was the worst one. About that time Professor Root bought an Essex. And I said, "Professor, what goes? Here you tell us and prove to us that an Essex crankshaft is the worst of the bunch. Yet you buy one."

He said, "It's cheaper." So he did have a sense of humor.

Later on, after his death, I talked to his widow. I told her that story, and she was amused.

---
*The Naval Postgraduate School moved from Annapolis to Monterey, California, in the early 1950s.

F. A. Edwards #2 - 150

Q: Was this course intended to make you an engineer yourself?

Captain Edwards: It was, I have to say, supplementary. We all had to be graduates of the academy, of course, and that was tough enough. But it was a general course. And then we all went to sea. I went to sea five years, four of which were engineering on the Henshaw, and then we had to request a PG course. Of the applicants, maybe 15 to 20 were selected for various PG courses. We went here to the academy for one year and a half, and then we went to various others schools for the next year. I went to Columbia. Some went to MIT, some to Penn State, some to Cal Tech, and so on--half a dozen places like that for various things.

Q: What was the objective of this course? Surely it wasn't just to prepare you to run engineering plants in ships.

Captain Edwards: The course was called mechanical engineering; about a third of it was electrical, and two-thirds was mechanical. The element for most of us was shipboard duty, but not necessarily. You weren't confined

F. A. Edwards #2 - 151

to that. But if you were going to engineering duty only, it was a limiting profession, but if you like it, you go for it. I went for it.

Q: Well, but wasn't part of the idea that with this additional knowledge you'd be able to design systems?

Captain Edwards: Yes. I had duty in design. For example, at Bremerton, before the war, I was the design superintendent for machinery. In fact, I loved design work. I did things which were based on experience, rather than book knowledge.

Q: Well, it was probably a combination of both.

Captain Edwards: Yes. Now, as a sidelight, I want to mention that the idea of gas-turbine engines came up in that PG course. At that time metallurgy hadn't advanced far enough to justify our going to gas turbines. Metals were eroding, you know, from all the hot gas and combustion particles. So I was more or less "agin" it, because I felt they weren't ready yet. Nowadays the new destroyers are all gas-turbine drive, but they should have a steam auxiliary plant for hotel services.

I told Arleigh Burke one day that you'd be able to hear that ship coming before you'd see it because of these noisy gas turbines. This was 60 years ago. They weren't ready yet for gas turbines for main propulsion. Nowadays I'd be for them.

Q: Well, they seem to have done very well.

Captain Edwards: Yes, they've done very well. There again, it isn't the designers. It's the metallurgists.

Q: Well, it's the advance of technology.

Captain Edwards: Sure, it's all connected. But I was asked back in the Twenties, and I said, "Not yet. They aren't ready yet metallurgically." If they ran them for 1,000 hours, perhaps the blades would be half thickness. They'd be eroded down.

Q: How challenging was the course at Annapolis, compared with Columbia?

Captain Edwards: The Navy's PG School was twice as hard. Columbia was easy.

Q: That surprises me.

Captain Edwards: We usually had classes in the morning,

and then in the afternoon we had laboratory work or time off. At Columbia we had several noted scholars giving us lectures. A fellow named Lucke was a noted mechanical engineer. He wrote the book. And then there was an electrical man who had invented the electric clock and other things. And then we had a cadre of a half dozen of these people. We had a metallurgical man; his name escapes me, but he was number one in the business at that time.

Q: When you were at Columbia, were you in the same courses with civilians?

Captain Edwards: There were eight or ten of us, I guess, and maybe two or three civilians in these courses. It was more or less a special course set up for the Navy, but we had full access to their professors. And they were all earning money as experts. If you had a gas explosion in a downtown Brooklyn building, they were called in to explain the percentage of oxygen and air and that sort of thing that caused the explosion. Or if you had a collision somewhere, they were called in to make expert testimony. So they were doing the best of both lives. They were teaching on one side and giving expert testimony on the other side.

Q: Well, so they must have been very capable also.

Captain Edwards: They were. As I say, they were nationally known at that time. At the PG school in Annapolis we also had civilian instructors, but they were not nationally known.

These people lectured to us, and we kept notes and had quizzes. This course was not half as hard as the Naval Academy. I told you last week that the Naval Academy was a hard, unrelenting course. I never felt I was ready for the recitation, but at Columbia it was relatively easy. We all took more hours than required for a master's degree. I got a master's degree in mechanical engineering; it's up there [on the wall of his office]. It's the lower one there.

They told me I had so many credits on the books for a Ph.D. if I wanted to take it. But I never took it because I wasn't going to teach engineering for a living. I taught once, two years, at the Naval Academy, and I was glad to. But I would not teach as a profession. If I were going to, I would have gotten a Ph.D., because then one gets a different pay level. No matter how much you know, or whether you're worth a damn or not, if you have a bachelor's degree, you get a certain pay level. Master's degree, certain pay level. Ph.D., why, you start in maybe half again as much or twice as much.

When I graduated from Columbia University, we all had to wear our uniforms for the ceremony. We had worn civilian clothes to class, but for graduation we all had to come out in white service uniforms. It was June. My wife was sitting back in amidst the audience when she overheard one of them say, "Here come the naval officers, busting out of their pants." We all, in two years' time, had developed another couple inches of waistline.

Q: What did you do once you got your diploma from Columbia?

Captain Edwards: After that came three months of visiting various companies, and that was most interesting. In the morning at these companies the man in charge of a division would give us a talk. And in the afternoon we'd go in his part of the plant and see what he was talking about. He might be making refrigerators. Or he might be making anything at all, but it was part of GE's or Westinghouse's work. We also went to the big power plants in New York City. As I recall, at that time the Hell Gate plant was the big one, and they were turning out fabulous amounts of electricity for the city.

Besides New York, we went down to the old Baldwin Locomotive Works in south Philadelphia. They were building big steam engines, tremendous steam engines. They made these huge steel castings for these engines, but they weren't getting as much business during the Depression as they wanted. Some wisecracker made a remark about that time. He said that the boss man--I forget his name now, Sam Somebody--would be very happy whenever the grass got less than a foot high down at his plant. Short grass or no grass symbolized full employment. Similarly, grass-covered railroad tracks indicated little or no traffic.

We went into a turbine plant, where Westinghouse was building turbines, not only for the Navy but also for civilian use. It was most interesting. They also were building electric generator sets--maybe 300- or 600-kilowatt generators for light and power aboard ship. Also, they were building high-capacity insulators, used both by the Navy and by power plants ashore. So that was most interesting.

There were no grades during this. It was just simply going to school, and we always showed up on time. We were happy to be there. I felt quite a few times--the Navy was at a low point then--of resigning and going into public utilities, power plants. In fact, I did own some stock in various companies, and I saw a list of some of these people there. Many presidents or chief engineers were Naval Academy graduates. They had resigned 30 or 40 years before. I felt I missed the boat, more or less. I don't regret staying in the Navy, but I still have a feeling I would have done better perhaps outside.

F. A. Edwards #2 - 157

Q: How actively did you consider that?

Captain Edwards: Well, I had a family then, a wife and two children in school. I had to have a paycheck, and I knew I couldn't get a job instantly. I'd have had to take a certain training course and maybe a year of breaking in. Even though you have all the experience, you still have to go into their schooling system and grow up with it. I never did, but I thought about it many times.

Another possibility involved these big diesel tugs they had on the Mississippi River and Ohio River. They were tremendous tugs, maybe six engines. They'd haul 15 to 20 barges, and the river was just full of them. They would tow down the Ohio and Mississippi rivers, down to New Orleans and Baton Rouge. I thought a lot about getting into the engineering end of that business. But, there again, I was a quiet mouse. I decided to stay where I was safe, which I did. But, I say, I had those inner feelings that I wanted to get into civilian engineering, where I might even get further, I hoped, than I did in the Navy.

Q: Did you talk it over with your wife?

Captain Edwards: No. I felt it was my decision and my job to support her and the family. We always lived on my salary--whether it was small or big. I feel that's the way to raise a family. Right now more women work and have children--school children. It's bad. No matter how good the parents are, the kids turn out sour. They're neglected during those formative years. And that's bad. That's why we have so many, I'll say, failures or casualties right now.

Q: Well, a lot of them turn out fine. It depends on the circumstances.

Captain Edwards: Too many of them turn out wrong. I know some very fine ones, but I know some very bad apples, largely due to the fact that they were neglected. They didn't have a father around or didn't have a mother around. They were latch-key kids, and that's likely to be bad. I don't want to damn the whole system, but, I mean, too many of them are victims of that system.

Q: Is this a convenient place to break?

Captain Edwards: It is, I think.

Q: Well, let me ask you then one more question. What was New York like to live in during that period? The Depression was getting started then.*

---
*The Great Depression began in October 1929 with the stock market crash. It lasted throughout much of the 1930s and resulted in widespread unemployment throughout the nation.

Captain Edwards: I was at postgraduate school in 1929 to '30, and the people were jumping out of windows down in Wall Street. I was not affected by it at that time. A year or so later, maybe two years later, they cut our pay 15%. Well, I was lucky. I was promoted two or three weeks before the cut came in, so my cut was on the new promotion to lieutenant, rather than on the old one. Some of the ensigns' wives who were having babies had to go home and live with Mama and Papa, because they could not afford to live separately during that time.

Interview Number 3 with Captain Frederick A. Edwards,
U.S. Navy (Retired)

Place: Captain Edwards's Apartment, Annapolis, Maryland

Date: Tuesday, 18 February 1992

Interviewer: Paul Stillwell

Q: Captain, last time we talked about your time at the postgraduate school, then your tours of the various manufacturing plants. That brought you up to reporting to the new heavy cruiser, USS Augusta.* What do you recall about her?

Captain Edwards: She was built at the Newport News Shipbuilding and Dry Dock Company, which I was generally familiar with. I'd asked for one of the heavy cruisers, because they were the latest big ships under construction at that time. Fortunately, it turned out, I was ordered to the Augusta. I reported in September or October 1930. We fitted out until commissioned in January 1931.

I served under two very interesting officers. One was in the class of 1917, Lieutenant Commander Huschke.**

_____
*USS Augusta (CA-31) was commissioned 30 January 1931. She had a standard displacement of 9,050 tons, was 600 feet long, and 66 feet in the beam. She had a top speed of 32.7 knots and a main battery of nine 8-inch guns. She served as flagship of the Scouting Force, May 1931-October 1933, and of the U.S. Asiatic Fleet, November 1933-November 1940.
**Lieutenant Commander Paul W. F. Huschke, USN.

Although he was raised in America, he had been born in Germany. Therefore, during World War I they wouldn't order him to sea duty. That hurt his pride, and understandably so, but he turned out to be a very fine officer. His number two was Lieutenant G. L. Schetky, class of 1919.*

Q: Were they assigned to the shipyard?

Captain Edwards: No, all of the ship's officers were assigned to the naval inspector of machinery for temporary duty in connection with fitting out. I was number three when I reported, and I was initially assigned as the prospective electrical officer of the ship. Later, after Schetky, the senior assistant engineer officer, was relieved, I fleeted up to number two. So I was the senior assistant engineer officer for about two years out of the three.

The engineer officer was Huschke, and he was a smart guy who stood number ten in his class. He had some detractors because of his background. He was rather hard to get along with at first, but I got along with him fine later on. He married at about that time, and his wife and my wife got along, so that was fine.

The _Augusta_ was one of the 8-inch-gun heavy cruisers. She was officialy a 10,000-ton cruiser, but actually she

---
*Lieutenant Gerald L. Schetky, USN.

was overweight. Initially, lightweight bricks were installed in the boilers, in order to reduce some of the overweight. However, they soon spalled and had to be replaced by standard-weight bricks. That required the installation of heavier brickpans to support the additional weight of bricks.

Those cruisers were really very good ships, but engineering-wise they had some faults. They had a cruising turbine which gave us an awful lot of trouble. It was connected to the high-pressure turbine via a reduction gear. Three-fourths of our problems, I think, occurred because of this unit. At high speed, this cruising turbine would turn idly, maybe 10,000 RPMs. Either the gear or the turbine eventually failed in service, so that was a mistake in design.

Q: How sophisticated was that plant, compared with the one in the Henshaw?

Captain Edwards: Well, it was an improvement, but not too much--50 pounds more boiler pressure. It was not a sophisticated plant. Now, the Mahan class, which I later put in commission, had a sophisticated plant. It had only 400 pounds of boiler pressure, but it had a lot of new things in it. It was a Gibbs & Cox design.

F. A. Edwards #3 - 163

Q: We'll get to that later on.

Captain Edwards: The boiler steam pressure in the Augusta was only 300 pounds per square inch. They'd been considering 400 pounds but actually were built with 300 pounds.

These were, generally speaking, very good ships. They acquitted themselves very well during the war. The Augusta, as you know, had an interesting career as flagship, temporary, of the Atlantic Fleet. Churchill and Roosevelt and their staffs had a meeting at Argentia on board the Augusta.*

Q: She was also the flagship for the Normandy invasion.

Captain Edwards: Yes, that's right. So, I say, she acquitted herself well during that period.

Now, just preceding that class were two other 10,000-ton cruisers, but they weren't as good militarily as the Augusta and her sisters.

Q: Pensacola and Salt Lake City.

---

*The Augusta was flagship of the U.S. Atlantic Fleet from May 1941 to January 1942. Admiral Ernest J. King, USN, was fleet commander in chief when Prime Minister Winston Churchill and President Franklin D. Roosevelt met on board in August 1941 as part of the Atlantic Charter discussions.

Captain Edwards: Correct. They were the two. They called one of them the "Salt Lake Maru" because she and her sister had certain lines which more or less suggested a Japanese design.

Q: The nickname that was hung on a number of these ships was the "tin-clads" or the "treaty cruisers."

Captain Edwards: They were the treaty cruisers.*

Q: Was there a perception of vulnerability because of the armor?

Captain Edwards: They were very thin, thin-clad.

Q: Did you have a concern about that?

Captain Edwards: Well, there wasn't anything you could do about it. As I recall, the deck armor was about two inches; the side armor was almost four inches.** They were expendable, more or less, as ships. We just simply disregarded the fact that we might get sunk. That was a

---

*The Washington Naval Treaty of 1922 limited battleships to a displacement of 35,000 tons; aircraft carriers to 27,000 tons; and other warships, thus cruisers, to 10,000 tons.
**By comparison, the Baltimore (CA-68)-class cruisers had the same main battery as the Augusta, but their belt armor was six inches thick; their armored decks were 2.5 inches.

secondary thing. The thing was to sink the enemy first.

Q: You deal with that when you come to it.

Captain Edwards: Right, yes.

Q: For an engineer what were the steps involved in taking an inert ship in a shipyard and getting her out operating in the fleet?

Captain Edwards: Well, first of all, way back when, comes a design of the ship as a hull and also the parallel design of the machinery to go into that ship. There has to be close coordination there, particularly for the main machinery that goes into a hull. The auxiliary machinery comes from everywhere where it is built. DeLaval in those days built a lot of our pumps. They had a plant at Trenton, New Jersey. Then we needed very good coordination for the piping. Piping was like cables; it was all over the ship--not only steam piping but oil piping, water piping, and hydraulic piping. There's an awful lot of design work before they even lay the keel. It's practically designed then, but from then on, why, it's installation. And then finally come tests.

F. A. Edwards #3 - 166

Q: What do you remember about the damage-control capabilities in that era?

Captain Edwards: Relatively poor. It wasn't until we got into the North Carolina class that we had a good capability of damage control. The Augusta wasn't bad; she was better than a lot of her predecessors, but still she had an intermediate type of damage control.

Q: What types of improvements did you see that came along later?

Captain Edwards: Well, the facility for pumping liquids from one side to the other to counterbalance whatever damage there was. And then centralized control. Before that they usually had a sparsely equipped damage control center. Pumping capability was secondary. The North Carolina and the later ships had full possible control over shifting the liquids and communications between control areas.

Q: What about the business of shoring? Was that something you practiced back in the Thirties?

Captain Edwards: It was just a name. I was on that ship three years, and I don't recall any shoring practice.

Q: How capable was the fire-fighting technique?

Captain Edwards: Well, limited. The fire-fighting schools weren't established till World War II came along. They got a lot of civilian fire-fighters in that program, and then it became very effective. The school was at the Philadelphia Navy Yard. Then we really had some effective fire-fighting capacity.

Q: What do you remember specifically about running the plant in that ship?

Captain Edwards: As I told you, our troubles, such as we had, were due to this cruising-turbine arrangement. Other than that, the engineering plant was quite good. I, as the senior assistant engineer officer, was not required to stand a watch, but I arbitrarily put myself on watch every day--say, the 4:00 to 8:00--to familiarize myself. We didn't change the watch rotation; those people just fell out.

Q: I'll bet they loved you for that.

Captain Edwards: Yes, but that wasn't the point, to be loved. I wanted to acquaint myself with the plant personally. I'll tell you one bad time. We were down in Ponce, Puerto Rico, on the shakedown cruise. The chamber of commerce invited the officers to a big party up at some place in the hills there where you overlooked the ship. The ship looked like a toy boat in a bathtub. They had all kinds of food and liquor--too much liquor. We got to the point at this party where we had bottles of champagne. We'd ease the cork out about halfway and then train it at an overhead light and BANG, knock out the light. We were having a big time. Well, we'd been to sea for two or three weeks. We would be going again and needed to relax.

I got back aboard ship around midnight. Then we got under way at, I'd say, 7:00 o'clock in the morning, and I had the 4:00 to 8:00 warm-up watch. The temperature down below was over 100 degrees, and I had too much liquor in my belly. And we changed the clocks one hour to a different zone time. That made it an extra hour. My relief was not able to relieve me on time, which added another half hour or so. I was walking around in a daze. I was the watch officer, trying to run the plant, which I did, but that was one of my worst days. That was very exceptional, understand. That was one of the few times I ever recall that I felt the effects of liquor. I didn't get it aboard ship; I got it ashore.

Q: It was legal there, wasn't it?

Captain Edwards: Oh, yes.

Q: What else do you recall about being ashore?

Captain Edwards: One time the Augusta was in Charleston, South Carolina. I was the right seniority to be in charge of the shore patrol for our week there. It was a very eye-opening experience. We had to inspect all the whorehouses and make sure that our boys weren't getting into fights or trouble with the police.

Q: Anything specific you remember about those eye-opening experiences?

Captain Edwards: Well, I went into one place, and up came my chief electrician's mate. He was quite embarrassed, and so was I. I caught him unawares; he had just been serviced and was on his way out. He had a sheepish look on his face. I was being taken around by the senior district shore patrol officer, a friend of mine. So he led me by the hand around and showed me all the sights I should see.

Q: Your first skipper was J. O. Richardson, a very capable officer.* What do you recall about him?

---

*Captain James O. Richardson, USN, eventually became a four-star admiral and served as Commander in Chief U.S. Fleet, 1940-41.

Captain Edwards: Everything good. We used to say in the wardroom, "If we have a war, we want Joe to run it." And we meant that. He was a very down-to-earth guy. He was a level-headed, around-the-clock sort of a skipper. In fact, that's why we said we wanted Joe to run it. At that time he was a little bit apprehensive about air power. When we'd go out to shoot a practice, we were supposed to have planes to do the spotting; the damn planes would never arrive on time. Joe was rather critical about that phase of cooperation between air and ships. Of course, aviation proved itself later.

Q: Was there hostility in that era between aviators and surface officers?

Captain Edwards: I won't call it hostility, but we still had our differences. There is a story to indicate that. At that time white-wall tires on cars came out, and they were very few and far between. One morning a certain officer drove down the dock in a car with white-wall tires. The remark was made that "Only niggers and aviators can afford to have white-wall tires." That was an off-color story, but it was true.

I never served in a carrier; I've been aboard as a passenger. Shipboard officers--the engineer and the first lieutenant and people like that--were more or less second-class citizens. The aviators, of course, were the first-class citizens. But I think that was overdone. Maybe the executive officer should be a ship's officer, and the skipper, of course, would be an aviator.

Q: What was the relationship between the aviators and the ship's officers on board the Augusta?

Captain Edwards: There it was very good, because the aviators were secondary. We had planes on there only for scouting and for gunfire spotting. Aviators were second-class citizens on board there. [Laughter] Those were elementary planes, you might say, but they did a job in the prewar Navy. They spotted our long-range firings. The Augusta stayed on the East Coast for about one year and then went around to the West Coast.

Q: Any more that you remember on J. O. Richardson? What was his personality like?

Captain Edwards: He was a calm, nice guy to work with. He never got excited. I don't believe I ever heard him bawl anybody out or get too excited. He was a very fine skipper, the kind of a guy one needs under stress.

Q: It sounds like he inspired a lot of confidence.

Captain Edwards: He did. Yes, he did.

Q: Did Richardson have a sense of humor?

Captain Edwards: Well, I don't say he didn't have one, but it was moderate, shall we say.

Q: I gather that Richardson was a friendly, fatherly type.

Captain Edwards: That's a good word--fatherly type, yes.

Q: Do you remember any specifics along that line?

Captain Edwards: Well, yes. On the West Coast we got under way one morning at 7:00 o'clock or thereabouts. And a certain ensign had recently reported aboard. As we got under way, we saw a shore boat coming toward the ship, hell-bent. And, sure enough, it came alongside, and up came this ensign. He had slept late. So he reported to the exec, of course, and the captain later on. The captain said, "Well, now, I want you to stay aboard until you feel you're rested up."

After about a week, this ensign came up and told the skipper that he thought he was rested up. Much, much later he became a vice admiral.

Q: Who was that?

Captain Edwards: Lloyd Mustin. Not the fellow who just retired but his father.* Lloyd's a good guy.

Q: Yes, he is.

Captain Edwards: Very good guy. He was class of '32. We got about six of them at that time. Now, Eph Holmes, who later became CinCLant, was also on board.** When I was later the material officer on the Atlantic Fleet staff, he was communication officer on the staff. He was then a commander and a nice fellow, very good. I'd pick him if I had the chance.

Q: Can you see the potential in men like that as junior officers?

Captain Edwards: No. Once in a while, you can see a lemon. But with the rest of them you cannot tell who's

---
*Ensign Lloyd M. Mustin, USN. His son, Henry C. Mustin, also retired as a vice admiral.
**Ensign Ephraim P. Holmes, USN, who later served as Commander in Chief Atlantic Fleet from 1967 to 1970.

going to be the favorite son. I'm sorry to say I couldn't.

Q: Maybe because they're all just starting from the same level at that point.

Captain Edwards: That's right. Now, there were half a dozen people. I would have picked any one of them. They were all about the same. Good guys, but they were without any experience at that time. They were just fresh out of the academy.

Q: The Augusta had a flag on board, didn't she?

Captain Edwards: Yes. Commander Scouting Force. That was Vice Admiral A. L. Willard.* He was very much imbued with his own importance, let me say. He had a big cabin, and he had shipfitters drilling holes all over. He had scores--I mean scores--of pictures of him with FDR, with this person and that person, or ships he'd been in, and so forth. My electrical people got involved because the admiral's bunk was on the side of the ship, and he didn't want to have to roll over in order to ask for things. So he had a call bell for everything: a call bell for the messboy, a call bell for the chief of staff, etc. It looked like a shotgun had shot through the bulkhead where

---
*Vice Admiral Arthur L. Willard, USN.

we had drilled holes to mount pictures.

We referred to the admiral as "Puffy." The <u>Augusta</u>'s officers' quarters were forward, on the upper deck. We had a double gangway, twice the length of an ordinary gangway. Willard was a rather overweight man, a little obese. He'd get up to the top of the first gangway and puff, get his breath back, and then he'd come up the second stage. So we called him "Puffy" offstage.

Willard was an almost typical pre-World War II senior officer. He was a spit-and-polish boy. Nice guy and all that, but he was not a technical person in the sense that we now have.

Q: What, in your opinion, was the value of that spit and polish? Did it have a value?

Captain Edwards: Yes, it had a value, which probably was overdone, but it had a value. Now I think we don't have enough of it. Somewhere in there should be an average.

Q: What was the value of it?

Captain Edwards: Pride in self and pride in ship. The ship had to be polished. If it wasn't, why, God help you. So the same way with the men. Their uniforms were wonderful. Their haircuts were good, and they looked good. They were good. But, I say, I think they probably overdid it. Now, in World War II it completely went the other way. I think we're coming back slowly, but I'll say maybe too slowly. I say that without any real knowledge but with what I've observed and I hear.

Q: How were the uniforms cleaned for the officers and enlisted men?

Captain Edwards: All the big ships had a laundry, and they did what I consider a fair job. But things like stiff collars or special things we sent ashore when we could. In fact, on the Augusta I was ship's laundry officer besides, an odd job. Well, there again, they had a collar machine that wasn't very good, so when we'd get in port we'd send dozens and dozens of collars ashore. They were all marked, of course, with black ink so we wouldn't lose them. Or things that had to be pressed, we sent ashore. Just run-of-the-mill items were done aboard ship.

Q: This is back in the era of detachable collars.

Captain Edwards: That's right.

Q: In this emphasis on cleanliness, do you remember any

problems with blowing tubes topside?

Captain Edwards: Yes, we had to wait until we got a cross wind. If we were under way in formation, we would tell the officer of the deck we wanted to blow tubes, and he'd give us a break. So whenever we could change course, he did change course 45 degrees or more, and then we'd blow tubes. He'd also tell us when to stop blowing them. Otherwise, you'd soot up the topside.

I remember once when the *Augusta* was anchored near Newport. Somebody blew tubes on the midwatch, and the soot went all inshore and got on some of those peoples' porches and roofs over in Jamestown. All hell broke loose. A man in the engineering department had blown tubes without getting permission from the officer of the deck. I had to be very careful about that.

Q: What do you remember about the ceremonial aspects of the *Augusta* as a flagship? What did it require of you as an in-port officer of the deck?

Captain Edwards: It was the same as on a battleship. The officer of the deck was the master of ceremonies, you might say. He had to be sure that the Marines and the sideboys were in place and on time and that the whole ship was alert. And he had to make sure that some guy in his underwear didn't come running out on the quarterdeck at the time a ceremony was going on.

Q: The bugler was an important man in that too.

Captain Edwards: He was very important, and so was the boatswain's mate. He piped important visitors aboard. That was a throwback to Nelson's time.

Q: That's right. Do you remember any especially interesting incidents in that regard?

Captain Edwards: There were certain formal calls which had to be made and returned. When you went into port, the captain had to go ashore. It depended on who was ashore. Was he an ambassador, or was he just a consul or whatnot? And they exchanged calls. The officer of the deck, of course, was in charge of all that. He had to have a boat alongside on time, and the crew had to be in proper dress, and the ship had to fire the correct number of guns and that sort of thing.* It really was quite a meticulous thing. You could live or die by your performance as the officer of the deck.

---

*Navy Regulations prescribe the number of guns to be fired in saluting civilian dignitaries and high-ranking military officers. The number of guns is always an odd number.

Q: Mistakes would be noticed.

Captain Edwards: Oh, yes, on high.

Q: What sorts of operations was the Augusta involved in once she got to the West Coast?

Captain Edwards: Well, she was the Scouting Force flagship. We made several trips out to Hawaii and south of Hawaii on pre-World War II task force operations. That's where the task force organizations were developed before the war. Augusta was the flag, and we'd have a couple of other cruisers and many destroyers. We'd go maybe 1,000 miles out, south of Hawaii, and then head back to the coast. Then we'd contact another "enemy."

Q: Battle problems.

Captain Edwards: Problems, yes. We engaged in those quite often.

Q: I'm sure that those were taken very seriously.

Captain Edwards: They were.

Q: My guess is that the morale was pretty high in the

Augusta.

Captain Edwards: It was very high. Let's see, the skipper I was with, Joe Richardson, was relieved by Chester Nimitz just about the time I was detached.*

Q: Did you have any contact with Nimitz?

Captain Edwards: No, he was about to relieve Richardson.

Q: What do you recall about the quality of the enlisted men in the ship?

Captain Edwards: It was excellent, except they didn't have the high technical education and skill that Navy men have now. Nowadays the average sailor is probably a high school graduate, and some of them may even have one or two years of college. But in those days they were excellent, up to a point. Morale-wise and job-wise, they were excellent. They lacked some technical knowledge.

Q: But the Navy, because of the Depression, was able to pick the cream of the crop on the applicants.

Captain Edwards: Sometimes we had 80-85% reenlistments.
_____
*Captain Chester W. Nimitz, USN, commanded the Augusta from October 1933 to April 1935.

That is unheard of these days. If you get 40 or 50%, you're really doing something very well. There was a lot of laughter, though, about reenlisting. One story was, "What are you going to do, Joe, when you get out?"

One of them said, "I'm going to take an oar in my right hand and start walking inland. And when someone says, 'What is that thing?' I'm going to retire right there." [Laughter]

That was a sailor story.

Q: Where did you go after you wound up on board the <u>Augusta</u>?

Captain Edwards: I went back to the Naval Academy as an instructor in engineering. I didn't want to go, and I almost asked for a change of duty. I didn't want to be an instructor, because I wanted to learn by association with a new plant--not to "give" to mids. But then I thought, "Well, I better take it and see." So I took it, and I'm glad I did, because it gave me some very good reviews in various subjects. I had that job two years, and I moved up with the class of '35. During my first year there they were second classmen. Then the next year, of course, they were first class. I, at my own request, moved up with them in order to review different subjects.

I'll tell you a funny story. One day a midshipman asked me a certain question, and I gave him an answer. He said, "Sir, that isn't what you told us yesterday."

I said, "Young man, you have a lamentable lack of confidence in your instructor." [Laughter]

It was a pleasure teaching midshipmen, though, because you could tell them what to do. That is, you had them under your thumb. So, I say, we had a pretty controlled class. It wasn't like out at a college or civilian school, where they raise hell and all that sort of thing.

Q: Any of the midshipmen you especially remember?

Captain Edwards: Yes, Buzz Borries.* One of the subjects I taught was thermodynamics, which the midshipmen called "thermo-goddamnics." Thermodynamics deals with the physics of heat. Buzz was class of '35 and, for one month at least, was in my class. During the classroom discussions, I could see the fog just gathering around Buzz. But we were very charitable, and during the football season he got a 2.5 or 2.6 to be eligible to play. But after the season was over, we put Buzz on the "tree" to wake him up.** He turned out to be a very good practical

---

*Midshipman Fred Borries, Jr., USN, was an all-America football player on the Naval Academy team.
**The "tree" was Naval Academy slang for the list of those midshipmen who were academically unsatisfactory.

F. A. Edwards #3 - 183

aviation line officer.*

Q: Were there others that you helped out that way?

Captain Edwards: Well, one fellow named Hinckley was not an athlete.** I used to give him many hours of extra instruction. He was the son of a senior commander in OpNav at that time. The son did very well in World War II, commanding a destroyer minesweeper. I remember him very well, because I spent many hours with him out of the classroom, pulling him through a knothole.

Q: Did you spend more time with him than with most of the students?

Captain Edwards: Yes.

Q: Was that because his dad was a friend of yours?

Captain Edwards: No, I just felt he needed help. He was a nice guy, but he didn't have 100% acuity in mathematics. No, his father was just a casual acquaintance, really, not a friend.

---
*Borries served 26 years of commissioned service, retiring as a captain in 1961. As a lieutenant commander in 1944 he was air officer of the escort carrier Gambier Bay (CVE-73) when she was sunk in the Battle of Leyte Gulf.
**Midshipman Robert M. Hinckley, Jr., USN. During the Okinawa campaign in 1945, as a commander, he was commanding officer of the USS Butler (DMS-29).

Q: How difficult a subject was thermodynamics?

Captain Edwards: It is the most difficult of the engineering subjects, but the average person who applies himself can get by. It's about on a par with mechanics, which we also had in the postgraduate school. Mechanics was so difficult in PG school that we were more or less told that our questions would be taken from maybe 50 basic questions. We might be tested on five out of the 50, so we would know where to spend our time.

Q: When you were an instructor, did you give hints to the midshipmen what they might expect on tests?

Captain Edwards: No, we had this slip system, which I described before. Maybe about 15 minutes out of the hour would be discussion, but we never told the students what they were going to have on an exam.

Q: What was the general approach on a marginal student? How did you decide which ones to try to pull through?

Captain Edwards: We gave a reexamination for those who failed the first exam. If a man failed the reexam, he either was turned back to a later class or kicked out. It also depended on his other marks. If he did well in other subjects but not too well in this particular subject, he, of course, got more consideration in passing.

Q: Well, and it might also depend on his "grease mark" and how good an athlete he was.*

Captain Edwards: Well, being an athlete didn't come in as important as you might think. There were exceptions, and I just gave you a good one. But most of the athletes were treated about the same as the rest of the midshipmen.

We had an extra-instruction hour maybe two or three times a week. People who weren't doing too well would come over voluntarily for extra instruction. The instructors were assigned that duty in rotation. Whenever possible, I gave marginal students the benefit of the doubt. If someone showed promise and actual interest, I gave him more time.

Q: What do you remember about Borries's personality?

Captain Edwards: Well, he was a very non-reg type person. I won't say he was sloppy, but he was unmilitary looking.

---

*The "grease mark" was the grade in the area of aptitude for service, a combination of conduct and leadership.

Q: I've heard he walked with a slouch.

Captain Edwards: He did. He preferred the slouch. I remember one time at an Army-Navy game at Philadelphia, he was the safety, playing way back. He would stand there, more or less on one foot, apparently not interested. But when that ball was kicked, just like a flash, he ran to where the ball was going to land. He was an exceptional athlete, but he was not the normal midshipman type. Everybody liked Buzz. He was such a nice guy that you had to make allowances for him. Also, they needed his help athletically. We could use several Buzz Borrieses right now.

Q: Well, kind of a happy-go-lucky type.

Captain Edwards: Exactly.

Q: What do you recall about Slade Cutter?* He was another football man in the class of '35.

Captain Edwards: Slade was a great, big husky guy-- entirely different-looking person than Borries. I had him

---
*Midshipman Slade D. Cutter, USN. Cutter, who retired as a captain, was one of the most successful U.S. submarine skippers of World War II, sinking some 20 Japanese ships while commanding the Seahorse (SS-304). His oral history is in the Naval Institute collection.

in class several times, and he gave me the impression of having everything a successful person should have. And he was smarter academically than Buzz. We gave him no particular assistance in getting through.

Q: He was an outstanding submarine skipper in the war.

Captain Edwards: Yes. Obviously, he was going to be a successful officer. Buzz, you weren't too sure about. Slade was a good guy, and I was very happy to see him succeed.

Q: Was the teaching method essentially what it had been when you were a midshipman?

Captain Edwards: Yes, but we opened up a little bit. A midshipman, a young fellow, wants to outsmart the instructor. So he wants to tell you, "Sir, I couldn't work problem [so-and-so]." He also wants to get you to work the problem to kill time. That's what I ran into. I was aware of that, so they didn't "take" me for anything. I always asked them to show me any homework that they had done. Of course, in most cases, they didn't have any homework to show me. So I didn't answer the question.

F. A. Edwards #3 - 188

Q: Did you find that the postgraduate education you'd had yourself made you a better instructor?

Captain Edwards: Yes, because, for example, I had calculus the second time over. I had calculus as a midshipman. As a postgraduate I had calculus the second time over. And so when I went to teach, I was much better prepared.

Q: Were you given any specific instruction on how to be a teacher?

Captain Edwards: Very little. Maybe a couple of hours they'd have us sit in a room for a lecture. But you were mostly on your own. By that time we were in our early 30s, 10 to 12 years out of the academy. By that time we were mature. The head of the department was Captain Bryson Bruce, who later became a rear admiral, EDO. He had some midshipmen in for coffee and whatnot, because he couldn't have them for drinks. He pumped them, and one of the questions he asked them was who was their favorite or best instructor. Well, one of them was kind enough to say I was. Captain Bruce later told me, and I felt very good about that.

Q: How much practical work was there along with the

classroom instruction?

Captain Edwards: About three times a week we'd have laboratory work. One summer, after the first class had graduated, and when other classes were on cruises, we had nobody except when we got some plebes in. To kill time, more or less, we'd indoctrinate them. And one summer I completely rewrote all the laboratory exercises for the second class. I didn't have to. I wasn't asked to, but I rewrote them. I just felt I had to do something, and that was it.

Q: What sorts of things were covered in these laboratory works?

Captain Edwards: Well, for the gasoline engines, for example, we had a test engine. As you put various grades of gasoline in, you'd find out when they began to knock and when they had power surges. We also had a test boiler, about the size of this room, and we ran tests like on a regular big boiler. We also looked at pumps of various kinds, heat exchangers, and units like that. Everything mechanical that was covered in class was also covered in laboratory.

Q: So these midshipmen could get a pretty good

understanding of the steam cycle, for example.

Captain Edwards: If they didn't, it was their fault. The laboratory work counted as a fraction, maybe one-fourth or something like that, of the whole year's mark.

Q: But that would be extremely important, because they would be dealing with this equipment when they got aboard ships.

Captain Edwards: That's right, but, of course, they went to sea every year in summer, and there they were with full-scale machinery.

Q: They could apply what you had taught them.

Captain Edwards: That's right. I thought they had a good understanding of what it was all about.

Q: What was the social life like for you and your family in Annapolis?

Captain Edwards: Well, I was there two times. Once was poor because my son had an ear infection. He had to have an operation in Washington and required extended care. So that was rather poor. The second time, when I was an instructor, was rather good. In those days we had lots of athletics, of course, that we attended and lots of social affairs.

Q: We've talked about your son's birth back when you were in the Henshaw. When did your daughter come along?

Captain Edwards: That was '33. This is a rather personal remark, but, like most families, the first child was an accident. Our second, our daughter, was intentional. Because there were, after all, seven years between the children. We felt if we were going to have another child, we'd have to do it right away. So that was it.

Q: What's your daughter's name?

Captain Edwards: Suzanne Elizabeth--Elizabeth after her mother. Bess picked the name Suzanne because she liked it--a French name.

Q: Well, you know, the joke on that is the first child can come at any time, and the rest of them take nine months.

Captain Edwards: That's right. We felt we could not educate or care for more than two children with the kind of life we were living--moving around and all that sort of thing.

Q: Did you have dealings with any of the superintendents during your time as an instructor?

Captain Edwards: When I joined the staff, there was a reporting-in cocktail party, so the wives and husbands all went over and met the admiral and his wife.

Q: Did you have a fair amount of fellowship with the other members of the faculty?

Captain Edwards: Yes, the mix was about 50-50--civilians and naval officers. I got along fine with them. The civilians, of course, were better prepared than we were. They were professionals, and we weren't. So we often went to them about problems, to help us out. It was very good camaraderie with them. I never had any problem with civilian professors.

Q: Well, it was sort of like a closed system. You were dealing with these people with whom you worked every day. Did you have contacts out in the community?

Captain Edwards: I had almost no community contact. It wasn't my fault, or it wasn't their fault. There was no

F. A. Edwards #3 - 193

opportunity.

Q: It was the nature of the system.

Captain Edwards: The system; that's right. In fact, we had almost no contact at all with people out in town, except our neighbors.

Q: The world situation was getting worse then with Mussolini and Hitler and so forth. Did you have a foreboding sense of what was coming?

Captain Edwards: Well, we knew it was coming, but the question was when and where. Nobody knew that.

Q: Was that in any sense a motivational factor in dealing with the midshipmen, that they may well have to fight?

Captain Edwards: No, I don't think we ever stressed that point. Of course, whoever makes the graduation speech always says that sort of thing, you know: "You're going to carry the ball." But that was just the routine admonition that the speaker gave the graduates.

Q: Well, that's appropriate, considering what line of work they're going into.

Captain Edwards: That's right, but, I mean, there was no pressure at our level saying that, "You're going to be in a shooting war here in five years or less." They read the papers, just like we did.

Q: How did you come to get assigned specifically to the Mahan after your tour at the Naval Academy?

Captain Edwards: I asked for it. My long-range plan was engineering duty only. I wanted therefore to be associated with the latest and best available, state-of-the-art machinery. So I went over personally to the Bureau of Navigation in Washington. I sat down with the detail officer and told him what I wanted. He got me ordered to the Mahan.* That same thing had happened when I went to the Augusta. I personally went down to the bureau and told the detail officer I wanted the latest thing in engineering. I put four new ships in commission for the reason that I wanted to be with the most up-to-date machinery.

Q: You were mentioning earlier that the Mahan had quite a

---

*USS Mahan (DD-364) was commissioned 18 September 1936. She had a standard displacement of 1,450 tons, was 341 feet long, and 35 feet in the beam. She had a top speed of 35 knots and a main battery of five 5-inch guns and 12 torpedo tubes. She was eventually sunk by Japanese aircraft near the Philippines on 7 December 1944.

few advances over the <u>Augusta</u>. What specifically were those?

Captain Edwards: Well, one small thing was the steam pressure. It was designed for 600 pounds per square inch, but they got cold feet and brought it back to 400. Both main engines, both turbine sets, were installed in the same space to cut down total machinery space. Normally in destroyers there were two boiler rooms and two engine rooms. Here they reduced the two engine rooms to one and installed the machinery very tightly.

They had a vacuum-type condensate system. Also, they installed an automatic throttle control. That works fine for a passenger ship, say, going day after day or hour after hour at the same speed. But in a destroyer we would have to have a throttleman there anyhow all the time because of the need for frequent speed changes. So that was a great mistake. They installed a tremendous main steam line steel casting which we had to eliminate eventually. We didn't take it out of the ship because we couldn't, but we just didn't use it.

Q: How would an automatic throttle control work?

Captain Edwards: You set it at whatever speed you wanted, and it automatically would open or close the main steam valve. It would automatically adjust to maintain a set speed--just like a cruise control on an automobile.

Now, we also had "Bain" metal piping for our steam and main feed lines. After we installed it in the ship we found out that to make any repairs to it we had to send it back to the factory. So a couple of times when we went to the New York Navy Yard, we removed sections of main steam or feed water piping and sent them back to Pittsburgh to have them altered. Well, that's no way to run a railroad. Also, we had cone-union joints instead of flanges on many of the small lines. Sooner or later they leaked, so we had to take them out and install flanges with gaskets.

Another thing was that they put the evaporator plant above our emergency diesel generator. Eventually we had to have a special shelf installed, with a drain on it, so the drips of water from the evaps wouldn't get on the diesel engine. Also, we had cone unions installed behind the main electrical switchboard in the engine room. We had leaks and moisture back of the main switchboard. Arrangements like that showed obvious lack of experience and understanding by the New York City designers.

They had a vacuum-type sealing system of all the condensate valves, and it was unworkable. If vibrations occurred, they started vacuum leaks, and we'd have to go around and tighten up on them. And they had a lot of copper piping, spaghetti-like piping, leading over to the condensate pumps. It simply was not a Navy type of installation.

Q: Why would the Navy accept that kind of design?

Captain Edwards: The Bureau of Engineering had a reputation of being fuddy-duddy, so it wanted to get an outside design. The job was given to Gibbs & Cox, which designed the United States later on.*

Q: Well, they also designed changes to the Leviathan when she was made into a passenger ship.**

Captain Edwards: They did several design jobs for the Navy, including other destroyers besides the Mahan class.***

Q: Gibbs & Cox had a good reputation. How would you account for these problems?

---

*SS United States was a 53,329-gross-ton, 990-foot-long passenger liner that went into service in 1952.
**USS Leviathan (SP-1326) was a former German passenger liner seized by the United States and used as a transport during World War I. After the war she was a commercial passenger ship for United States Lines, 1923-37.
***Gibbs & Cox did design work on the Sims (DD-409), Gleaves (DD-423), and Fletcher (DD-445) classes, as well as a number of post-World War II destroyers.

Captain Edwards: It was a good general reputation, but it was not experienced in naval work at that time.

Q: Were there other difficulties in the Mahan besides just in engineering?

Captain Edwards: We had other problems. In the hull, for example, the forward stack was so close to the forward superstructure that under certain relative wind conditions we got a swirl of gases. You couldn't even stay on the bridge, it was so bad. So they installed a big shield on the forward stack. Also, they installed wing doors on the open bridge, so that if worse came to worst you'd be protected from the gases coming in around the bridge. But most of it, 75% or more, was killed by the big shield on the stack. That was one thing.

They had built the ship with square access hatches to the machinery spaces. The Flusser went to sea in rough weather one time, and she came back with cracks around her square hatches.* Later, all the ships of that class got these round manhole-type hatches. That was another thing.

Also, the forward fireroom bulkhead was right up against the oil tanks. So we had to put in a spacer, a void, between that row of oil tanks and the forward fireroom. Otherwise, you had the fireroom heat up against

---

*The USS Flusser (DD-368) was a sister ship of the Mahan.

those tanks. Such design errors would drive you wild when you would see them. They were the result of inexperience. We were in the yard six months getting some of these major alterations.

Q: One of the disadvantages to that type of machinery space that you described is that you wouldn't have as much protection against flooding as it would with more compartmentation.

Captain Edwards: That's right, and the machinery was very crowded. For example, you might have one pump in front of another pump. If something happened to the inboard pump, you had to take out the outboard pump to get to the inboard pump. It was just not well designed to meet our requirements.

Q: So you'd lay a lot of this at Gibbs & Cox.

Captain Edwards: Yes, with all due disrespect. [Laughter]

Q: How did the sailors adapt to this plant?

Captain Edwards: I'd say we had to make do. That's all there was to it. When a major problem came up, we had to go to a yard and have them help us with it. I remember one time we had to lift up a whole deck plate to take a turbine out. That was a Navy yard-type job. I had my office in that space, so I was "unhorsed" for several weeks while we were putting in this new turbine.

Q: Why did you have to change turbines?

Captain Edwards: Blading failed.

Q: What advantages did you get from the higher steam pressure, over what was before?

Captain Edwards: A few percent more efficiency; that's all. But it's greatly over-exaggerated for a ship like a destroyer. A destroyer goes up and down, up and down in speed. Therefore, you cannot avail yourselves of the advantages of higher steam pressure. Now, if you had a passenger ship going across the Atlantic, or if you had a power plant ashore, where you put the boiler on the line for 30 days or 60 days, that higher steam pressure would give a great advantage. But if you have to cycle it back and forth, you destroy the advantage of the higher steam pressure. So at best the Mahan class was a poor design. In fact, Captain Joe Evans, chief engineer on the InSurv Board, wrote in his report that this ship should not get more than three days away from a Navy yard.*

Evans was the senior engineer and a damn good one, by the way. I followed him around on these trials with my tongue hanging out, because he worked day and night on everything he took part in. Another fellow on that InSurv team didn't do so well. They wanted to get in a secured fireroom, so we went in there, and it was 160 degrees. I was then a lieutenant. Half an hour later I walked out, but the commander on the board was carried out. He never went back to active duty; he had a heart attack.

Q: I wonder if you had built up a tolerance to it.

Captain Edwards: Probably had, yes.

Q: With all these problems, I suspect that a lot of things were learned in that class that were beneficial later.

Captain Edwards: Oh, yes--things not to do.

Q: Any other examples?

Captain Edwards: Let's see. Well, the main deck was not high enough. There should have been another couple of feet of height on the main deck freeboard, because when we went

---
*Captain Joseph S. Evans, USN, Board of Inspection and Survey.

to sea we often had water sluicing across the main deck. You had to watch the waves and run to the next deckhouse. Later on, in the DD-445 class, they put a closed centerline passage, fore and aft, see.*

Q: So you didn't have a way to go fore and aft inside the ship?

Captain Edwards: No. You had to run for it, from the bow area to amidships and aft, where the crew lived. You just had to watch the waves and make a run for it. If you got caught, you just grabbed the overhead under the motorboat stowage. You jumped up there and hung on. Your feet might be off the deck, but if you didn't grab something you could go overboard.

Q: Anything specifically you remember about the reduction gears or the propeller shafts?

Captain Edwards: No, the reduction gears were all right. Also, the propellers and propeller shafts were all right.

Q: Who was the first skipper of the Mahan?

---

*This is a reference to the Fletcher (DD-445) class of destroyers that began going into service in 1942.

Captain Edwards: J. B. W. Waller, class of '14.* His father was a more or less noted Marine Corps officer in the Spanish-American War. And this fellow had a feeling that some of that rubbed off on him. He was a Dr. Jekyll and Mr. Hyde.

For example, we had an officers' motorboat and a crew's launch. He took over the officers' motorboat for himself. The officers, except himself, rode in the open launch. Many times we got wet going ashore, so we turned around and went back to the ship. Also, we had a division commander's mess up on the upper deck, in case we had a division commander embarked. The captain would have guests out for a special dinner, in which he and his guests were the only people at that table. We in the wardroom paid the bill.

That bastard was just a very hard person to live with. For example, Waller sat in the wardroom at the end of the table. The exec was to his right and then the engineer to his left and so on down. There were eight officers. It was customary in ships at that time, when the skipper or the exec was at the head of the table, to use a "buck." It might be a napkin ring or something comparable that we'd rotate around so that everybody got a turn at being served first. Not Waller. Waller always was first--always. I was over on the left side, so I was always last.

---

*Commander John B. W. Waller, USN, son of Major General Littleton W. T. Waller, USMC. At the turn of the century his father became well known for his service during the Boxer Rebellion and the Philippine Insurrection.

I guess he didn't like engineers or something. He gave me an additional duty as the ship's service officer, which was a very petty, laborious job. I'd sit up nights counting the chits and so forth. I finally told him, I said, "Captain, I want to be either the ship's service officer or the chief engineer. I can't do both." So he assigned that job to somebody else. While I was still ship's service officer he said my accounts had to come out to the penny every month. Well, nobody comes out to the penny every month. If you come out to the nearest $10.00 or $20.00, you're lucky. But he had a supply officer come down from the Navy yard to investigate me. The supply officer told him it was impossible to come out to the penny.

The captain's personality depended on the situation. Ashore, with women around, he was the life of the party. When the ship was at Barbados during our shakedown cruise, I met a certain very nice woman there. We went out on a swimming party Sunday morning, and she said to me, "How do you like your skipper?" She looked at me, and I looked at her, and I didn't say anything. She said, "I understand." He was just a bastard. It was ironical that our midshipmen sons became good friends.

Q: How was Waller operationally?

Captain Edwards: Satisfactory is the word--nothing special.

Q: How well did that class perform tactically in comparison with the four-stackers?

Captain Edwards: They performed better. They had more power and more rudder control. The four-stackers were peas in a pod, you know, out of World War I. And you knew one, you knew them all. They were very fine training-type ships, but as warships they were second-class.

Q: Well, they could mount a sonar, which was certainly an advantage.

Captain Edwards: Yes, and during World War II the Navy converted quite a few of them into other types. One was the APD, in which they took out the forward fireroom and made it into troop quarters. And then we had a couple of others--minesweepers and minelayers, etc. So they served a very useful purpose but not all as they were originally intended. Later, after the war, some were sold, and a few of them became banana boats. They had one engine room and one fireroom in that configuration.

Q: What do you remember about the Mahan's antiair and antisubmarine capabilities?

Captain Edwards: We had the usual torpedo tubes, but some were mounted on the centerline, as I recall. Sonar was improved. As sonar went, it was elementary, but it was state of the art at that time. We had depth charges. So they were good, all-around destroyers but turned out to be not the tops.

Q: How did the Mahan ride in heavy seas?

Captain Edwards: Rough. We were under way to Trinidad from New York one November day with a Northeaster blowing. It hit us right on the port quarter. When I was talking to somebody, she took a deep roll. I got up and stood on my porthole till she came back.

Q: So it went over at least 45 degrees.

Captain Edwards: A quartering sea is bad for any long, narrow ship. They had an approximate 10:1 length-beam ratio. Even in the four-stackers, when we went into a quartering sea, you could stand on the bulkhead.

F. A. Edwards #3 - 207

Q: Did you have any sense that the ship was top-heavy?

Captain Edwards: No, that came in later with that class after I left it. They installed 40-millimeter and 20-millimeter guns and new radars.

Q: What else do you remember about that shakedown cruise in late 1936?

Captain Edwards: We went to Trinidad, where we met the Indianapolis, which had FDR on board.* We had been outfitted to take the President on a fishing trip at Trinidad, but it didn't happen. We had all kinds of things fitted out for him. For instance, we had a low shaving mirror and a long ramp from the upper deck level forward to the main deck level aft for his wheelchair. As I say, it so happened that he didn't transfer over to the Mahan, but we used that authority to no end. Anything we wanted, we put in a requisition for it because it was to be the President's ship. We left the Navy yard with about a dozen brand-new movies that hadn't even been shown ashore yet. They were still in the cans, and every night for about five nights or so we showed three movies, from dusk until dawn, seeing these beautiful--in those days--color movies.

---
*President Franklin D. Roosevelt was on board the heavy cruiser Indianapolis (CA-35) from 18 November to 15 December 1936 for a "Good-Neighbor" cruise to Brazil, Argentina, and Uruguay. The cruise went via the Caribbean.

F. A. Edwards #3 - 208

Q: That was very rare in the Thirties.

Captain Edwards: Yes. Well, they were just brand-new and for the President. So to be sure of satisfaction for him, we showed them ourselves!

Q: What do you remember about the Mahan's operations, once you got the shakedown done?

Captain Edwards: Well, they were, I'd say, routine. You never had a good day. There was always some damn thing; something was going to happen. You could never write night orders and expect them to be carried out, because something would happen in the meantime.

Q: I wonder if you could go into more detail on your duty as ship's service officer. What sorts of things did you sell?

Captain Edwards: Well, mostly candies, tobaccos, and soft drinks. When we went down to Rio on our shakedown cruise of the Mahan, we took 1,200 bottles of Coke, which we put in the bilges, because we had nowhere else to put them. They took care of our crew. Also, when we had guests we served Cokes. The visitors were very appreciative because they didn't get Cokes in town. In fact, at that time I thought if I were smart I would resign my commission and get the Coca-Cola concession for Brazil and be a multi-millionaire in no time. But I didn't have the guts, so I didn't do it.

Q: Did you have a gedunk stand per se?

Captain Edwards: No, it wasn't a big enough ship. We just had a great big locker amidships which we opened up a couple of times a day, morning and afternoon. Candy bars in those days were five cents. We bought them for 3.3 and sold them for five.

Q: Did you have a means of cooling the Cokes?

Captain Edwards: Yes, we had an ice machine and a freezer aboard, and so we put ice cubes in them.

Q: What about necessities like soap and shaving cream and razor blades?

Captain Edwards: We sold those things too. We had a whole range of toiletries. We ran into salesmen alongside a dock, anytime, day or night. In those days they weren't selling too much stuff ashore, so we were real welcome.

Q: What did you do with the profits from this operation?

Captain Edwards: Welfare and recreation. It went into athletic gear primarily. We bought baseballs and bats and footballs for the crew. It was entirely nonprofit. We had to make a report, though, but there was no profit.

Q: But the benefits went back to the crew.

Captain Edwards: That's right.

Q: The destroyers from that era, the new ones, were known as the "gold-platers." Did some of the older destroyer sailors envy you?

Captain Edwards: Well, yes, because, after all, we had the state of the art. World War I ships were elementary compared to the ones we were on.

Q: Did you also do underway refueling in the *Mahan*?

Captain Edwards: Yes. The oiler had an overhead crane which held up the hose in a great big loop. We hauled it aboard and put it into a fueling trunk about 18 inches in diameter. From the first tank we fueled the other tanks.

F. A. Edwards #3 - 211

To facilitate that process, before we refueled we arranged all of our oil in order to empty the largest number of tanks. So we could fuel in maybe 45 minutes or so. We'd be able to fuel and get clear. That was routine.

Q: How much did the Bureau of Engineering and the Bureau of Construction and Repair pay attention to your operations because the ship was so new?

Captain Edwards: Well, the Board of Inspection and Survey was the one that really counted. I prepared alteration after alteration for these Mahan-class ships and gave them to the board. And then the board got the Bureau of Engineering to make the changes. And same way with the hull. I wrote up most of the hull alterations for that class of ship, although I was an engineer. Then the Board of Inspection and Survey put the bee on the bureaus to authorize these things. That's where we got most of our leverage.

Q: Any specific memories you have of that period when the ship was being constructed?

Captain Edwards: I was only there in connection with fitting out. I had little or nothing to do with the basic construction. I prepared the alterations that seemed warranted. In most cases they were approved. But the Bureau of C&R in those days was rather unfeeling, I'll say, of ships. If you wanted something that was obvious, the answer came back no. So we did a lot of things ourselves, and the hell with them. We did get the shipyard's help on some things, as long as it did not affect the safety of the ship or people.

Q: How do you account for that attitude on the part of the bureaus?

Captain Edwards: Lack of connection with the ships, with the seagoing Navy. The constructors in those days were the "upstairs" boys.

Q: Ivory tower.

Captain Edwards: Ivory tower. The C&R people had little to do with the nuts and bolts, and they had very little understanding. So I used to do things with the permission of my skipper, to improve the ship, knowing full well that I couldn't get C&R to approve it. But that's why, I guess, they went eventually to the "con-engineer" concept and the Bureau of Ships, rather than Engineering and Construction and Repair.* We used to call it the "Bureau of

_____
*Captain Edwards discusses the combined constructor-engineer (con-engineer) in a later interview in connection with the merger of the two bureaus.

Destruction and Despair." [Laughter] There was a lot of feeling in those days, but it did subside as time went on.

Q: Did Gibbs & Cox show a willingness to stay in touch and learn from their mistakes?

Captain Edwards: I doubt it, because most of their money came from civilian jobs. They were also expensive. They got a contract later on to design a bunch of destroyers--just design them. J. J. Henry, my boss, said he thought the price included the building of the first ship--they were so expensive.* He told me he'd do the design for half the price, but there were a lot of internal connections there that Henry couldn't fight. He was an outsider.

Q: So Gibbs & Cox had an in with the bureau?

Captain Edwards: That's right, with bureau people. I felt at one time I would resign my commission and get myself a writer, a hatchet man, and go to town on Gibbs & Cox and the bureaus. That's how badly I felt. But I didn't. I took it lying down.

---

*J. J. Henry & Company was a civilian naval architecture firm for which Captain Edwards worked in the late 1950s, following his retirement from the Navy.

Q: What do you remember about the <u>Mahan</u>'s performance in operation? Did you operate with the fleet?

Captain Edwards: Yes. Of course, our first trip was the shakedown cruise. We were supposed to go to the Mediterranean, but at that time the Spanish Civil War broke out, and we were shunted to the Caribbean and to South America. Other ships already on station near Spain took care of the refugees; there were a lot of American refugees who had to be gotten out. So I didn't get there at that time.

We stopped first at Trinidad, where we met the <u>Indianapolis</u>, which had brought down the President and Cordell Hull.* Then we went over to Barbados to kill some time while the President's party went on down to Rio, then back to Trinidad. After the <u>Indianapolis</u> returned and went on north, we went to Rio ourselves. Then we came up to Guantanamo and then home. Following the cruise we were in the New York Navy Yard for six months to install some of these alterations. The ship was torn apart, really, getting these alterations. We were the guinea pig for that whole class of destroyers.

We spent two weeks down at Rio; that was very nice. The Brazilian liaison officer was a lieutenant commander

---

*Cordell Hull was the Secretary of State, a participant in the President's goodwill cruise to South America.

named Suzano, who later became head of Brazil's Navy.* I didn't know him later, but in 1936 he and his wife were very nice to us down there. We stayed two weeks, and they took us to the Copacabana Beach, nightclubs, and that sort of thing.

Q: It sounds very appealing.

Captain Edwards: I felt that I wanted to go back again, which I did. I've been back four or five times since then under different circumstances--as a tourist.

Q: Well, for that crew at least, it fulfilled the recruiting pledge: "Join the Navy and see the world."

Captain Edwards: And we got a good idea of the ship's capabilities.

Another thing that happened in Rio was that we fueled the ship, and that caused several problems. I'll tell you a funny story; it's a dirty story. We were fueling from a barge while at anchor. Waller, the skipper, insisted that I fuel to 100% of the tank capacity. I said to him, "We should only fuel to 95%. You've got to allow a certain air cushion."

---

*In the early 1960s the Brazilian Minister of Marine was Almirante de Esquadra Pedro Paulo de Aranjo Suzano.

I said, "Aye, aye, sir," and we fueled. Pretty soon there was an air bubble in this line, which went "BOOP," and flecks of oil were all over the crew's bunking area. An enlisted man came to me and said, "Mr. Edwards, we had a fart in the fuel line."

On top of that, the captain was going to make me pay for all this. I said, "No, sir. I'm not paying anybody anything. It was your order, which I objected to." So we took it out of the ship's service fund to buy new mattresses and linen for the crew. I say, he was a bastard.

Q: That wasn't exactly kosher.

Captain Edwards: I personally objected to it, but we steamed 15 knots all the way to Guantanamo without a stop, which showed that class could operate that far and have plenty to spare.

Even though I didn't have to pay for the bedding, I did have to calculate how much the ship would pay for the oil, and that was a real struggle. For one thing, Brazil measures temperature in centigrade, and we, of course, use Fahrenheit. Their volume is liters instead of gallons. Their money is Cruzeiros, and ours is dollars. I had to reconcile these three things in order to sign an invoice for what we got. I had my engineer's manual out, and I sat down with this guy for a couple of hours at least. We dickered and dickered, and I finally signed that invoice. That's the only time I ever had to do that.

Q: Why would the difference between Fahrenheit and centigrade be a factor?

Captain Edwards: Oil is supposed to be delivered internationally at a certain temperature, 60 degrees Fahrenheit. Oil expands. If you took oil at 60 degrees, that's a certain volume. If you took it at 70 degrees, you'd have more oil because it expanded. You had to have a common denominator, a common base.

Q: Makes sense. Did you get out into the Pacific in that ship?

Captain Edwards: Yes. I left her in San Diego. We had an interesting experience on the way.

The cruiser <u>Omaha</u> had grounded near San Salvador.* We were ordered to stand by her and at high tides steam at full power in tight circles to build up waves. We went about 25 knots, which was as fast as we could go in the

---

*The light cruiser <u>Omaha</u> (CL-4) went aground near Castle Island Light in the Bahamas on 19 July 1937. She was refloated on 29 July through the combined efforts of tugs, beach gear, and artificial waves from five destroyers.

shallow water, trying to rock and roll the Omaha. At the same time, a tug pulled astern on her. Also, there was a barge there to take off ammunition and dry stores.

We spent several days there, going ashore between high tides. There were only two or three people ashore there, a family. Those poor devils were living in that place--fishermen, I guess.

Then we went around through the Panama Canal, and I was relieved at San Diego.

Interview Number 4 with Captain Frederick A. Edwards,
U.S. Navy (Retired)

Place: Captain Edwards's Apartment, Annapolis, Maryland

Date: Tuesday, 25 February 1992

Interviewer: Paul Stillwell

Q: Captain, we begin today with a discussion of your service in the USS New Mexico. How did that assignment come about?

Captain Edwards: My time in the Mahan was up. I had asked for battleship duty, and I got the New Mexico, which was my happiest ship; really, a wonderful ship. Everybody was a little casual, and yet they got the job done.

Q: Why do you remember her as such a happy ship?

Captain Edwards: Well, just people. Harry Power, class of '20, was my chief engineer.* Harry was a fine guy. I knew him when I was a plebe at the Naval Academy. After he graduated in 1919, he was kept over for the summer to train the plebes. Then, later on, he was in Destroyer Division 30 on the West Coast. My ship, the Henshaw, was one ship, and he was in the McCawley, one of the other ships of that

---
*Lieutenant Commander Harry D. Power, USN. As a captain, Power commanded the light cruiser Birmingham (CL-62) during the Okinawa campaign in 1945.

division. Later he was the chief engineer of the <u>New Mexico</u>. Harry was not an engineer. He was not a dummy by any means, but he was not a technical engineer, as I was.

Q: So he relied on you a lot.

Captain Edwards: So he relied on me, and we had no problems whatsoever.

Q: Was he sort of the front man for the department?

Captain Edwards: He was the front man, yes, and certainly a capable officer. He let me run the plant, and we just got along swimmingly. I knew him socially for many years after that. The other people, too, were very nice. Frank Jack Fletcher, who was later on in the Pacific was a task force commander, was our skipper at that time.*

Q: Well, please tell me more about him.

Captain Edwards: Well, I didn't know too much about him, because I just reported to him; that's all. I had no personal contact except to sit down at dinner with him on occasion, that sort of thing. I didn't really know him.

---

*Captain Frank Jack Fletcher, USN. Fletcher reached the rank of vice admiral during World War II. He commanded carrier task forces during the battles of Coral Sea, Midway, and Guadalcanal.

Q: What was Fletcher's reputation in the ship?

Captain Edwards: Good. He was a little bit austere but a good officer. But he was not a particularly friendly man. You wouldn't tell him an off-color story.

Q: Well, comparing the personalities between him and Richardson, what comparison would you draw?

Captain Edwards: Well, I would pick Richardson because I thought he was more a solid citizen. He had more experience, and I had more confidence in him. I knew Richardson well, and I didn't know Fletcher well, so that's maybe an unfair statement.

Q: I see.

Captain Edwards: So I won't want to stress that.

Q: Captain Fletcher was relieved by Captain Jacobs.* Do you recall him?

Captain Edwards: Yes, a very nice guy. He was not a top-

---

*Captain Walter F. Jacobs, USN.

flight naval officer as such, but he was a nice guy. His wife was also very friendly with the officers' wives. Frank Jack was aloof. Jacobs wasn't; he was very friendly.

Q: Was Mrs. Jacobs sort of a mother hen for these other wives?

Captain Edwards: Yes, she even had them call her by her first name, Winnie. She organized the rest of the officers' wives, took them places, and did things together. She was very well liked. I don't think I ever met Fletcher's wife. The Fletchers were more or less standoffish. That's not wrong, but it was just the way they were.

Q: What was it like taking over from Lieutenant Commander Rickover on board the New Mexico?*

Captain Edwards: I didn't take over from him in person, although I got his job as senior assistant engineer officer. He had just left the ship, and I reported a few days later. I did have to deal with the results of his reign.

Rickover had left a feeling of fear behind him. Men were afraid to talk if they had a casualty. When somebody

---

*Edwards's immediate predecessor was Lieutenant Commander Hyman G. Rickover, USN. Rickover eventually became a four-star admiral and for many years ran the Navy's nuclear power program.

opened or closed the wrong valve at the wrong time, why, nobody would admit knowing anything about it. They just clammed up. It took me most of a year to be able to talk to people and get them to admit they did something wrong-- the idea of using that as a training device. It wasn't to punish them; it was to learn from our mistakes.

He had made enemies on the ship. When I went to the "New Mex," the first lieutenant was a man in the class of '18, Sonny Sullivan.* I had been there about two days when he came in and started bawling me out. I said, "What's this all about?" In those days it was the first lieutenant who was in charge of the potable water, which the engineers had distilled. Well, there was a little friction about potable water being transferred up to the storage tanks. Sullivan said Rickover had sent up water that was too salty to drink, so Sullivan came in and started working me over. I said, "I'm sorry, I'm just new here, and I don't know what you're talking about." We made friends after that, but I had inherited the ill will Sullivan had developed from dealing with Rickover.

Rickover had the crew afraid. I made an inspection every evening before the 8:00 o'clock reports. As the senior assistant engineer, I would tour the engineering department and report on all the divisions to the chief, Harry Power. When I went into the evaporator room, the

_____
*Lieutenant Commander John R. Sullivan, USN.

watch stander came up with a dish full of new water and said, "It's three-tenths [of a grain of salt per gallon of water]" or whatever it was that night.

I said, "Who told you to do this?"

"Mr. Rickover did."

I said, "Knock it off." This was just a ritual that Rickover had installed to satisfy his ego.

I got these people so they were all on the same team--officers and crew alike working together. Rickover just had a reign of fear on that ship.

Q: Did he punish people whenever anything went wrong? Was that why they clammed up?

Captain Edwards: Oh, yes. We had four chief warrant officers, one in each division. The one in charge of the auxiliaries was a damn good one. Rickover had demoted him to tool-room keeper because he hadn't done something Rickover wanted him to do. I put him back on his regular job. Rickover didn't demote the man in rank; he demoted him in job. A tool-room keeper was a first class machinist's mate's job.

Rickover just simply was a discredit to the Navy and to officers and men in general. Yet he got what he wanted later on by kissing the asses of various congressmen and senators. They thought he was wonderful. Later it came to light that Rickover had presented expensive baubles to certain politicians' wives. He had extracted these gifts from contractors with whom he had business contacts.

Q: There are stories about extreme measures Rickover took to conserve fuel, like cold showers and inadequate lighting. Did you improve that situation?

Captain Edwards: Very much. I fitted out all of the washrooms on the ship with mirrors. We put in nickel or nickel-plated wash basins with hot and cold water. The men had been washing out of buckets before that.

We had a program to use but conserve electricity. The slogan was, "When not in use, turn off the juice." If you came out of a storeroom, turn off the light. If nobody is there, don't leave a light on. That's the sort of thing I'm talking about. We had the full cooperation of the crew, because they had hot water any time they wanted it, and they also had facilities that they hadn't had before.

Q: I'm surprised that it would be the engineering department's responsibility to provide the washroom and head facilities.

Captain Edwards: Well, it wasn't our responsibility, but

we offered because we cooperated with the first lieutenant. That was the first lieutenant's job, but we did the plumbing work. In fact, we did it for the engineers. They were so enamored of it that word spread, and then we did it for the whole crew.

Q: Was there still the interest in fuel economy during that era when you were the assistant chief?

Captain Edwards: Yes. The chief would have one ensign a month assigned, among other things, to make up the daily fuel reports. Then the ensign gave them to me to accept or reject. This is a peripheral thing, but any time I objected, he had to give the chief a cigar as "punishment" for not doing it correctly. So he got a lot of cigars. It was called Form H. It was a horrible thing like an income tax, a nasty form. But as a veteran, I knew all about it.

Q: Did you stand bridge watches in that ship?

Captain Edwards: No, I did not. I was the assistant engineer, so I would take the watch down below at times just for my own education.

Now, we had four boilers out of the battle cruisers which were scrapped.* These were big White-Foster

---
*In 1916 Congress authorized construction of six battle cruisers. Work began on all six ships of the Lexington (CC-1) class, then stopped because of the Washington Naval Treaty of 1922. Two of the six were completed as aircraft carriers: Lexington (CV-2) and Saratoga (CV-3).

boilers, and they had the same capacity as the six Bureau Express boilers in the <u>Mississippi</u> and <u>Idaho</u>, the <u>New Mexico</u>'s sister ships. When the <u>New Mexico</u> was modernized, the yard installed these leftover boilers, one boiler per fireroom.* The Bureau "Cox" boilers in the <u>Idaho</u> and <u>Mississippi</u> were four-drum type, two steam drums and two water drums. The <u>New Mexico</u> could make full power on only three boilers. And we could make 18 knots, which was usual operating speed, with only two boilers. That annoyed the hell out of the engineers in these two sister ships, because we didn't have to light off any more boilers. We could steam on two boilers at 18 knots, no problem at all.

Q: If you could make full power on three boilers, why did you have four?

Captain Edwards: In case we had a casualty, it was a standby. Suppose you had some brick work fall out of your firebox or something. Or suppose you had a tube blow out. Well, you had another boiler. But, I say, these boilers had over-capacity for the <u>New Mexico</u> class. The ship had three engine rooms. The wing engine rooms had one engine only, and the center engine room had two engines.

---

*The <u>New Mexico</u> was modernized by the Philadelphia Navy Yard from March 1931 to January 1933. Besides the engineering changes, her cage masts were replaced by a tower foremast, and she got anti-torpedo hull blisters.

Q: That was pretty standard battleship design of that era. I know the Pennsylvania class just before that had the same arrangement.

Captain Edwards: Yes.

Q: Did you have any speed advantage over the Idaho and Mississippi?

Captain Edwards: Not really. They were 21-knot ships. We may have had two- or three-tenths or maybe half a knot. We could produce more steam than the turbines could take, so we made the maximum speed that the turbines would take.

Q: Had the ship gotten new turbines when she was modernized?

Captain Edwards: Yes. She was originally electric drive. They took out those big generators and motors and put in Westinghouse geared turbines. They were excellent turbines, by the way. No problems.

Q: Was that an indication that the turbo-electric system didn't work as well?

Captain Edwards: No, it was an indication that if you had a casualty--say, a flooding--you were in trouble. If a generator or motor flooded, you had to rewire it aboard or take it completely out of the ship and take it back to the factory for rewiring. So electric drive fell out of favor at Pearl Harbor.

Q: How reliable was that overall engineering plant in the New Mexico?

Captain Edwards: Very reliable, very reliable. Initially they had some turbine blades fall out, but they corrected that. After that we had no problems at all with it.

Q: One thing I've been struck by--looking at pictures of those three ships--is that they were almost identical--more similarity than almost any class of ship you'll see.

Captain Edwards: That class, after their modernization, was, I felt, the best ships that we had.

Q: They were in the late Thirties certainly.

Captain Edwards: They had heavy armor--deck armor and special interior armor. They were beautiful ships. We called them solid citizens; they were dependable ships.

Q: The New Mexico's slogan was "The Queen."

Captain Edwards: That's right.

When I was a midshipman, I was in Seattle on board the old Michigan in 1920. I took time off and went over to see the yard as a spectator. The New Mexico then was tied up at the Navy Yard, Puget Sound, Bremerton. I had no idea that 17 years later I would be in that ship.

Q: She still had the cage masts at that point.

Captain Edwards: Oh, yes. That was to get the visual gun range, which we didn't need later on because we had planes. We had these little observation planes on board. And still later radar took over.

Q: The New Mexico class, when modernized, didn't have a maintop, which meant that they had to depend exclusively on airplane spotting.

Captain Edwards: That's right. So, as I said, by that time we didn't need the basket-type masts. I had a warm spot in my heart for the New Mexico. She was a very happy ship. Everybody on there was very compatible.

F. A. Edwards #4 - 231

Q: Well, I've heard something that's attributed to old Navy veterans, that ships have personalities. Some have good ones and some have bad ones.

Captain Edwards: I've heard that too, but it's the personalities of the persons, not the ship. We were kidding all the time. We had a good happy ship.

I remember one time we were in Panama. In Panama they had "silver" employees; they were the natives, blacks. And "gold" employees were the whites. Well, one morning at breakfast there was a commotion out in the wardroom pantry. The paymaster was in charge, and he was out there settling them down. Somebody said, "What's going on?"

The answer was, "'Pay' has had a little trouble with his silver employees."

Q: When was that?

Captain Edwards: Oh, gee, that was probably '38, when we went through the canal both east and west.

Q: Probably on a fleet problem, wouldn't it have been?

Captain Edwards: Yes. At that same time we were headed north from Panama to Norfolk Easter morning. The exec was Commander J. J. Brown, class of '12. We called him Jiggy

Jig Brown.*

Q: You told me he was one of the duty officers at the Naval Academy. How was he as an executive officer? Was he the same way he'd been at Annapolis?

Captain Edwards: Well, he was sort of an annoyance at times. He was always inspecting this and that and always looking in the dark corners. His wife was semi-mentally disturbed, and she was a pain in the neck. I shouldn't say that, but it's true. Brown was respected, but not as much as his relief, Commander Pickhardt.** The latter was calm, quiet, and above petty practices.

Q: Well, inspecting to detail was the Navy way. It sounds as if Brown went a little beyond the norm.

Captain Edwards: He did. I'd say he was on the smaller side. He got all the small things done right, but I don't think he did the big things properly. I'll give you an example of something small. For Easter that year he decided he was going to increase the morale of the ship. He had a lot of Easter eggs painted in the galley. They ended up being distributed around the ship. Easter morning

---
*"Jig" was the word used for the letter J in the phonetic alphabet of the time.
**Commander Adolph von S. Pickhardt, USN.

about 9:30 or 10:00 o'clock, I happened to be standing on deck when an order came over the loudspeaker, "All hands on deck for Easter egg hunt." I was standing next to a first-class boatswain's mate, big ham-handed guy. He said, "I'll be goddamned. On a battleship, an Easter egg hunt."

Another time we had a happy hour there at Guantanamo, and there was a tall, gangly Negro mess attendant watching boxing tryouts there. Jiggy Jig said to this kid, "Why don't you try out for boxing? You'd be like Joe Louis."*

This coon said, "Well, Commander, suh, I'se not a fighter. I'se a lover." So that became a watchword from then on--"I'se not a fighter. I'se a lover."

We had a lot of happy hours. We went over to Port-au-Prince about that same time. They had a fleet review for the President of Haiti, a big, tall black guy.** A cruiser picked up the President down at Port-au-Prince and brought him to Gonaives Bay, where we were anchored. Then the cruiser steamed between the rows of ships at anchor for inspection. In our hearing the band on this cruiser was playing "Black Bottom," which in those days was a popular song. Fortunately, he didn't know what it was.

During that trip we dry-docked the New Mexico at Balboa, Panama. They had a big dry dock down there, which had been there since they built the canal. It had very

---

*Joe Louis was a talented black heavyweight boxer of the period. He won the world title in 1938.
**Stenio Vincent was then the President of Haiti.

limited facilities for the crew, including no hot water. After we docked there, I wrote a letter that went up the chain of command. In it I spelled out what they needed for better crew's facilities and also for ship facilities. Believe it or not, some of those things were actually done a couple of years later.

Q: Was this a graving dock?

Captain Edwards: Yes, and it took the <u>New Mexico</u> with no trouble.

Q: I had not heard about repairs being done in Panama.

Captain Edwards: Well, they had the Panama Railroad shops there. They did certain emergency repairs, small repairs, but this was dry-docking.

Q: Could you tell a difference in speed and fuel efficiency after the bottom was scraped?

Captain Edwards: Oh, yes, it was obvious. You were supposed to use so many RPMs for a certain number of knots. Well, if you had a foul bottom, maybe you'd need the RPMs for another half a knot in order to make the same overall speed over the ground.

Q: Well, and presumably you would have a lower maximum speed too.

Q: That's correct. Another thing we did to remove barnacles from the <u>New Mexico</u> was to list ship. For instance, when we were in Pearl Harbor, we would list the ship maybe 12-15 degrees and then scrape that exposed belt. There was a belt there, anywhere from three to five feet, covered with barnacles. We'd scrape them all off and paint the hull. Then the next day we'd roll over to the other side and do the same thing.

Q: Did you list the ship just by pumping fluids internally?

Captain Edwards: Yes. With fluids, which we controlled, of course. We had permission, so everybody knew we were going to do this and that we weren't going to capsize.

Q: You'd have to have a fair number of empty tanks to be able to do that.

Captain Edwards: That's right. We'd flood voids. I may be wrong about the number of degrees, but it was a healthy list. Everybody griped and groaned.

Q: You were a fairly senior officer on board the ship. What were the living accommodations like?

Captain Edwards: I was a lieutenant commander then. The heads of departments were on the main deck. The chief engineer was on the starboard side of the main deck. I was on the deck below, aft; I had a good room. By rank I was where I belonged, down there with the lieutenants and lieutenant commanders.

Q: Did you have any collateral duties?

Captain Edwards: I had just been promoted, and by the ship's regulations the junior lieutenant commander had to be in charge of the landing force. Well, I knew nothing about a landing force, so I boned up on it. When we got to Guantanamo, we had landing force drills and inspection. I spent a lot of time preparing my officers for what their jobs were and so forth. We got along splendidly with 400 or 500 men in the landing force.

I recall another time when my rank fitted an extra duty. When the ship was up at Frisco once, I was sent as senior shore patrol officer. I reported to the chief of police. The police took me by the hand and took me all around and showed me some of the evening sights that I didn't know existed.

Q: What did they include?

Captain Edwards: At one place they had a bunch of men dressed up as women, putting on suggestive dances and whatnot. At a distance you couldn't tell them from real women. That was news to me. And they also took me down to various houses of prostitution. That was really a sight to see. I was just a country boy. Even when I was in my late 30s, I was a country boy.

Q: What was the Navy's method of dealing with venereal disease in that era?

Captain Edwards: Well, they gave men the various prophylactic treatments. They warned them and all that sort of thing. They made speeches, but you cannot talk certain people out of certain things. They'll listen to you, but they'll do something else. Before they went ashore, they could get these shots; after they came back, they could get these shots. Our junior doctor was there to help them.

Q: What was the home port like, living there in Long Beach or San Pedro?

Captain Edwards: Well, it was all right, except we weren't there too much. We made an annual cruise, usually south or to the East Coast. We'd be gone anywhere from two to five months. And then we had an overhaul every 18 months, which was three months long, usually at Bremerton. We had various tactical exercises, at least once a month when we were in there. We were out for long weekends, four and five days, on tactical exercises. So it was nice when we had it, but we didn't have it too much of the time.

Q: The general pattern when you were in home port was to go out on Monday and come back on Friday and have the weekends in port.

Captain Edwards: That's right. That was it.

Q: How capable a job did Bremerton do in supporting the New Mexico?

Captain Edwards: Excellent. Bremerton is an excellent yard. In fact, I think it's the best yard we have.

Q: That really was the specialized battleship yard.

Captain Edwards: Yes. I overhauled five times in a

destroyer, and I got the same kind of treatment.

Q: Did you ever get technical consultation with the manufacturers' representatives, like Babcock & Wilcox or so forth?

Captain Edwards: Yes, they would drift through, maybe once a month or once a quarter, to see if you had any troubles. They'd like to also sell us something if they had something new to try out. For example, we bought some excellent pressure-reducing valves that one of those companies had. They gave us a sample, which we bought some more of later on, because they were very good. Steam pressure went from 300 pounds down to maybe 150 or whatever you wanted for an auxiliary. A pump couldn't take 300 pounds; it would only take maybe 100 pounds. A reducing valve would bring the pressure down.

Q: What do you remember about the fellowship in the wardroom of the New Mexico?

Captain Edwards: Excellent; it was excellent. That's why I say it was the happiest ship I was ever on. And everybody was mindful of the other fellows' jobs and their positions.

Q: Did you bring your family on board when you had duty days?

Captain Edwards: Sometimes for dinner on weekends, Saturdays or Sundays, but not on weekdays. It was just reserved for Sundays.

Q: So they'd have dinner and maybe watch the movie.

Captain Edwards: Yes, and it was just a way to kill a weekend.

Q: Well, and it's interesting to see dad's office. That's a lot different from most office buildings, which don't have guns on them.

Captain Edwards: Well, dad's office, which was the engineering log room, was a working office--not very pretty--with standard Navy furniture, which was not pretty. I shared it with Harry Power. He and I had adjacent desks.

Q: One of the junior officers in that ship later became a famous aviator, Butch O'Hare.* Did you know him?

---
*Ensign Edward H. O'Hare, USN, had graduated from the Naval Academy in 1937 and served in the <u>New Mexico</u> prior to reporting for flight training. In February 1942, he became the Navy's first fighter ace of World War II.

Captain Edwards: The O'Hare I knew was sort of overweight and I thought not a 4.0 officer. He didn't impress me too much. Nice guy, but he didn't impress me. Now, we had another fellow named Bob Erly, who later made rear admiral.* He was a fresh-caught ensign at that time.

Q: He and O'Hare were classmates.

Captain Edwards: They were both there at the same time, but I didn't realize that he was the O'Hare who became an aviator later.

Q: What do you remember about Erly?

Captain Edwards: Well, he was a nice guy and on the ball. He was always willing and able to do things, and I thought well of him.

Q: From my listening to his descriptions, he was a real go-getter.

Captain Edwards: Well, he was. He was a go-getter, always able and willing and full of beans--that sort.
    Now, O'Hare was not. He was a passive type. Nothing

---

*Ensign Robert B. Erly, USN. Erly's oral history is in the Naval Institute collection.

against him, but he was sort of passive and did not impress me.

Q: At lunch we were mentioning the role of the blacks in the Navy of that period. In the New Mexico I presume they were the steward's mates and mess attendants.

Captain Edwards: We had both Filipinos and blacks. They were all right, but they're still what they are. They were a necessary evil, let me say. We had to have them, but they were not top-flight people. I remember once the mess treasurer looked in the wardroom at, say, midnight, and here was a black with a big ham bone, turning it around and eating it just like a drumstick or like rotating a typewriter roller.

We had two ways of handling the mess attendants financially. In one option they were on the mess. We took their food allowance and combined it with our own money. Or we put them on their own allowance and fed them beans and whatnot out of that. I saw it both ways. I preferred their eating out of their own allowance. That is, they and the other enlisted men were allowed so much a day for food. Then they could feed themselves out of that money and have a separate mess, instead of belonging to our mess. If it was a combined arrangement, they ate our mess food, and they always ate about twice as much as we ate. So, I say, it was better financially for us to have them on their own mess. If we took up their allowance and then fed them off our mess, they were eating better food at our expense.

Q: The steward's mates also took care of the officers' rooms, didn't they?

Captain Edwards: Yes. Each officer didn't have a separate boy, but a boy would take care of several rooms.

Q: Clean them and make the beds and what have you?

Captain Edwards: That's right.

Q: Did you have a feeling for how the black sailors and the white sailors got along?

Captain Edwards: Well, they had separate quarters. Once in a while there'd be a fight, but nothing to write home about.

Any sailor who got into a fight was sent up on the forecastle to finish it--black or white or brown. The fighters had to go up there and be supervised by the chief master-at-arms and finish their fight. People came up as spectators.

F. A. Edwards #4 - 244

Q: So that was entertainment?

Captain Edwards: That was entertainment.

Q: Is there anything else you wanted to mention on the <u>New Mexico</u>?

Captain Edwards: This is a funny story. When she was modernized, they put in some inside staterooms, right near the boiler uptakes. Those rooms were almost unbearable. So whenever we had a visiting representative from the Bureau of C&R, which had designed that change, we put him right away in one of the new rooms so he could enjoy the "pleasure" of an inside room. Those are some of the petty things that went on between constructors and ships in those days.

Q: Did you leave the <u>New Mexico</u> reluctantly since she was such a happy ship?

Captain Edwards: Well, no. I won't say I was glad to go, but it was time to go. One can overstay his leave sometimes when other people change. I reported to the Navy yard up at Bremerton, and that was a very happy experience.

Q: What was your specific job at Bremerton?

Captain Edwards: I was the engineering design officer. My boss was the design superintendent. He was a naval constructor, W. R. Nichols, who stood number three in the class of '18.* I was his first and principal assistant, engineering design.

Q: But you were officially still a general line officer at that point.

Captain Edwards: Yes. I didn't become an engineering duty only officer until late '41.

Q: That's interesting.

Captain Edwards: I remember one time I finished a project at Bremerton that I started aboard the New Mexico. When I was still on board I'd asked the Navy yard for copies of a lot of the ship's plans because we were missing them. When I got to the Navy yard, the job was still undone, so I did it for the ship. Otherwise, it wouldn't have been done. Harry Power was very grateful for that. By accident I'd been able to answer the same letter which I had written some months before. I ran off a couple of hundred plans.

---
*Commander William R. Nichols, Construction Corps, USN.

Q: What sort of facilities did you have for copying drawings there?

Captain Edwards: Well, at Bremerton they were very good. They had the CB method. They had a big machine; it was more than three feet wide. They'd run an original plan through it and make as many copies as wanted.

Q: Did the yard have a complete library of plans for each ship?

Captain Edwards: Supposed to have, yes. If she changed yards, they were supposed to ship that ship's plans over to the new yard.

Q: Did the yard also have a crew of draftsmen to keep them up to date?

Captain Edwards: Yes. Bremerton had at least 100 draftsmen, because we were doing not only that kind of work, but we were doing new design work. We designed the YTBs; those were yard tugs, diesel drive, about 100 feet long. They built them like peas in a pod, about 100 of them. The plans went to various yards. Most of the tugs were sold after the war to towing companies for a song.

During that same period also we did the AVPs, small

seaplane tenders. We were building the first two ships of that class.* They were commissioned a few months after I left. They were named after bays, inlets, and so forth. Other yards built AVPs later.

Q: So you then had to supply copies of all the plans to the other yards?

Captain Edwards: That's correct, and it was no problem at all, because they had these big machines to run them off.

Q: Well, there's also the matter of lessons learned. How do you incorporate those as you go along?

Captain Edwards: Alterations. In the lower righthand side there was a space where one wrote in all the alterations. And as we made alterations, we sent copies to these other yards that had the same plans.

Q: Did those yards send representatives to watch your construction?

Captain Edwards: On occasion, yes. Nothing planned; it

---

*The early ships of this type were converted minesweepers built during World War I. The first of the new type was the Barnegat (AVP-10), Her keel was laid at the Puget Sound Navy Yard in October 1939, and she was commissioned in July 1941. Later the Biscayne (AVP-11), Casco (AVP-12), and Mackinac (AVP-13) were built at Bremerton also.

was just casual. And if they didn't have the proper people, the plans would suffice.

Now, we lost some people when the Lake Washington Shipyard built a private plant over near Seattle. They robbed the Navy yard of some talent to get going. One of them was an officer named E. B. Colton.* He was an EDO, commander, and he got himself a job over there at twice as much money, of course. Then they took a lot of our civilian help. They got more money, so they shifted over to that place. After the war, they were out of a job, because they had been shortsighted. In the short run, they won, but in the long run they lost.

Q: Who did the preliminary design on those AVPs? Did that come from the bureaus?

Captain Edwards: Yes, C&R and the Bureau of Engineering. They gave them to us, and we developed the working plans.

Q: You did the detail design.

Captain Edwards: That's correct.

Q: Any details that you remember on that class?

---

*Commander Ernest B. Colton, USN, who had stood fourth of the 199 graduates in the Naval Academy class of 1918. He retired from the service in May 1941.

Captain Edwards: Well, we found out that the diesel engines were longer than the engine rooms.

Q: That's a problem.

Captain Edwards: So on the centerline we ran aft on one side, three feet. A bulkhead was jogged over to give us so much space for these diesel engines. So that was one thing. Another thing was that we completely redesigned the tool-handling facilities. For example, the ship had to have an aviation machine shop. It had to have a ship's machine shop. It had to have an electrical shop. So I put them all together with different windows, and a metal tag system so that if you checked out a tool you would give a metal tag. I combined them and saved a lot of space and a lot of headaches that way. And it was interesting work; I loved it.

We did a lot of other adjustments and changes as necessary as we went along. In order to have the crane overhead to pick up, say, airplane engines, we had to shift the crane location so we could get a direct lift. An airplane engine weighs, I don't know, a couple of thousand pounds. We had a direct lift right down into the stowage area. Then they had to have overhead trolleys to run them from the lift point to the stowage point--that sort of thing.

A minor thing was the water distilling plant in the AVPs. It required I don't know how many valves, 15 or 20 valves of different kinds, to run a distilling plant. Well, I brought all those valve controls into a common watch station, where they were connected with the valves themselves by long reach rods. The job was to consolidate them into one watch station so that one man could stand there and "play the piano." But the original design was for a valve here and a valve there. The watch stander would have to be stumbling and fumbling all over the place to run the plant.

I designed the machinery spaces and the hull arrangements. My boss, Commander Nichols, said I'd been aboard ship many years, and he hadn't, so he told me to arrange the living quarters and all that sort of thing also. I got a lot of fun out of that. I put things into those ships which weren't in the book. One of my classmates was skipper of one of the AVPs we designed. He was an aviator, and I asked him one day how he liked his ship. He was kind enough to say that it was wonderful. He didn't know at that time that I had anything to do with it.

Q: Did you talk to any aviators to get their inputs?

F. A. Edwards #4 - 251

Captain Edwards: Yes, we got some inputs, especially from the crew that came to fit out the ship. They gave us ideas. We also went over to the nearest AV, a large seaplane tender. She was there at Seattle, so we got ideas from her.

Q: Do you remember anything specific from the AV?

Captain Edwards: The important things were plane handling and weight handling.

Q: What is the satisfaction in seeing a ship that you've drawn on paper develop into steel?

Captain Edwards: It's a good feeling. Even though you are not directly credited, it's a good feeling. I'm not bragging now, but a lot of the ideas I advanced went into those ships. But that was just my job. I wasn't any hero; I was just doing the job I was trained for.

Q: Even so, that's a very tangible result of your efforts.

Captain Edwards: That's right. It gave me a good feeling inside.

Q: What other kinds of ships were involved in that job at

Bremerton?

Captain Edwards: We also built some destroyers, and that was mostly keeping up with alterations. They were designed by another yard, and we were building them, subject to alterations which were being made from time to time. On these destroyers we were a following yard, not a lead yard. For these YTBs and AVPs we were the lead yard, which meant a lot, design-wise. We were responsible for keeping the building yards informed of the proper plans and alterations. And we ordered the special materials. For example, when we ordered turbines or boilers, we ordered maybe ten. Two of them would go to one yard, and two of them would go to another yard, and so forth. So we were the lead yard in that respect.

Q: Assembling a ship is like putting together a giant jigsaw puzzle.

Captain Edwards: That's correct. But I was a paperwork boy only. I was only in design; I was not in construction. The construction people were entirely separate. They'd come and ask us, "How about this or how about that?" They were up there every day asking questions. We merely did the design.

Q: Was that yard increasing in employment as a buildup to the war?

Captain Edwards: Yes, and those people were mostly local residents. They had a better personal interest in that job than if they lived in Seattle or somewhere else, so we had a large local employment level, which was good. There was one ferry that came over bringing 300 or 400 people from the Seattle area. They'd catch the 6:00 o'clock ferry and be at the yard by a quarter to 8:00 or so.

Q: Mostly you'd been working with officers and enlisted men up to this point? What was it like now dealing with civilians?

Captain Edwards: Well, I got along fine. I dealt mostly with a chief engineer there named Finnegan, a good Irishman.* He and I got along fine. And, again, like with enlisted men, I did not normally deal with draftsmen personally. I dealt either with Finnegan or one of his subordinates who was in charge of a section. Anyhow, dealing with hull matters was Nichols's primary job. Now, all those plans had to be approved by Nichols as design superintendent, and so they'd bring in maybe 10-20 in the

---

*L. L. "Larry" Finnegan began work at the Puget Sound Navy Yard in 1917 as a draftsman and became a marine engineer in 1932. He worked at the shipyard for more than 40 years.

afternoon and lay them out on a large table. Nichols would sit down and talk to these people about the plans, or he'd make changes. That was routine.

Q: How much training did these draftsmen have? How good were they?

Captain Edwards: In general they were very good. The senior ones had been there 25-30 years. Of course, we got a new crop with the war coming on, college graduates who had come in. Like anywhere else, you have young people coming in at the bottom and being trained on the job.

Q: Well, you needed people also who were more than skilled draftsmen. They have to understand the engineering of it.

Captain Edwards: The senior people were all design engineers, but they first had become draftsmen. They had to be engineers first and then become designers. So these senior people were all design engineers, and then the younger people were just draftsmen. They had to qualify later on to fleet up.

Q: How harmonious was the working relationship in the yard?

Captain Edwards: As far as I know, good. I heard of no disturbances of any kind or consequence.

Q: What kind of a place was it for you and your family to live? Some people really like the Pacific Northwest.

Captain Edwards: Good. It's God's country six months out of the year, and the devil could take it for the other six!

Q: Why do you say that?

Captain Edwards: Moisture. They claim that the total rainfall up there per year is no more than at New York City. That could be true, but a whole lot there comes down week by week and day by day. Sometimes you'll go three and four days without seeing the sun. So they say you're growing web feet. But in the summertime it's just delightful; it's wonderful. I often thought I would like to live in that area. I thought about it seriously. It so happened I was able to rent a very nice little brick house which had just been vacated by a naval constructor who had been ordered away, so we fit right into this particular house.

Q: Was it in Bremerton itself?

Captain Edwards: Well, up on a hill overlooking Bremerton. So our life there was very pleasant. They had a nine-hole golf course, which I used to try out on holidays and weekends. We had a lot of entertainment there, self-entertainment at the club. Every Saturday night they had a big show. When it came our time to entertain, we had 125 people to dinner and dancing at the officers' club. That was our entertainment for the period. So we all took turns producing the entertainment.

Q: That was a good-sized affair.

Captain Edwards: It was. It was very nice; we loved it. We had live-in help, which I could not afford later as a captain. I was then a lieutenant commander, but I could not afford it later as a captain. So that's what inflation had done to us.

Q: Well, that was one advantage for those who had jobs, I guess.

Captain Edwards: Well, it was a delightful period. That was my best shore duty, at Bremerton. In fact, I thought so much of the area that I thought I might want to live up there. Sometimes you go day after day before you see the sun again. But in the summertime it's absolutely remarkable. We drove all around that country at various times. I had shipboard overhaul there five times in the Henshaw. Then I was there in the New Mexico once, and then I had duty there two years, so during that time I got well acquainted with it. My wife also had relatives up in that area, so they took us in tow and showed us what it was all about. We drove to Port Angeles, out to the ocean, down the coast to Oregon, and back around--all in one trip. We went out to the Grand Coulee Dam on another trip.

Another time we drove up to Vancouver, Canada. Canada is a cut above the United States in cleanliness and general living. Vancouver is a beautiful city; I've been there many times. One can't even find a cigarette butt on the sidewalk, even on Sunday morning after Saturday night. It's just beautiful. And the people there are good people. You don't have these so-called minorities and all this, but they do have Chinese. There's quite a colony of Chinese there. In fact, they say that's the second largest Chinese colony in the Western Hemisphere, Frisco being number one. But they stay to themselves, more or less. You seldom see them, unless you go into their area. But you don't have blacks or all other kinds of minorities. That's beautiful country.

Q: Do you remember there being tighter controls on classified information after the war started in Europe in

1939?

Captain Edwards: Yes. Once a week we had to burn plans that had been superseded by newer versions. We had to get rid of them by fire. We could not tear them up, because they might be reassembled. So we had a truck come down, and we took maybe a ton of plans at a time to be burned in a big incinerator.

Q: Anything else along those lines?

Captain Edwards: One time I was contacted by a lieutenant named Frost from the 13th Naval District security office.* He said that there was a chief petty officer on board the Pennsylvania who was playing footsie with the Germans. Also, we had a draftsman in our design section who was playing footsie with this petty officer. Frost said to me, "He's going to ask for leave; give it to him and treat him normally, because he's going out to photograph the Northwest hydro-electric power plants." The idea being to wreck them, I guess, eventually.

So I watched this draftsman's desk; when he was out for lunch I would search his desk drawers for anything suspicious. Also, we were getting letters from the post

---
*Lieutenant Daniel A. Frost, USN (Ret.), had been recalled to active duty in connection with the national emergency and was serving on the staff of the commandant of the 13th Naval District in Seattle.

office addressed to him and also to this fellow on the Pennsylvania. We were opening letters, and we were copying them. I was playing spymaster on these two people, and we got both of them eventually. The petty officer and the draftsmen were members of an espionage ring that went up and down the coast, but this was the part of it that we were interested in.

Q: Did you find incriminating things in his desk?

Captain Edwards: Yes, there were letters there which referred to these power plants, and we knew damn well he was only interested in them for one reason--eventually to wreck them. These two people were specifically interested in Grand Coulee Dam, which in those days was just being built.* It was fitted out with hydro-electric turbines.

Q: Was the FBI called in?

Captain Edwards: I don't know. I only dealt with the Navy security office. They, in turn, probably contacted the FBI, but I was involved only through this fellow known as Jack Frost. He contacted me because we had known each other as midshipmen. He was in the class of 1921, and I

---

*The Grand Coulee Dam on the Columbia River in Washington state is 550 feet high and 4,173 feet long; completed 1942.

was "his plebe." Jack came to me, and he gave me the dope. I didn't even tell Nichols, my boss; I didn't tell anybody. I just dealt with Frost, and he told me what to expect and how to handle these people.

Q: In 1940, while you were at Bremerton, the Bureau of Ships was established, and the Construction Corps and the Engineering Corps were abolished. What had been the relationship between those two corps up to then?

Captain Edwards: They were separate entities.

Q: How well did they get along with each other?

Captain Edwards: It depended upon the persons. Generally, they were standoffish, except maybe certain people got together. It was good that they pushed them together to form the Bureau of Ships; that was an excellent idea. But we kept our own trades. Later on they put them together; that was not too good perhaps. You're neither fish nor fowl, neither engineers nor constructors. They called them "con-engineers." It took us a lifetime to become engineers, and it took them a lifetime to become constructors. I don't think they can become the same quality people if they push them together and spend half the time on each. Now, I'm perhaps on the outside, but that's my personal opinion. They should retain them but marry them together on duty. When we had a constructor in charge of a section, his number-one assistant was an engineer and vice versa.

Q: Well, you, as an engineer, though, had to have some basics on ship design and construction.

Captain Edwards: Oh, yes.

Q: How did you get that?

Captain Edwards: Well, we had a course in naval construction, but that was secondary. At Columbia our primary course was mechanical; our secondary was electrical. In the PG school here in Annapolis our primary was mechanical, and our secondary was construction.

Q: You still needed to know something about hull design, because you had to know what was feasible to go in that ship.

Captain Edwards: That's correct. But you have an emphasis, a priority.

Q: Was there any rivalry between those two groups?

Captain Edwards: Yes, unfortunately. We engineers felt that the constructors didn't have enough sea duty to make good advisers, let me say. And constructors felt we didn't have enough construction duty to make us good ship designers. But we had to marry it halfway. We got along, but I still think that saying they are "con-engineers" is a mistake. They are neither fish nor fowl. Nobody asked me, but that's it.

Q: Well, I asked you, so now I got an answer.

Captain Edwards: I'm thinking of that section in the Proceedings: "Nobody Asked Me But . . ."

Q: About that same time President Roosevelt declared a state of national emergency. What do you recall about that?

Captain Edwards: That was sort of a semi-war, and it was the key that war itself was coming. That's when I put in for sea duty, because that was the thing to do. I didn't hear anything about my request for six months. Nothing. Then, all of sudden, I got dispatch orders to report to the New York Navy Yard in connection with fitting out North Carolina. That was sort of a surprise.

It was then winter, and I hitched up the horses and in a matter of two or three days we packed up and drove across country. We started south on the West Coast to get out of the snow and ice, and then turned eastward at Las Vegas and continued across the Southwest and up to Ohio, where my mother lived. After several days there, we continued on to New York City. And on the second day of January '41 I reported in for duty. I didn't know that Texas, New Mexico, and Arizona had snow in the wintertime. We ran into snow somewhere a foot deep. I was completely baffled by that. I thought it was summertime down south.

Q: We can get started on the <u>North Carolina</u> the next time. Any final thoughts on Bremerton?

Captain Edwards: Well, it was and probably still is our best yard, with all due respect to the other yards.

Q: I look forward to hearing more the next time. Thank you very much.

F. A. Edwards #5 - 264

Interview Number 5 with Captain Frederick A. Edwards,
U.S. Navy (Retired)

Place: Captain Edwards's Apartment, Annapolis, Maryland

Date: Tuesday, 3 March 1992

Interviewer: Paul Stillwell

Q: Captain Edwards, we talked the last time about your tour of duty at the Puget Sound Navy Yard, and then you got orders to the North Carolina. Whom did you report to, with the ship not yet in commission?

Captain Edwards: My orders were to the Commandant Third Naval District and then, in turn, to the Commander New York Navy Yard.

Q: I would think that that would really be a plum assignment for an engineer at that time.

Captain Edwards: It was. There was another engineering officer at New York who had duty in connection with the building of the ship. I thought he would be the chief engineer of the North Carolina. I expected to go to the Washington, which was being built at Philadelphia. Instead, I found out suddenly I was selected for the North

Carolina, the first ship of that class.*

Q: Did you have some connections that helped out on that?

Captain Edwards: I think Earle Mills was probably responsible.** I had known him for years and had talked to him intimately about going engineering duty only.

Q: How had you gotten to know him?

Captain Edwards: I first met him on board the Mahan in 1936. He was a representative of the Bureau of Engineering, and I was the prospective engineer officer during the ship's trials. From then on, I talked with him occasionally.

Q: Well, maybe the fact that that was the lead ship of a class had something to do with it, so he knew you were familiar with trials.

Captain Edwards: Yes, that was the third new ship I had ridden on trials.

---

*USS North Carolina (BB-55) was commissioned 9 April 1941. She had a standard displacement of 35,000 tons, was 729 feet long, and 108 feet in the beam. She had a top speed of 27.5 knots. The main battery comprised nine 16-inch guns; the secondary battery was 20 5-inch guns. After World War II service, the ship was decommissioned in 1947.
**Captain Earle W. Mills, USN.

Q: What was the status of the North Carolina when you reported there? That was about three months before commissioning.

Captain Edwards: She was being finished in a frantic manner. It was six and sometimes seven days a week, around-the-clock work. They were so busy getting the ship completed that we, the prospective ship crew, had to be prepared at any time to witness the tests of various pieces of machinery. We were watching these tests on Sundays, Saturdays, midnight, any time. The pressure was on. I had to have officers and/or men present with the yard people to accept or not accept the tests of the machinery.

Q: What would be an example of one of those tests?

Captain Edwards: One was the fresh-water distilling plant, the evaporators. It was being operated entirely independent of the main engines. We had to be present to accept--or to reject in part--the tests of the plant. The manufacturers' people were there too; it was a joint operation.

Q: Did you actually put salt water in and see if it worked?

Captain Edwards: Yes, they ran it.

Q: How good was the equipment that you got?

Captain Edwards: Well, it was good, except inadequate. The requirements for the crew were such that we could not make enough low-salinity feed water for the ship. So they installed a 12,000-gallon-per-day plant in one of the firerooms to distill feed water only, entirely independent of potable water, which was a higher salinity.*

Q: What percentage of the crew reported early to help out in that process?

Captain Edwards: Perhaps 10%. These were senior people, enlisted and officers, who were there to witness these tests.

Q: Were the rest of the people off being trained?

Captain Edwards: Yes. A number of people were in schools for their particular parts of the ship.

Q: Well, this was a lot more sophisticated ship than the
_____
*The distilling plant produced feed water for the ship's boilers and potable water for drinking, cleaning, cooking.

West Virginia and much more modern equipment.

Captain Edwards: Yes.

Q: For example, did you have radar yet at that point?

Captain Edwards: Yes, but in some people's minds it was so secret that we weren't to mention the word "radar" outside of our own people.

Q: How much awareness did you have of it yourself?

Captain Edwards: I knew it existed, but I knew nothing about the details of it. Finally, The New York Times printed that radar was being installed on the North Carolina. So Tom Hill, our gunnery officer, who had a good sense of humor, went to the exec and said, "Is it all right now to say that dirty word?"*

Q: Did all this equipment put any additional demands on electrical power?

Captain Edwards: Yes, we had four turbo-electric units, and they were rated much more than on prior ships.** They

---
*Lieutenant Commander Tom B. Hill, USN.
**The North Carolina was equipped with four 1,250-kilowatt ship's service turbo generators. By comparison, the West Virginia had been equipped with six 300-KW generators.

were very good plants. We also had four 850-kilowatt emergency diesel generators.

Q: How much assistance did you get from the manufacturers in these installations?

Captain Edwards: They had people on board or available all the time. They were manufacturers' representatives, and they were on good terms with the ship and the yard.

Q: Did they provide training for the prospective crew as part of that?

Captain Edwards: They went from ship to ship to represent the company and to ensure that we were informed and well trained about how to run their equipment. And many of these manufacturers had schools at their factories for the senior enlisted men and junior officers. I had nothing to do with that, but those people came back to the ship on commissioning.

Q: That's comparable to your experience in the West Virginia when the people went to the Ford Instrument Company for training.

F. A. Edwards #5 - 270

Captain Edwards: That's right, yes.

Q: Where did the prospective crew members live while the ship was being completed?

Captain Edwards: The officers lived out in town, but the enlisted men lived in a barracks right across the street from the Navy yard.

Q: Did your children go to local schools?

Captain Edwards: No. You've perhaps seen some movies or TV programs about school conditions in New York City. They're just terrible; they're jungles. You have to have a gun on your hip or be ready to slug somebody or be slugged. Our daughter Suzanne was then high school age, and people told me she shouldn't attend New York schools. So we sent her to Packer Institute, which is a private school in Brooklyn. And we sent our son Fred down to the Admiral Farragut Academy in New Jersey. We went down to see him about once a month.

Q: What do you remember about the sense of patriotism in the New York area at that time?

Captain Edwards: I would say superficially that it was poor. Civilians weren't interested. They were not looking for a war; they were just worried about their jobs, their entertainment, and continuing their normal lives.

Q: I've heard later, during the war itself, people were very accommodating, buying drinks for sailors and what have you.

Captain Edwards: Not at first. This is jumping forward a little bit, but after Pearl Harbor we all had to wear uniforms. I was on a subway one day when I was accosted by some character who berated me for Pearl Harbor. He talked as if it was my fault that Pearl Harbor had been attacked.

Q: That's interesting--as if you had anything to do with it.

Captain Edwards: One morning I was coming from home, and there was quite a large group of civilian workmen ahead of me, going through the gate to be checked in by the Marines. I was in uniform, of course. I had to delay to show my ID card, but these characters ahead of me just seemed to walk on through. We got maybe a block inside the yard when one of these men turned around to me, a dirty-looking character, and said, "Hey, buddy, where's the pipe shop?

This is my first day here." So there was little or no control over those randomly employed people coming in.

Q: This was after the war started?

Captain Edwards: Yes, after.

Q: What do you recall about the quality of the workmanship from the New York yard?

Captain Edwards: It was probably as good as average, nothing superior perhaps, but it was acceptable. It had to be. Years ago, it was poor. This is backtracking, but it did improve. The shop masters and other top people were excellent, but the lower echelons were run-of-the-mill people.

Q: What is your assessment of the design of the North Carolina?

Captain Edwards: The design of the engineering plant was excellent. We had a problem, though, of vibration. The underwater part of the hull was divided into sections aft by skegs because we had four shafts and twin rudders. When the water came from the propellers, it would strike these skegs. That caused a lot of unexpected vibration. So we had to change propellers. Instead of five blades, we experimented in some cases with four blades or three blades. In fact, we had vibration experts ride with us and advise us what to do. We did have vibration points in the speed range. We had to go through those points quickly in order to minimize the vibration.

Q: I know the Washington had a lot of problems with that also.*

Captain Edwards: Same. I think we solved it better. They tried tying machinery units down with big restraining straps. But we changed propellers; that did the same job without all that mechanical work.

Q: How did changing propellers help?

Captain Edwards: It changed the vibration points from lower speeds to higher speeds. And in some cases it reduced the amount of the vibration. It changed the whole range of vibration, so if we were increasing to full power we had a certain spot where we would go right through fast, rather than slowly.

---

*For details on the Washington's vibration problems, see Ivan Musicant, Battleship at War (San Diego: Harcourt Brace Jovanovich, 1986), pages 14-18.

Q: How much help did you get from BuShips in trying to solve that problem?

Captain Edwards: They had a vibration expert with us. It was a completely unexpected trouble to everybody concerned. It was all due to this unusual contour of the underwater after body of the ship. It was due to the fact that we had two rudders and four shafts.

Q: Do you think those skegs served a useful purpose?

Captain Edwards: Yes, the idea was to separate the flow of water from each propeller without having side interference.

By the way, this expert was a reserve officer who wrote the book on vibrations. I had gotten a library of technical books from the Bureau of Ships, and one of them was on vibrations. So when this officer came aboard, I couldn't believe it. I just reached up and got his book.

Q: So you had a fair amount of confidence in him.

Captain Edwards: Yes. He was a very able gentleman.

Q: The North Carolina was known as "The Showboat." What do you remember about the amount of attention she got?

Captain Edwards: Well, being the first ship of the class, she got more attention than Washington. Also, we had a more showman-like group of people on board. For example, we invited USO shows; we were the first to get those.* And we had a lot of important people come aboard and entertain us. Andy Shepard, the exec, was probably most responsible for that.** He'd had duty in New York City. He knew a lot of the show people and got them aboard.

Q: Even so, dealing with all that when you were trying to get the ship ready had to be a headache.

Captain Edwards: Well, I'll tell you. The day we were commissioned, they had teakwood planking down on the starboard side where the guests came aboard to go aft to the fantail for the ceremony. Yard workmen were still installing the wooden deck on the port side, hammering and pounding over there.

Q: What do you remember about the commissioning ceremony itself?

Captain Edwards: Well, it was quite good. I've got a

---

*USO--United Service Organization, which did a great deal to provide for the welfare and recreation of U.S. military personnel in World War II. Included was the sponsorship of traveling entertainment troupes and the establishment of centers where service people could relax while off duty.
**Commander Andrew B. Shepard, USN.

picture of it here. The Secretary of the Navy, Frank Knox, was there. The CNO, Admiral Stark, was there; he had been the exec of the West Virginia when she was commissioned in 1923.

Q: I imagine there was a great deal of pride on the part of the crew.

Captain Edwards: Oh, yes. We felt we were the chosen people, which we were, in effect.

Q: Well, that makes the skipper's job easier in building morale.

Captain Edwards: Yes. The skipper was Olaf Hustvedt, a very fine gentleman, class of '09.* I never knew him before, but I respected him highly. He was a very fine man. In fact, I felt we could not have gotten along as well as we did without him.

Q: What qualities do you especially remember in Hustvedt?

Captain Edwards: If we made mistakes, he was forgiving and understanding and reasonable. He was an excellent manager and further, more or less a father confessor of the
___
*Captain Olaf M. Hustvedt, USN, commanded the North Carolina from 9 April 1941 to 23 October 1941.

operation. We all had great respect for him.

Q: How much was he involved in this pressure situation you've described, to get the ship finished?

Captain Edwards: Well, how much he was under pressure from the Navy Department, of course, I don't know. But he never pressured us, except to give us the facts of what had to be ready by a certain date. He was kind enough to say later that he would not have picked others to be his heads of departments.

Q: You mentioned before the tape started that several of you showed up on the same day.

Captain Edwards: One was Tom Hill, the gunnery officer. The first lieutenant was Red Thackrey, class of '21.* We were the three senior heads of departments. We almost jammed into the doorway, arriving at the same time from different parts of the country.

Q: Did you have regular department head meetings to keep up to date on this progress?

Captain Edwards: Yes, they were at least weekly, sometimes oftener, depending on what the situation was.

---
*Lieutenant Commander Lyman A. Thackrey, USN.

Q: In keeping with that "Showboat" theme, there was press on board for the ship's trials, including Hanson Baldwin from The New York Times.*

Captain Edwards: Including Walter Winchell.** In fact, he edited our first ship's paper, the Tar Heel. I have a copy of issue number one, dated Saturday, April 12, 1941.

Q: He was an old Navy man, wasn't he?

Captain Edwards: In World War I, I think he was an enlisted man. So we got to hear Walter and see him in action.

Q: Did he talk on the public address system of the ship?

Captain Edwards: Yes, and also he had a wardroom meeting for the officers. He was quite a guy. He put a frantic tinge to his delivery. He always seemed to be out of breath.

---

*Hanson W. Baldwin graduated from the Naval Academy in 1924 and served at sea before becoming a newspaperman. His two-volume oral history, including recollections of the North Carolina trials, is in the Naval Institute collection.
**Walter Winchell was one of the best-known personalities of the day, a syndicated newspaper columnist and popular radio commentator.

Q: That was his style on the radio. It sounds like he did the same thing.

Captain Edwards: The same thing exactly.

Q: Any recollections of Baldwin specifically?

Captain Edwards: No. In fact, I don't recall Baldwin on board, I'm sorry to say. I did see him on board the _Augusta_ many years before, but at that particular time I don't recall Baldwin.

Q: What do you remember about the trials themselves and how the plant worked?

Captain Edwards: Well, we went out, of course, several times. One was when we fired all the guns at one time, main and secondary batteries, which was a terrific test of the ship's hull and the ship's machinery. The ship seemed to jump sideways about three feet when all 9 main-battery guns and all 20 5-inch/38-caliber antiaircraft guns fired.

Q: Was there any damage inside the ship from that?

Captain Edwards: Superficial damage. We lost a lot of

light bulbs and stuff like that, but there was no structural damage.

Q: The North Carolina had a very capable antiaircraft battery.

Captain Edwards: Very capable. We had ten twin 5-inch/38-caliber mounts. I first saw them in action off Cape May. They sent out drones at 12,000 or 13,000 feet, and--bing, bing--we shot down those drones. That was the guns' extreme range. That was really an eye-opener to me because we'd been using those 5-inch/25-caliber guns in earlier ships, and they had only 5,000-7,000 feet max vertical range.

Q: You probably had some 1.1-inch in the North Carolina also.

Captain Edwards: We went in commission with 1.1s. We didn't get the 40 millimeters until the second overhaul. We got some of them then. Then the ship got more when it went to the West Coast.

Q: I haven't heard people say much good about those 1.1s.

Captain Edwards: They were very unsatisfactory guns.

Q: Where did you go on the trials?

Captain Edwards: We called it the "break-down cruise," instead of the shakedown cruise. We did not have an overseas trip because of the war coming on. These trials were just off New York, out to sea for 100 miles or so. After the war ended, the log of a certain German submarine came to notice. She had reported sighting the North Carolina there, and fortunately we were then at peace--on paper. Otherwise, there would definitely have been a problem. At that time we did not have a destroyer escorting us. Of course, when the war came along we always had destroyers escorting us anywhere.

After we were commissioned, we went to Guantanamo Bay for some additional trials, including running the measured mile there. They had an onshore range for trials. We also fired guns. It was a strenuous period.

Q: What do you recall about the process of taking on fuel and ammunition in the North Carolina?

Captain Edwards: We took fuel on quite rapidly because we had a series of--I'll call them nests of tanks, which were fed from a central tank. So we'd put oil down a trunk, into the master tank. From then on, the other tanks filled automatically with the valves open. Then we'd go to another master tank, and we'd do maybe two or three of them at a time. So we fueled in perhaps half the time the earlier ships had fueled to the same capacity.

Q: What was the role of the oil king in all that fueling process?

Captain Edwards: He was in immediate charge of taking on the oil and telling his people which valves to open and close. He was a very valuable person, usually a chief water tender or a water tender first class in most ships.

Q: Without him you could have a tank overfilled or any number of untoward things.

Captain Edwards: That's right. He would station a man on each tank to keep sounding it, to make sure he knew what the level was. And that way, he would not overflow a tank. I once was explaining that process to somebody during dinner in the wardroom. Just about that time I got an emergency call that they had overflowed the tank in some compartment. That was the only time it ever happened, but it happened just as I was explaining how it couldn't happen.

Q: Sort of embarrassing.

Captain Edwards: It was.

Q: Did you take any precautions against sabotage to the plant?

Captain Edwards: No, because it was manned all the time. When we were at anchor we had a man in each machinery space.

Q: I presume you still had locks on the reduction gears.

Captain Edwards: Well, yes, but we still had a man stationed and on watch in every single machinery space, even including the shaft alleys, to make sure there'd be no outside access.

Q: How crowded was that ship?

Captain Edwards: Oh, it wasn't crowded, as I recall. Compared to other ships, there was plenty of room. We were continually funneling off senior ratings to ships being built and then bringing in more junior ratings. That was routine. We were, in effect, a semi-training ship by funneling off these senior people. If we had an allowance

F. A. Edwards #5 - 284

for ten chief electrician's mates, we had 12 or 15.

Q: That was the practice out in the Pacific Fleet too, where the Bureau of Navigation deliberately overmanned ships for training purposes before the war.

Captain Edwards: That's right. We were overmanned purposely, but we kept funneling them off to new construction.

Q: I'm surprised you didn't have a crowding problem with this overmanning.

Captain Edwards: The ship was built for I don't know how many people, but we had adequate space, I felt.

Q: Was this completely with bunks, no hammocks in the North Carolina?

Captain Edwards: I don't recall any hammocks. Completely bunks.

Q: This ship was substantially faster than any previous U.S. battleship. How well did that machinery work?

Captain Edwards: Excellent. Except for that vibration,

which first showed up on these trials, there was no problem. In fact, the ship made 120,000-some horsepower. The speed was supposed to be 27-and-a-half knots or thereabouts, which we made or slightly exceeded.

Q: When was the correction period for working on the vibrations?

Captain Edwards: We went back to the Navy yard to get alterations and corrections, including the propeller changes. We tried different propellers on different shafts. Maybe the outboard propellers would be five, and the inboard would be four, and so forth. That was purely experimental.

Q: What happened after you got those problems worked out and went into operation?

Captain Edwards: No more difficulties. When I was transferred from the ship in March '42, I reported to the captain that the engineering plant was ready for war in all respects. I was satisfied with the plant. So my "reward" was to be shipped off to the Bureau of Ships. I did not request it, but I was ordered.

Q: Was that a disappointment at that point?

Captain Edwards: Well, no, I'd gotten everything technically that I could get out of the ship. That is, she was ready for war, and the rest of it was going to be operational routine. So I felt the job was over technically. They ordered a general-line classmate of mine, Al Murdaugh, to relieve me.* He was not an engineering specialist. He was mad as hell, and I was too. But shortly after that he was ordered away, and my former assistant fleeted up to engineer officer.

Q: Who was he?

Captain Edwards: Maxwell.** Maxwell was a former Russian, so that was not his original name. He had been picked up on the dock at Vladivostok in World War I by a ship whose chief boatswain was named Maxwell. He adopted this kid, gave him his name, and sent him to school and all that. My assistant still had some Russian characteristics.

Q: Such as what?

Captain Edwards: Well, he was moody at times. He was on top of the world, and then he'd be on the bottom. I used to tell him, "For God's sake, forget about it. Relax."

---
*Commander Albert C. Murdaugh, USN.
**Lieutenant Commander William S. Maxwell, USN.

Q: Was he a mustang?

Captain Edwards: Yes, and he eventually went to the postgraduate school, where he had to take an extra year because of his lack of the language.*

Q: What role did the warrant officers serve in your engineering department?

Captain Edwards: We had a chief warrant officer for each division in engineering. They were good ones. In fact, one of them, Tom Doyle, the main engines warrant officer, became a lieutenant commander later on.** He was one of the succeeding chief engineers of the Missouri. Maxwell was the first chief engineer in the Missouri, and then Doyle was one of the later engineers. He was a very good one. He was the best of the bunch in the North Carolina, and he was excellent.

    Before that, he was a machinist's mate first class on board the West Virginia when she was commissioned. Lieutenant Bob Strite, Doyle, and myself were the only

---

*Maxwell, who joined the Navy around the end of World War I, served initially as an enlisted man, then a warrant machinist, and finally as a commissioned officer. He reached the rank of captain on active duty and eventually retired as a tombstone rear admiral.
**Chief Machinist Thomas H. Doyle, USN.

three people who were in the commissioning crews of both ships, the West Virginia, and 18 years later, the North Carolina.* In the West Virginia Strite was a jaygee. He later resigned and then came back as a reserve officer in World War II. Of course, Admiral Stark was executive officer of the West Virginia in 1923 and CNO in 1941. He was part of the North Carolina's commissioning ceremony.

Q: What do you remember about the ship's operations once the trials were over and you went into regular service?

Captain Edwards: The war started, of course, in December. Bess and I were down to have Sunday lunch with our son Fred, who was going to the Admiral Farragut prep school in New Jersey. After lunch he went upstairs and came back and said, "Hey, Dad, somebody's attacked Pearl Harbor."

I said, "Forget it." But I started listening to the radio, and, sure enough, that was it, so we rushed back to New York. I took my wife home. Then I went back to the ship, and we were busy for some time. We redoubled our efforts to get the yard work done so we could go to sea.

Then we went down to Norfolk, and there we formed a task force with the Washington, North Carolina, Hornet, a couple of the cruisers, and maybe a half dozen or more

---

*Lieutenant Robert Strite, USNR, had been in the first crew of the West Virginia as a lieutenant (junior grade), USN.

destroyers. It was a training-type task force. We operated offshore and then went down to the Caribbean and the Gulf of Mexico for about a month. It was seven-days-a-week training. The task force commander, Rear Admiral Wilcox, was lost on board the Washington later.* Captain Mitscher commanded the Hornet.**

We had a submarine scare during that period. I can't tell you much about it, but we had a submarine attack, so they said. Planes dropped bombs on it, and destroyers dropped depth charges. Whether the target was sunk or not, I don't know. But that was only once. Reveille came early in the morning--5:00 o'clock--and then we had to stand to for an hour or an hour and a half. That was just the beginning.

After breakfast we had drills--always more drills. We were drill-happy.

Q: That early general quarters was a typical feature in ships during the war because of the submarine threat.

Captain Edwards: That's right. The logical attack time for an enemy was, of course, just at daylight. So we were all at general quarters before daylight.

---
*Rear Admiral John W. Wilcox, USN, Commander Battleship Division Six. While the USS Washington (BB-56) was at sea en route to Britain on 27 March 1942, Wilcox was lost overboard under unexplained circumstances.
**Captain Marc A. Mitscher, USN, was the first commanding officer of the carrier Hornet (CV-8). He became famous later for his command of the fast carrier task force in Pacific operations in 1944-45.

Q: Were you standing watches during that period?

Captain Edwards: I was in charge, essentially standing watches in the engineering spaces. I was down there hour after hour after hour. Sometimes I'd be there 16-18 hours a day. There was the regular watch officer besides. I was down there communicating directly with the captain on the bridge about what he wanted to do next.

Q: Lending a fatherly presence.

Captain Edwards: Well, I was hardly a father, but it was an overall presence anyhow. It was so enervating that we ate salt tablets and drank water all the time. I had most of my meals brought down to the control engine room. I didn't have time to change clothes and go up to the wardroom for meals.

Q: Well, at other times, when you did eat in the wardroom, how formal an affair was that?

Captain Edwards: Well, it was reasonably so. We all were in uniform. We had mess attendants who served us. It was approximately the same as prewar. Of course, nowadays, I understand that they have cafeteria-style meals. Thank God I'm retired.

The <u>North Carolina</u> was the first battleship I was on without a JO mess. We had these 30-some newly commissioned ensigns, and they were thrown into the wardroom. That created some problems for me during one period of a couple of months when I was the mess treasurer. One of the jobs as mess treasurer was to handle the money, of course, but also to arrange the menus. We had two different sets of appetites, so I had to have two menus. The young studs wanted meat and potatoes, and the old fuds wanted salads and lighter food.

Q: Well, they probably sat by seniority, so they'd all be by themselves.

Captain Edwards: That's right. The executive officer and heads of departments were all at one table. And we had an intermediate table. Then there was a JO table. It was a big wardroom; it went clear across the ship.

Q: How strict was the protocol in that era?

Captain Edwards: Well, I'd have to say it was reasonably strict. There wasn't anything exhausting. We still had the ordinary respect of rank for rate and rate for rank.

Q: Was there a chasm between officers and enlisted, a gulf, in that period?

Captain Edwards: No, I don't think so.

Q: What do you remember about Commander Shepard as executive officer?

Captain Edwards: Andy was a very good executive officer; he had a good sense of humor. He was a member of the gun club and therefore gave favored assignments to the gunners. But I wouldn't be pushed around. For example, once one of his assistants was assigning shore patrol duty off the ship. Some of my officers were being assigned, so I said, "How come?"

"Well, the executive officer wanted them."

I said, "Well, I'll assign them. If you want three lieutenants from me, come to me. I will assign them. I don't want somebody outside my department assigning my people to jobs." So I kept them straight. It was the engineering department, not everybody's department.

Andy had almost a daily sitdown with the heads of departments. When he left, he said he was damn glad to go because he knew Oscar Badger was coming as the new skipper.* He said, "As for you guys, I'm sorry." Badger

---
*Captain Oscar C. Badger, USN, commanded the North Carolina from 23 October 1941 to 1 June 1942.

was the son of Admiral Charles Badger, who had been Commander in Chief Atlantic Fleet just prior to World War I. Oscar was, I guess, a good officer, but he was very hard to live with. In fact, he gave me 4.0 fitness reports, but I had to take a lot of guff along with the reports.

Q: In what sense was he hard to live with?

Captain Edwards: He was, I should say, difficult to communicate with ordinarily. You had to do all the listening, practically no talking. I remember that many times he'd call us heads of department up to his cabin at midnight or thereabouts. Then he would parade back and forth with his hands behind his back, talking as he went, bawling out each one of us in succession. After we were released, we went back to bed if it wasn't time for the morning antisubmarine alert.

One day Badger omitted me in his harangue, and Tom Hill, who was the gunnery officer, said, "Captain, can't we get the engineer for something this morning?" [Laughter]

Q: Share the misery.

Captain Edwards: I wasn't standing bridge watches, but on

the bridge he was known to get excited and jump up and down, even on his cap. One time I was told by Tom Hill that Badger threw his cap on the deck and jumped up and down on it because there was a near-collision. I was spared a lot of that guff because I was the engineer. I didn't have to listen to it too much, but most of the boys had to take it as routine. I guess he was a capable officer. He later on made vice admiral, but he was just difficult personally.

Q: Another part of the problem, I understand, is that Oscar Badger thought he knew everything.

Captain Edwards: That's correct. He told me he had been first lieutenant and gunnery officer of the Maryland. Gunnery was really his specialty. I doubt if he knew the way down to the engine room. If he did, it was just to qualify for promotion. We had to have rotational duty in various departments in those days to be qualified for promotion.

I remember one time, Christmas of '41, we went down to Norfolk from New York, and he made a speech to us in the wardroom that if any officer's wife showed up down there in the time it took for the North Carolina to go down to Norfolk, which was one day, he would be court-martialed.

Well, when we arrived down there, we had Christmas dinner aboard. Who should be our guest but Mrs. Badger? And she said she just happened to go down to Norfolk for vacation, and she looked out the window one morning, and here was the North Carolina. Surprise, surprise, surprise.

Q: What a coincidence.

Captain Edwards: So, I say, we took that with a grain of salt. It was all right for him, but for us it was a general court-martial if any of us had broken our silence as to operational movements, to have our wives down there for Christmas.

Q: Sounds kind of hypocritical to me.

Captain Edwards: That's right. Well, she was a nice person. I just met her socially. But Oscar, I say, was just a tough guy. He thought he knew more than he did, but we were not in a position to tell him so.

Captain Edwards: Badger got where he was by virtue of his father's position and thereby his connections. During the war I was in a driving squad to the Navy Department, and one day we picked up a certain captain aviator.*

---
*"Driving squad" was the term used then for what is now known as a car pool.

F. A. Edwards #5 - 296

Somebody said, "Let's pick up Joe and give him a ride." So Joe got aboard and told us Oscar Badger was his skipper a while back. He said, "You take Oscar, and I'll take Manila." That's before we liberated the Philippines. So he was known as a screamer and a shouter and that sort of thing. And, I say, he got his positions primarily because of connections.

Q: What do you recall of Tom Hill? He was a very capable officer.

Captain Edwards: Tom was class of '22. I liked Tom very much, and we got along fine. I was just trying to think of a story about Tom. When Andy Shepard was about to be transferred, the heads of departments were called informally into his office. Tom said to him, "Andy, as bad as you are, we hate to see you go." He had a good joke at Andy's expense, and Andy took it well. Andy was a good guy, but he was primarily a gunner. He told me once that he was in the Bureau of Ordnance before the war, and a man came into his office with a suitcase full of plans for the Bofors 40-millimeter gun. And that's how the U.S. Navy got the Bofors gun. I guess this man had to be paid off. I don't know what the arrangement was, but from then on, we shifted from the 1.1-inch rapid-fire gun to the 40-millimeter and 20-millimeter guns.

Q: The bureau chief, Admiral Blandy, was instrumental in getting the Bofors and the Oerlikon installed.*

Captain Edwards: Well, I think Andy went in to see Blandy.

Later on, I had the pleasure of being the material officer under Blandy. He was then Commander in Chief Atlantic Fleet.

Q: It was more than a year from the time of commissioning until the North Carolina got into combat. Was there a sense she was not ready before then?

Captain Edwards: No, she was assigned to the East Coast. There was a threat of the battleship Tirpitz and the German battle cruisers getting out into the Atlantic. So the North Carolina was held on the East Coast until those things cleared up. Then she was sent to the West Coast. It was not a question of not being ready. In fact, the Washington was sent overseas to the British Home Fleet for several months.

Q: At what point in this whole sequence did you become an EDO?

---

*Rear Admiral William H. P. Blandy, USN, Chief of the Bureau of Ordnance, 1941-43.

Captain Edwards: In those days you had to have 15 years straight line-officer duty before you were eligible to be selected for engineering duty. Well, I started putting in for the old Engineering Corps the month I finished the engineering PG course. Down at the bottom of the fitness report was a place you could write your desired duty. I always put down engineering duty, even though I knew they wouldn't talk to me about it for several years yet.

In fact, for about the first half of my time as an officer, I did nothing but engineering duty on special assignment. After a while that was a problem for promotions. To be selected for two and a half or three stripes, one had to have general duty: navigation, gunnery, engineering, and so forth. That's proper, I think, but I didn't want that. I wanted engineering duty, but I didn't want to be kicked out of the Navy before I had a chance to get it.

Because of this situation, the Bureau of Engineering wrote to the Bureau of Navigation, which handled personnel matters in those days. The letter pointed out the fact that several of us were doing engineering duty for the good of the Navy and so forth, and we should not be passed over because of lack of other duty. Well, that saved me and several others, because I made lieutenant commander in 1937 and commander in 1941 with nothing but engineering duty.

If it hadn't been for that letter, I would have been thrown out and of no further value to the Navy, because I didn't have gunnery and first lieutenancy and all that sort of thing on my record.

Sometime early in 1941 Earle Mills came up from the Bureau of Ships to New York to see the North Carolina. He visited us there and escorted somebody around the engineering plant. Of course, I went along and I talked to him then. I knew Earle well enough to call him by his first name.* I said, "Earle, I've got all this engineering duty. If I'm not selected this year, I'll forget about engineering and go back to general line and get myself a job as exec of one of these CLAAs." These were the Atlanta-class antiaircraft light cruisers that my Naval Academy class was then going to. That October I was selected for engineering duty only. I don't know whether my conversation with Earle Mills had anything to do with it or not.

Q: Anything else to remember about the North Carolina before we move on?

Captain Edwards: Well, she was a splendid ship, and I was very happy to be in her. In our lingo, we say "in" a ship, and we don't use the word "the." It's "in North Carolina."

---

*In the summer of 1941, Captain Mills was assigned to the design division of the Bureau of Ships.

But, of course, I realize that's a fetish.

Q: It's a matter of individual style.

Well, then you went ashore to the Bureau of Ships.

Captain Edwards: I wanted the battleship desk, because I just came from a battleship. Unfortunately, a fellow named Bill Dolan, class of '25, got there the day before, and he got the job.* I reported to Captain Broshek, who later became a rear admiral.** When I got there, he asked, "Have you ever been in destroyers?"

I said, "Yes, sir, for six years--four in one and two in another."

He said, "You're it."

That's how I got the destroyer and DE type desk, and that was the busiest time of my life. For the next three years I did nothing but six days a week-plus. I'm glad I did, because it was a very, very busy desk. I couldn't do it now physically. I worked from 8:00 A.M. till 6:00 P.M., then went home and had supper. I worked for two hours at home.

Q: Why was it so demanding?

---
*Lieutenant Commander William A. Dolan, Jr., USN.
**Captain Joseph J. Broshek, USN, who was head of the Maintenance Division of the Bureau of Ships. He was promoted to rear admiral during the course of the war.

Captain Edwards: So many ships. We were eventually getting out seven and eight destroyers a month in '43 and maybe 35 or 40 DEs a month. They involved an awful lot of paperwork and other work.

Q: Did the pressure ever let up during the war?

Captain Edwards: No. It was unrelenting pressure. I had my full day at the office, and I took things home in my briefcase and continued the fight after supper. In '43 I had one day off, and that was Christmas.

Q: When you reported in the spring of 1942, how far along was the destroyer escort program?

Captain Edwards: It was just getting under way. The first keels were laid early that year. They had, as I recall, four different machinery types. The FMRs were the Fairbanks Morse diesel type. Then there was the WGT type; that was the Westinghouse geared turbine type. Then they had two electric types; there was a GE type and a Westinghouse type. So we had four different machinery plants. All were building at the same time. In my opinion, the WGTs, Westinghouse geared turbines, were the best.

Q: Why do you say that?

Captain Edwards: Well, they were steam turbine and rugged. While the diesel-drive ships had the required rated speed, they couldn't produce it for sustained cruising. Otherwise you had excessive wear. And the electric ones were always breaking down--always something wrong with them.

Q: Whose responsibility was it to get the crews trained to run these engineering plants?

Captain Edwards: It was the Bureau of Personnel, in connection with the Bureau of Ships and the Bureau of Ordnance.

Q: Were you involved in any degree?

Captain Edwards: No. They set up training schools. The DEs had one at Miami, Florida, and so on. I was not involved in that training program. I was merely involved in getting these ships running and replacing parts, things that were falling apart or they didn't have. For example, I had a telephone bank with connections all over the world. I was getting calls in desperation: "We want this and we want that." For example, when a destroyer down in Rio had to retube a boiler, we had to get the tubes for the boiler, get an airplane, and fly the tubes down to Rio.

At the Battle of the Komandorskis up in the Aleutians, a destroyer had an engine room flooded.* She had to have certain replacement turbines and machinery. We had to divert machinery from new construction over to the ship. And, there again, usually it was an airplane, if possible, or it was a freight car. That freight car was monitored all the way across country. We knew when it went to Chicago and when it got through Denver and so forth. That was a busy, busy time.

You will recall that two destroyers, the Cassin and Downes of the Mahan class, were in dry dock number one at Pearl, ahead of the Pennsylvania, at the time of the Japanese attack. Due to damage from bombing, a lot of oil was spilled and then caught on fire, so they flooded the dock at least part way, and these two destroyers were very badly damaged. However, the main machinery was almost intact. The damage was to the hull primarily.

Q: And machinery was in very scarce supply.

Captain Edwards: Right. The question came up, of course, what to do with these two ships. Should they be repaired,

---

*The Battle of the Komandorski Islands, 26 March 1943, was one of the few daylight surface gunnery battles of the Pacific War.

should they be scrapped, or should they be made spare parts for other ships of the class? I carried the ball in the bureau's name to restore those ships to their original or near-original condition. The yards at Pearl Harbor and Mare Island were very much against it, because they were doing new-construction work, which would, of course, interfere with the logical flows of labor and material for fleet maintenance or new construction. But I felt that the history books would read much better years later if all those ships—both these in particular—went back to active service.

They were broken up and shipped in pieces to Mare Island for restoration as the original ships. As I said, the machinery was in relatively good condition. The yards at Pearl took off what I'll call the hard parts: bows and sterns, the doors and hatches, and things like that. They were all cut out of the plating and shipped back. Then, of course, new plating was used at Mare Island.

Q: Could some of those pieces and parts be used in the new hulls?

Captain Edwards: Yes, they were. That was the idea. These hard parts were removed from the old hulls and shipped back for the new hulls that went back into active service during the war. I carried the ball for that. That was one of those incidents which I felt good about.*

Q: Are there any further examples you remember of coping with battle damage during the war?

Captain Edwards: The Shaw was in dry dock there at Pearl Harbor at the same time. She had her bow blown off. So we welded a stub bow on, a new bow, and sent her back to Mare Island, where they put on a replica, a duplicate of the original bow.

Then the Abner Read, one of our new Fletcher-class destroyers, had her tail blown off by a mine up in Alaskan waters. We had to bring her back to salvage her.**

Q: The forward areas were doing more and more repair and maintenance. How much did you keep in touch with those people?

Captain Edwards: We were in touch continually, usually by correspondence. OpNav decided where to send the ships after first consulting the Bureau of Ships. BuShips

---

*For details of the damage to and reconstruction of these two ships, see Commander John D. Alden, USN (Ret.), "Up from the Ashes--The Saga of Cassin and Downes," U.S. Naval Institute Proceedings, January 1961, pages 33-41.
**USS Abner Read (DD-526) was patrolling off Kiska in the Aleutians when shaken by an explosion on 17 August 1943. She lost 70 killed and 47 wounded. The ship received temporary repairs in Alaskan ports, then was towed to the Puget Sound Navy Yard for extensive restoration work.

suggested the best places to send them so the workload would best be distributed, as well as maintain the active, working Navy.

Q: Did you have to arrange for naval constructors or EDOs to go there and repair parts and all that?

Captain Edwards: We had EDOs out there. Roy Cowdrey was one; he was class of '20, a constructor.* He was there on the spot to advise them what to do temporarily. These places had lots of what I'll call scrap iron--railroad rails and all sorts of plating--from which they put in temporary crude repairs. These were enough to get the ships back to the West Coast or Hawaii, where they could be properly repaired.

Q: You'd probably have to send plans and other things out to the forward areas.

Captain Edwards: Well, the yards already had them. And they especially sent materials. If a ship needed a winch, for example, or a steering gear, or whatever was missing, it would be available. They might even need an engine room, if they had a whole engine room full of machinery missing that had to be replaced. In some of those ships we

---
*Captain Roy T. Cowdrey, USN.

would replace the original equipment with new machinery, even if it was different from the other engine room and from the sister ships. If a suitable alternative was available, we couldn't fool around having the original manufactured.

Q: Was the Bureau of Ships then in the Navy Department on Constitution Avenue?

Captain Edwards: Yes, when I first reported, it was the old Navy Department building. It was built during World War I and served overtime as the Bureau of Ships headquarters. Now, there was also a similar building which housed the War Department. It was a duplication, practically, of the Navy Department. The War Department abandoned that site when it moved over to the Pentagon.

Q: Those old buildings weren't torn down till the Nixon administration.

Captain Edwards: That's right. They were tough customers; they were concrete and hard to get rid of. Sometime in late '42 BuShips moved to some wooden shanties, I'll call them, on the Washington Monument grounds and stayed there until 1945. After the war was over, we moved back into the concrete World War I building. The wooden temporary buildings were easy to demolish, so they were soon torn down.

Q: What do you remember about the new Fletcher-class destroyers coming in?

Captain Edwards: Well, I'll have to say beautiful. I attended the trials of the first, the Fletcher itself. They were the best destroyers we'd had up to that time. I always felt it was the Fletcher class that won the war. There were 175 of them. I don't have time to detail the characteristics of the Fletcher class. However, those ships were superior to earlier destroyers in every respect. They were the heart and soul of the small-ship Navy.

Q: What do you remember about the trials for the Fletcher?*

Captain Edwards: The trials were very abbreviated. In fact, I went aboard up at Federal Shipbuilding, where she was built. We spent time inspecting her and sitting down in the wardroom and going over their list of requested alterations. I was not aboard when she actually got under way.

---
*USS Fletcher (DD-445) was commissioned 30 June 1942. She had a displacement of 2,100 tons, was 376 feet long, and 40 feet in the beam. She had a top speed of 36 knots and a main battery of five 5-inch guns and ten torpedo tubes.

Q: That was only six years since the Mahan had been commissioned. There were a lot of changes in destroyer design in that time.

Captain Edwards: A lot, yes. In the meantime, we had the Sims class. They had a single big stack. Otherwise, the machinery was generally the same as in the Mahan. Also, they had no closed-in, fore-and-aft access. You had to jump for it in case you were in a seaway.

Q: So that was an advantage of the Fletchers, certainly.

Captain Edwards: Yes, they were much more habitable, in rough weather particularly. The arrangements were improved throughout the ship over the predecessors.

Q: Do you have any observations on the Sumner and Gearing classes in comparison with the Fletchers?*

Captain Edwards: Well, yes. There wasn't time to design and build new engines, so we used the 445-class engines in the 692 class. That meant they were slower than the Fletchers because the 692s were bigger ships. Later they

---

*The USS Allen M. Sumner (DD-692) was commissioned 26 January 1944 and the USS Gearing on 3 May 1945.

cut them in two and put oil tanks amidships to give them more range. We called them long-legged types. <u>Gearing</u> was the first one.* They were much better ships than the <u>Mahan</u> class or thereabouts.

Q: How would you rate the various yards that were building destroyers then?

Captain Edwards: Bath Iron Works was always number one. After that, I hate to damn anybody, but Bethlehem Steel ships were the worst, I'm sorry to say. Federal Shipbuilding at Kearny, New Jersey, did a good job. As far as I know, the Navy yards did a good job. But, unfortunately, Bethlehem had the poorest reputation of all. I hate to damn them, but they had problems that the other people didn't have.

Q: What was so good about the Bath ships?

Captain Edwards: The workmen were local people. And they had pride in their work. In fact, their whole living depended on that job. There was no other job in town of that nature. In a big city you get medium to average labor.

---

*The <u>Gearing</u>-class ships were 390 feet long, compared with 376 for those of the <u>Allen M. Sumner</u> class.

Q: Well, perhaps in Bath it was generation after generation in the same trades.

Captain Edwards: That's correct. For example, I knew the boss man there, Pete Newell.* He was the number-one destroyer builder in both World War I and World War II. Then his son John took over after he retired. Later his son sold out, I'll have to say, to a conglomerate. I think that was a mistake.

Q: Did you get out and visit these various yards?

Captain Edwards: Very seldom. I was the kingpin there at headquarters, and I felt I had to be present. So I did it from the seat of my pants. I sent out people to get information.

Q: Was there any frustration in being tied to a desk when other people from BuShips were out on board ships?

Captain Edwards: Well, yes and no. I'd had that shipboard life. I knew what that was all about. I just came from a ship, and I felt I was doing more good in Washington than I could by being a single officer in some ship. That's the

---

*William Stark "Pete" Newell, president of Bath Iron Works.

way I felt about it. I was educated and paid for that job, so I gave them all I had.

Q: Well, I would think, though, that there would still be some satisfaction in getting out to shipyards and seeing the results of your handiwork.

Captain Edwards: Well, I did visit occasionally, but, I say, most of my information came personally from people I sent out to get that information. Usually they were lieutenants or lieutenant commanders who went out to see a particular yard and get the story. They'd come back with a whole fistful of papers.

Q: Was welding becoming more commonplace instead of riveting during World War II?

Captain Edwards: Oh, yes. I won't say it was 50-50, but they were using both.

Q: What were the advantages of welding?

Captain Edwards: With riveting you had to drill all these holes, and it took a longer time. And you had to very carefully get these plates aligned. Then there was all this banging of hot rivets. Welding was relatively quiet, and if you knew how to do it, you didn't have any warping. You couldn't just start at one end and go back. You had to start in the middle and work both ways on the plating in order not to get warping. So nowadays there are very few requirements for riveting.

Q: Well, presumably it would be lighter weight too because you don't have to overlap the plates.

Captain Edwards: That's right.

Q: How much did you get involved in looking at plans for ships that were coming down the line?

Captain Edwards: Only for the alterations and proposed changes. The ships had already been designed when I arrived there.

Q: Were you more involved in maintenance and repair than new construction?

Captain Edwards: Originally we had two desks for destroyers and escorts--construction and maintenance. When I started, I had the maintenance desk only, but then in 1944 they combined the two, so I had both. I had over 100 people in this one desk after the merger.

Q: Why were they combined?

Captain Edwards: Well, the war was beginning to level off. The construction people weren't too helpful to us as to the status of the ships, so I had to send out people to shipyards to get the status of the alterations of the ships--what was finished and what wasn't finished. It became obvious that we were in duplication, so the two desks were pushed together.

Q: Did you have a practice of bringing in lessons learned from combat to incorporate in future destroyers?

Captain Edwards: Well, I'll tell you, we learned during the war the hard way that the officers' quarters should be divided into two parts. In fact, I separated them in some later designs. When the Reuben James was hit by a torpedo, the senior survivor was the chief machinist's mate of the engine room watch.* The captain, exec, officers, chief petty officers, and most of the crew were lost. The only survivors were the people on watch in the machinery spaces. That's one thing we learned: split it up. So in later designs I put the executive officer, the chief engineer,

---

*The USS Reuben James (DD-245) was the first U.S. naval vessel sunk in World War II. She was torpedoed by a U-boat on 31 October 1941 while escorting a convoy to Iceland.

and a couple of others amidships so all your rank wouldn't be wiped out in one blow.

Also, I learned that you had to have a source of emergency power aft as well as forward. The emergency generator was forward, and if that was wiped out, you were helpless: no water and no light anywhere on the ship. So in the 692 class we had an emergency generator aft. I personally put it there as a major alteration.

Q: One practice I know they had in the combat areas was to build wooden mockups of particular spaces, like the bridge or the plotting room or turret. Did they do that for engineering spaces?

Captain Edwards: I had no mockups. They may have had mockups somewhere else, but in BuShips we had just drawings, blueprints.

Q: You mentioned that Gibbs & Cox had been doing design work for the Navy back in the Thirties. Did you deal with them also during the war?

Captain Edwards: No, I had nothing to do with them during the war. The designs were done before I arrived.

Q: What else do you remember about the maintenance and

repair process?

Captain Edwards: Well, in peacetime, the norm was two weeks alongside a tender and six weeks operating. During the war, that had to be put aside, and the ships ran until they practically fell apart.

Q: Did you have some kind of a regular program for voyage repairs after a convoy trip or something like that?

Captain Edwards: I can't say after a convoy trip, because I was not involved. But there was usually a period of at least ten days to two weeks between convoys, at which time they took care of body and soul, physical and inanimate.

Q: Well, it takes a fair amount of planning, I would think, to have repair parts at the right yard at the right time.

Captain Edwards: We scheduled that by working with the central parts depots. One was in Mechanicsburg, Pennsylvania, a suburb of Harrisburg. That was the center for repair parts on the East Coast. Out west we had a similar setup at Clearfield, Utah. We could shunt special materials out quickly from those central depots.

Q: Rickover was then a captain. I think he had a big hand in the electrical parts.

Captain Edwards: He was trying to run his own Navy. I had trouble with Rickover during this period. He was on the electrical desk, and he wrote letters to destroyers without even consulting me. And I told him that was a no-no. Destroyer matters came through me. Either in or out, I had to have control of destroyer matters. So we had an argument about that. He later more or less agreed but begrudgingly.

Q: How much did you work with the various suppliers on their quantities and specifications for equipment?

Captain Edwards: Well, we had certain low levels, and they were automatically renewed by, say, Mechanicsburg or Clearfield. They kept certain levels, and they ordered on their own.

Q: You probably weren't in the competitive bidding business.

Captain Edwards: No, there was no competition. It was produce or else. I was not in the contract business. I reviewed contacts, purely from the technical standpoint, but I had nothing to do with awarding them.

Q: What do you remember about the hierarchy within the Bureau of Ships and how it worked during that period?

Captain Edwards: Well, as I said before, the Bureau of Ships was a combination of the Bureau of Engineering on one hand and the Bureau of C&R on the other. And all those top people were pushed together. I had a feeling that the constructors were still running things, but I had no real proof of that. Cochrane was running the show, and Mills was his very able assistant, but he didn't call the shots while Cochrane was there. Later on Mills was the chief of bureau and, of course, called the shots.*

Q: Whom did you report to directly?

Captain Edwards: Admiral Broshek was in charge of the division. In between were a constructor and another engineer. Walter Christmas was the constructor, and I can't think of the engineer's name.** He was in the Philippines when the war started, but he escaped through Australia and came back to the bureau, and he was my

---

*As a vice admiral, Mills served as Chief of the Bureau of Ships from November 1946 to February 1949. He was deputy chief under Rear Admiral Edward L. Cochrane, USN, who was promoted to vice admiral during the course of his tenure as bureau chief, which was November 1942 to November 1946.
**Commander Walter F. Christmas, USN.

leading engineer; I reported to him directly. He and Christmas, in turn, reported to Broshek.

Q: Did you have much direct dealing with Admiral Cochrane himself?

Captain Edwards: No. On occasion I attended conferences, and once in a while talked. We were always on good terms.

The day Cochrane got the job, which was in 1942, I happened to be one of three of four people there talking to him at the time. I remember hearing him say, "I'd rather be design chief than I would be chief of the bureau." I thought that rather queer, but I realized later he was right. Just like I said, I'd rather be the chief engineer of a ship than the skipper, because the engineer is closer to the job. The reason for his reaction was that as head of the bureau, he'd be taken away from the nuts and bolts of the job. He and Mills sat down more or less completely flabbergasted to have just been selected chief and assistant chief of the bureau.

Q: Why was he flabbergasted?

Captain Edwards: He had been a technical man all his career, and that was his love. When he found out he had been selected, he and Earle Mills both expressed amazement that they were now in position as administrators and no longer technical people.

Q: Was he flabbergasted in the sense of being surprised?

Captain Edwards: Yes. He had no reason I know of to be picked as the one. He was eligible and all that, and lightning struck in the right place at the right time.

Q: Was it typical for the bureau chief and the assistant chief to change at the same time?

Captain Edwards: In this case it was necessary, because their predecessors had different attitudes and performances, let me say. Admiral Van Keuren went across the river to the Naval Research Lab at that time.*

Q: So this was the idea of pairing a constructor and an engineer.

Captain Edwards: Yes, that was common practice at all levels.

---

*Rear Admiral Alexander H. Van Keuren, USN, was Chief of the Bureau of Construction and Repair, September 1939-June 1940; Chief of the Bureau of Ships, February-October 1942; and Director, Naval Research Laboratory, November 1942-November 1945. Van Keuren's assistant chief in the Bureau of Ships was Rear Admiral Claud A. Jones, USN.

F. A. Edwards #5 - 321

Q: That brings me to another question. You had been out in Bremerton at the point when the Bureau of Ships came into being. Did you see any effect then at your level?

Captain Edwards: Not at that time. The people around me were more or less surprised that here, suddenly, we had a new bureau, the Bureau of Ships, which superseded the old Bureau of Construction and Repair and the Bureau of Engineering.

Q: Did people who were in the Construction Corps and the Engineering Corps feel somewhat disappointed at loss of that separate identity?

Captain Edwards: Yes, especially constructors. They felt they were an elite group, and now they'd been merged with the engineers, who were not so elite, in their opinion.

Q: Well, and not only that; people could no longer tell them apart from line officers just by looking at their sleeves.

Captain Edwards: They were now wearing the star, instead of an oak branch with an acorn. I was interested and all that, but it had no direct effect on me.

Q: How difficult was it to find a place to live in Washington?

Captain Edwards: We were very lucky. We spent one day looking around, and finally at the last minute, on the way home, this real-estate agent said, "Well, there's a new house over here."

So I said, "Well, let's see it." So we turned around and went back to see it. We liked it so well we said, "We'll take it." The owner had just built this very nice brick house, but he was going to sell it rather than live in it. The house was out in south Arlington, overlooking the Army-Navy Country Club. It was generally hard to get housing at that time, except for just pure luck.

Q: Were you exempt from the rationing that took place during the war?

Captain Edwards: No. Gasoline and food were rationed.

Q: So that's why you got involved in these driving squads, probably.

Captain Edwards: That's right. It was a necessity. They had a bus, but it was overcrowded all the time and not too

F. A. Edwards #5 - 323

reliable at times.

Q: What was the setup for schools for your children?

Captain Edwards: We sent our daughter Suzanne for one year to Western High School, which in those days was all white. Then she went to Holton Arms for the other three years. That was probably the best private girls' school there. Our son Fred came from Admiral Farragut Academy down to Washington and went the next year to George Washington University as a freshman. Then he took examinations and entered the Naval Academy after that. He graduated there in the class of 1950.

Q: You must have had fairly decent pay as a commander to be able to put both children in private schools.

Captain Edwards: Of course, a dollar went a lot farther in those days than it does now. I had a car, but I couldn't use it there very much, only on weekends.

Q: When were you promoted to captain?

Captain Edwards: May '43. A whole bunch of us were promoted at the same time, just by block. The Navy was increasing so fast, they didn't bother about individuals.

They just went to blocks and maybe picked out certain people there they didn't want to promote, but the block as a whole was promoted. When I retired in '54 I was still a captain. That was 11 years I was a captain, a real old fud.

Q: What sorts of things did your wife get involved in during the war?

Captain Edwards: Red Cross. She put in, I guess, it was 1,000 hours; she had one of those pins. That was at the Pentagon.

Q: Doing what sorts of things?

Captain Edwards: Well, running a blood bank and looking out for unfortunate or underprivileged families, the sort of thing that the Red Cross did.

Q: Sort of like the Navy Relief does?

Captain Edwards: That's right, same idea, only on a bigger scale.

Q: Did you have a concern about your health? That kind of seven-day-a-week job can be very demanding.

Captain Edwards: Well, I was in my early 40s. That's supposed to be about the peak of one's physical life, and I had no problem. I couldn't do it now.

Q: Did you have any means of relaxation during off-duty time?

Captain Edwards: Practically none. I worked on my yard and that sort of thing. I built a fence to fence off my lot from another lot, but that was not recreation. That was a job I wanted to get done. There was no fun in it.

Q: How much opportunity did you have to keep track of the war from a strategic or tactical point of view?

Captain Edwards: I saw a daily batch of dispatches--a whole fistful of them. They had a special officer who did nothing but take these around to the heads of units, so I had all that. And I had all kinds of letters, official letters, coming in, action reports and everything. I was constantly reading. In fact, I used to cool off my glasses at the water cooler. [Laughter]

Q: What did you have in the way of a staff to accomplish all this?

Captain Edwards: My number one was a lieutenant commander constructor. And I had a couple of other lieutenant commanders who were general line. And I had perhaps four or five lieutenants. And I had a civilian staff of, altogether, about 50 people. They were very good. I got some WAVES finally, before the war was over, and they were very good.*

Q: What sort of work did they do for you?

Captain Edwards: Clerical, running files and taking care of correspondence. Of course, I had to make the decisions. Also, I'd read the incoming letters, and people would give me proposed answers. I either okayed the replies or changed them to suit myself. One time a fellow said to me, "You know what they call you upstairs?"

    I said, "No."

    He said, "They call you 'The Butcher.'"

Q: Why was that?

Captain Edwards: Because I was always butchering up letters. Generally, technical people are not good writers or authors, so I gave them some help.

---

*WAVES--Women Accepted for Voluntary Emergency Service.

Q: Did you maintain a material history on each individual ship?

Captain Edwards: Yes, we had a file. That's before computers came in. In fact, that's what I say about a computer. It's another four-drawer file cabinet.

Q: You would have to work in very close concert with the shipyards to keep these histories up.

Captain Edwards: For each ship we had a file, and we kept those files in whole racks of file cabinets. We had a total of probably 800 or 900 ships altogether--destroyers and escorts. Now, the converted types were farmed out to another desk. These included the DMs, DMSs, APDs, and AVDs.* But we had to give them consultation. On alterations, the people involved with those types came to us and asked us what to do, and we gave them copies of our alterations. In '43 my desk issued, I think, a little over 300 shipalts.**

One wartime shipalt I remember involved portholes. OpNav put out an order to the whole Navy to weld over portholes in the hulls of various classes of ships. We

---
*DM--destroyer minelayer; DMS--destroyer minesweeper; APD--high-speed transport; AVD--destroyer seaplane tender.
**Shipalt--ship alteration order.

issued the detail order to do it. Well, many of the destroyer officers were annoyed no end. They'd come in and bawl us out. So we'd just sic them onto OpNav and let those people give them the sad news. These destroyers were not cool, but they were much better than the older ships. With the portholes closed, of course, the ventilation situation was worse.

Q: What was the rationale for covering over the portholes?

Captain Edwards: Trying to keep out light so that submarines would not sight these ships at night.

Q: Did it have anything to do with structural integrity?

Captain Edwards: No, no, no. Because these platings were relatively light, and this was just a question of blocking out the light, giving away their existence.

Let me say that to issue a shipalt was just not a stroke of the pen. There was an awful lot of background work. We had to find out where the material was and arrange for it to arrive. We had to have the plans prepared and that sort of thing. Having something like the current Xerox machines would have been a godsend back then. Instead, we had to use a duplicating machine like a ditto or mimeograph, because we often ran off 400 or 500 copies of a given shipalt.

Q: You probably had to work in coordination with the other bureaus also.

Captain Edwards: Yes, particularly the Bureau of Ordnance. If you wanted to add a new gun, you didn't just put a gun on. You had to find out what the weight was, what wiring was required, and all that sort of thing for the gun. Then the shield or whatever the protection it had--that's weight, so we were in constant communication with Ordnance particularly and the Bureau of Supplies and Accounts.

Q: Probably most of the places they wanted to put things were topside, so you get concerned about top-heaviness.

Captain Edwards: That's right. And then we used to say that we needed to have a bulkhead stretcher if it was a new radar or a new gun. We might have to add electronic equipment or a new magazine, so we had to stretch the bulkhead to put it in or take out something else. There was constant coordination between these two bureaus.

Q: What uniform did you wear to BuShips during those war years?

Captain Edwards: Mostly khakis. I never got to gray. Ernie King specified the gray.* They called him "Clothes Horse Ernie," because he had decreed that we'd have one of these gray uniforms, without even consulting the fabric people, who didn't have the fabrics available. So they skirmished around to get that gray cloth available from which to make all these uniforms. However, toward the end of the war, I had word from a member of the board that they were going to do away with them, so I didn't buy any. I was under the gun, but I took a chance and won.

Q: King was one of the few people who did like the grays.

Captain Edwards: Somebody said they made officers look like milk-delivery men.

Q: Bus driver was another description I heard.

Captain Edwards: That's correct. They were very unpopular with officers. Khaki, however, was very popular and a very good uniform.

Q: Anything else about that tour of duty before we move on?

---

*Admiral Ernest J. King, USN, was Chief of Naval Operations and Commander in Chief U.S. Fleet during World War II.

Captain Edwards: I used this expression--it's almost true--that I am the most undecorated officer of World War II. After the war was over--this is petty--the Secretary of the Navy's office sent me over a green commendation ribbon.* I took it down to the chief of the bureau, Admiral Cochrane, and I told him that if that was the Navy's opinion of my value to the bureau, I didn't want it. Would he please take it back. He refused to take it back; he said it would be insulting the secretary, that sort of crap. So I kept the damn thing and put it in my pocket. We had people there, some of them reserves, with all due respect, who were given red ribbons, Legions of Merit. They did their jobs as required but had no responsibility. The Navy gave them going-home-happy ribbons, red ribbons. I wasn't after a ribbon of any kind, but it annoyed me when some of these people of secondary value were given red ribbons, the next higher grade.

Q: Did you eventually put it on your uniform?

Captain Edwards: Yes, I had to, but without any pleasure.

One last job of interest was the preparation and shipment of a destroyer engine to the Naval Academy for

---

*The Commendation Ribbon was authorized in January 1944 to recognize meritorious service The award distinguishes the individual from those performing similar services. In 1950 the award became the Navy Commendation Medal.

permanent display in the engineering building. With the war winding down, I arranged with the department head, Murray Stokes, class of '22, to salvage the engine and its auxiliaries from a battle-damaged Fletcher-class destroyer at the Norfolk Navy Yard.*

Q: How did your next assignment come about?

Captain Edwards: When the war was coming to an end, I was about to be transferred to the Pacific Fleet as destroyer maintenance officer. In fact, the orders were written for me. But then they suddenly decided the war was too far along, and the orders were canceled. So then BuPers decided it was going to send me to the East Coast as fleet maintenance officer.**

I also, for several months, headed up a desk to decide what excess machinery to retain. For example, the Navy built many more diesel engines than it had hulls for, and it had built many more propellers and shafts and so forth. So I sat down with some people and decided what to retain in storage and what to get rid of. When the Korean War came along, they built an awful lot of LSTs and other landing craft, which required diesel engines of the World War II type. Here we had a couple of thousand engines in

---
*Captain Thomas Murray Stokes, USN.
**BuPers--Bureau of Naval Personnel.

stock, which they were able just to pull out and put into these hulls. So that was one thing I felt good about. Otherwise, I could have scrapped the whole damn bunch, and then they would have had to build new engines, taking more time and more money.

Q: Where were they stored in the meantime?

Captain Edwards: Various places: Mechanicsburg or Clearfield, and in some cases, Navy yards.

Q: Were you involved in any way in the mothballing of the fleet after the war?

Captain Edwards: No, fortunately I was shorn of that duty, because it's just a headache. It has to be done, and somebody has to do it. I'm glad I wasn't involved.

Q: When did you report to the Atlantic Fleet staff?

Captain Edwards: October 1946.

When I was leaving BuShips to go to the Atlantic Fleet staff, Admiral Cochrane told me how to get along with line officers. I said, "Well, thank you very much." I said, "Admiral, I've been with these people for 18 years. I hope to get along with them." Here he was, a constructor, telling me how to get along with ships' officers. I liked Cochrane, but he was a little bit unrealistic, let me say. I don't want to detract from him, but as a person he was not down-to-earth as much as he might have been. Now, Earle Mills was his assistant and a down-to-earth guy.

Q: It sounds like he was a good liaison for Cochrane.

Captain Edwards: Yes. And Mills relieved him afterwards. I knew Earle quite well, and he kept the thing on an even keel. But Cochrane also did a damn good job.

Q: Where was the fleet staff when you joined it?

Captain Edwards: The Pocono, which was the administrative flagship, was then down in Norfolk.* Admiral Mitscher was then Commander in Chief Atlantic Fleet.**

Q: Well, please tell me about him in that role.

Captain Edwards: He was then a sick man. He had had an operation for appendicitis some two or three months prior to that, and he was still recovering. But generally his

---

*USS Pocono (AGC-16) was commissioned 29 December 1945 as an amphibious force flagship. She was a 459-foot, 13,910-ton merchant-type ship equipped with an assortment of communication gear for the flagship role.
**Admiral Marc A. Mitscher, USN, served as Commander in Chief Atlantic Fleet from September 1946 until his death in February 1947.

system was weakened, so he relied on Burke a lot.*
Burke, who was a classmate of mine, was his chief of staff.
In fact, when I reported to Mitscher, I didn't report to
him in his cabin. He was over in an easy chair, talking to
Burke in Burke's cabin. So Burke had me come in and meet
the admiral there. He was sitting there in casual clothes.
He was a nice fellow, but he was over the hill; he really
was. He'd already given his pound of flesh to the Navy. I
won't go into that, because you know about his war effort
and his earlier career.

Q: I'd be interested in what you saw and how it affected
Admiral Mitscher's ability to do his job.

Captain Edwards: It did affect his ability. He was not
active. He was inactive, you might say. Burke did all the
active work. We did make one inspection trip north. We
went up to Newport first. Then we went to New London;
Boston; Portland, Maine; and then back to Norfolk. That
was the only time he went to sea at all after I joined up.

Q: Did you have headquarters ashore in addition to the
Pocono?

---

*Captain Arleigh A. Burke, USN. During World War II, in
the rank of commodore, Burke had been chief of staff when
Mitscher was Commander Task Force 58. After the war, Burke
reverted to captain before again reaching flag rank.

Captain Edwards: No, not then. Later we moved into what had been a World War II extension of the Naval Hospital Norfolk. The old hospital was still in Portsmouth, Virginia, but during the war they built a new brick annex over on the Norfolk side. It was being decommissioned at the time I came along. So perhaps six months later they took one of the wings of this big building and made that Atlantic Fleet headquarters ashore.

Q: What did you observe about the relationship between Burke and Mitscher?

Captain Edwards: Well, very fatherly. Burke was the son, and Mitscher was the father.

Q: Burke would have had quite a bit to do since Mitscher was not up to par then.

Captain Edwards: He was the active person; he had to be. Mitscher, I say, was sick and not active. Once I heard our fleet surgeon say that Mitscher's circulatory system was that of a man of about 90. That's how far advanced he was. In his conversations he would seldom complete a sentence immediately. He'd wait five seconds or ten seconds, swallow, and finish it. It was very difficult to carry on a conversation with him or even to listen to him.

Q: Did what he said make sense?

Captain Edwards: Oh, yes, it made sense. Nothing earthshaking, but it made sense. His was mostly a decision-making job, not an active inspection job.

Q: What sorts of issues did you report to him on?

Captain Edwards: Material. I prepared correspondence for his signature, and once in a while I'd go in with it and explain it to him or expand it. But I never bothered him, because he was a sick man. I tried to run the job the best I could, subject to Burke's okay.

Q: Did it help in your relationship with Burke that he was a classmate?

Captain Edwards: No difference. We got along fine. Arleigh and I were in different parts of the woods. He was the general line officer, and I wasn't--by my own choice. Now, Arleigh was already preparing himself for bigger jobs. I went one day to see him, and he was listening to a record of a speech he'd made out at Denver for Navy Day or some other naval occasion. He was playing it over, not to hear his voice but to try to improve himself. He was a good guy; he was a great guy.

Q: Anything else about Mitscher's personality?

Captain Edwards: I hate to use the word, but he was washed up by that time. He was just a husk of a man. He had been active all his life, but here he was, in the twilight of his life, unable to do the job actively. It was more or less an award for his wartime service. But all he had to do was make decisions, which Burke carried out.

Q: What do you remember about Mitscher's last days?

Captain Edwards: I had lunch at his table one Saturday noon in late January of '47. Afterward he went ashore on ordinary weekend liberty, as he thought, but that was it. He never came back to duty, because he had a heart attack during that weekend.* I, among many others, attended the funeral at Arlington. Ernie King was there; I saw him at the funeral.

Then Burke took the Pocono down to Trinidad to await the arrival of Blandy. Blandy had been selected to be the new commander in chief. We went alone down to Trinidad,

---

*Admiral Mitscher's heart attack was on Sunday, 26 January 1947, his 60th birthday. He died on 3 February.

and Blandy flew down and took command of the fleet down there.

Q: Since Blandy was a surface officer, I presume that an aviator came in to relieve Burke as chief of staff.

Captain Edwards: Yes, that was Dave Johnson, class of '21.* He was a very nice gentleman, very fine. Since he was an aviator, he and I didn't have too much technical to talk about. But he was a very good shipmate.

Later on, he was relieved by Hugh Goodwin, class of '22.** Hugh was not very popular with junior staff officers, including myself.

Q: Why not?

Captain Edwards: He was petty. One thing was that he was very picayune about the uniform. For example, he told me I had to wear a fabric belt over my khakis instead of a leather belt and just stuff like that. Also, I won't say he was a drunkard, but he was a semi-alcoholic who once went to a party in New York City and forgot who brought him home. He would make slighting remarks about the fact that I wasn't a full-fledged drinker--by his standards. Every day when we were in the Navy yard or in port somewhere,

---
*Rear Admiral William David Johnson, Jr., USN.
**Captain Hugh H. Goodwin, USN.

he'd go up to the club and get a snootful. I'd go up with him occasionally, but I'd only have one or two drinks, and that would annoy him no end. According to him, I was not one of the real guys who could stand and drink. Since I had only one or two drinks, I was a teetotaler by his standards.

I was told that Hugh once landed his plane on a carrier deck with his wheels up. So he skidded the length of the ship.

Q: You probably did more business with those chiefs of staff, didn't you, than with the admiral?

Captain Edwards: Yes. With certain important letters, I went up and explained them or talked to the chief of staff about them. But I didn't send too many up to the admiral. Most of them I signed myself, or the chief of staff did. It all depended on the admiral's condition and his attitudes and his schedule, that sort of thing.

Q: Admiral Blandy ran the show to suit himself, obviously.

Captain Edwards: That's right. Blandy was much more active, as I have said. I saw him many more times about material matters than I did Mitscher. Mitscher was just simply not able to deal with much because he was a sick man. I never bothered him unless I had to see him about something really important.

Q: Did you go along on any inspections on board ships?

Captain Edwards: Mostly they were staff inspections, not individual ships. We'd go up to a base or a flagship or something like that.

Q: Type commanders?

Captain Edwards: Yes. The type commanders made the individual ship inspections. Our admiral was only interested in the flagships and specifically the flag commanders and the bases, what they were doing or had troubles with and so forth.

Q: Did you have daily briefings for the admiral on material casualties and other topics?

Captain Edwards: No. He had a weekly staff meeting, and, frankly, unless it was really important, I didn't bother him with any of my problems. I'd go to him later, individually, about a matter rather than take up the whole time of these 15 or 20 people who were then on the staff.

Q: But I presume if there was some material problem, you'd keep him informed on it.

Captain Edwards: Oh, yes, but I kept that down as much as I could, because I felt he was too damn busy with fleet matters to worry about some of these lesser material matters.

Q: Well, of course, they're related, because if a ship can't operate, that affects the fleet.

Captain Edwards: If a ship couldn't operate, then that was a problem, yes. Then I'd have to keep him informed. But something that didn't affect the ship's ability to run, why, I didn't fool with.

Q: We who served later had a system called casualty reports. Did you have something comparable?

Captain Edwards: Yes, it was a matter of letter reports.

Q: How suitable was the Pocono as a flagship?

Captain Edwards: Very suitable, because she had all kinds of electronics, which a fleet commander required. That's why she was selected in the first place. She was an amphibious flagship.

Q: What kind of issues did you deal with as the material officer?

Captain Edwards: One was fleet repair money. The basic money came from the Bureau of Ships. They would give the Atlantic Fleet maybe a third of it or a certain percentage of it for us to dish out. So then I dished out that percentage to my people at the various type commands. Then if they needed extra money, I dealt it out to them. They had to tell me what the problem was. If I needed more money, I had to go back to the bureau to get it. I think one time the destroyer force got completely head over heels in debt. I think it was $19 million.

Q: How did that happen?

Captain Edwards: These administrative type commanders gave the naval shipyards block sums of money to overhaul or repair ships. But they were not getting reports on the allocations of that money until maybe three or four months after the ships had left the shipyards. After a while, the type commanders were dishing out more money than they had. So I wrote a letter which obliged the naval shipyards to give the type commanders a statement of costs--plus or minus 5%--within 30 days of a ship's leaving the yard. Then the yards would later give them the final figures. That made the money active again. As it was, it was being stacked up to go nowhere, just because the yards hadn't prepared their final bills.

Another cost was for emergency dockings or repairs. If a ship ran aground or had a turbine blade casualty, we'd have to send that ship into the yard. I had to arrange for the ship to move and the money to pay for the repairs. Also, if a ship had a serious material casualty, I went over and took a look and advised the ship's officers what to do. I know down at Guantanamo Bay one of the carriers had a steering-gear casualty, and they were afraid of operating it. So I went over and talked to them and advised them to keep the rudder angle down to 5%, unless they had an emergency, and to get a fleet tug to go along with them. So they went back to Norfolk with a fleet tug standing by them and using practically no rudder on the way up. Fortunately, it worked out that way.

Q: Who did the scheduling that various ships would go into specific yards at a given time for regular overhauls?

Captain Edwards: The basic plan was done in the Bureau of Ships. But then alterations to it necessarily were made by the fleet staffs. For example, in the Atlantic I made alterations to the schedule, necessarily, because if a ship had a casualty, they had to go into a yard. Or maybe a yard needed work to keep its work force intact. I was the guy on the fleet staff who took care of that. Of course, I had to talk to other people too, but I headed it up.

Q: The fleet was shrinking then. Did that cause any problems?

Captain Edwards: No. It had already shrunk a lot. There was no great problem. They were still putting ships out of commission. In fact, I remember the Wisconsin was put out at that time.* She came back from a junket on the West Coast of South America, and then they put her out of commission.

Q: But you would just monitor that instead of supervising.

Captain Edwards: I had no supervision at all. That went to the Navy yard and the bureaus concerned.

Q: Was there a supply officer in addition to the material officer?

---

*USS Wisconsin (BB-64) was decommissioned 1 July 1948 and put into the Atlantic Reserve fleet at Norfolk.

Captain Edwards: We had a fleet supply officer, yes.

Q: So you must have worked closely with him.

Captain Edwards: Yes, but the operations officer was the one I worked with most. We had adjacent desks, operations and material. We worked hand in hand. We also had an ordnance and gunnery officer, communications officer, supply officer, doctor, and plans officer. In fact, I've got a picture of that staff here among my pictures.

Q: Who was the operations officer you worked with?

Captain Edwards: The first one was Tom Sawyer, class of '24.* And he was relieved by C. H. Lyman, class of '26.**

Q: Were there any specific demands that came out of the origin of the Sixth Fleet and having to support those ships?

Captain Edwards: No, but when ships came back to the Atlantic Fleet after their five months overseas, the captains and admirals came over and reported to the

---

*Captain Merle A. Sawyer, USN.
**Captain Charles H. Lyman III, USN.

commander in chief. Frequently I would be at the lunch table when this went on. And it was really interesting how Admiral Blandy would very deftly extract information on the situation that was going on and what was about to go on. I was a very interested bystander in those sessions.

Q: Do you remember any specific examples?

Captain Edwards: No, I don't, except they were just simply telling what they did and what they thought was going to happen and what they recommended--just general, mostly operational. He really sucked these men dry when he had lunch with them.

Q: It must have been quite a change to get Blandy, whom you said was very vigorous.

Captain Edwards: Very dynamic person. I had perhaps 100 meals with him, so I got to know him pretty well. Also, when he went on inspections I went along with him. He was ten years older than I, but he had me panting and my tongue hanging out.*

He was physically a very rugged guy and a very smart guy. In fact, he stood number one in the class of '13. He also was the five-striper, midshipman commander. So he was

---
*Blandy was born 28 June 1890, Edwards on 19 July 1901.

quite a distinguished fellow. They called him the "boy admiral" because when they had selections for admiral they jumped over the bottom of the class of '12 and picked him as the last man. That was to show the boys that the rest of them were all passed over. They called him the "boy admiral."

Q: He made it way early when he got to be Chief of the Bureau of Ordnance.*

Captain Edwards: Yes, I first met him when he was chief of ordnance, way back when.

Blandy was the smartest man I ever met. And I say that with all due respect to everybody else. He didn't rub it in, but he just simply knew what he was talking about. He should have been CNO, but he opposed Truman as part of the admirals' revolt.** He also tried to keep the naval aviation intact, and, of course, that didn't go down well with people like Symington et al.***

I recall that in late 1947 Blandy and his staff went up to see Truman. His flag lieutenant told me the story that Blandy was interviewed by Truman for CNO. Truman also

---
*When he was made bureau chief in February 1941, Blandy was, at age 50, the youngest line flag officer in the Navy.
**The Navy's flag officers objected to the attempts to subjugate naval aviation during the administration of President Harry S Truman.
***Stuart Symington was the first Secretary of the Air Force following the unification of the services in 1947.

interviewed Denfeld about the same time.* Later on Truman was quoted as saying he saw no difference between the two, so he would appoint Denfeld, who was senior—class of '12 versus '13. Well, that's not true. He appointed Denfeld because Denfeld had been passive about service unification. Blandy had been very active in opposing this merger. That's why Blandy missed being CNO.

Q: Well, another factor was that Leahy was a strong supporter of Denfeld, and he was Truman's chief of staff in that role.**

Captain Edwards: I don't know the inside of it, but this commander told me he was present when he heard Truman tell him that he was going to pick Denfeld because, as far as Truman knew, there was no difference in their professional abilities or capacities. That was a political lie, I think, because there wasn't any comparison between the two people from the standpoint of a naval officer. Denfeld was a nice guy, but he didn't have half the gumption that Blandy had.

Q: Well, that's an interesting observation. What more can

---

*Admiral Louis E. Denfeld, USN, was then Commander in Chief Pacific Fleet. He served as Chief of Naval Operations from December 1947 to November 1949.
**Fleet Admiral William D. Leahy, USN, was chief of staff to the Commander in Chief, that is, President Truman.

you say about Blandy's personality?

Captain Edwards: He liked to tell a good off-color story, and he wanted one in return. He had a good sense of humor and was a very direct guy. And I mentioned these inspection tours. He'd come back and maybe change clothes and go out and play golf. I'd be probably having a cup of coffee and recovering.

Q: Do you have any other recollections of traveling with Admiral Blandy?

Captain Edwards: Yes, and, as I say, I was in a very enviable position of being a spectator in these comings and goings. For instance, in about 1947 or '48 the staff was up at Newport on an inspection trip. Admiral Blandy had been entertained by some of the local society people, and so he responded. He gave a cocktail party one afternoon, and I happened to be among those in the receiving line.

I especially recall seeing the Mrs. Vanderbilt, who had been the reigning lady of New York society, the grande dame.* She had a manservant who pushed her around in a wheelchair. That's as close as I got to the rich and famous. A few of them still go to Newport for the summer.

---

*The grande dame was Grace Vanderbilt, widow of Cornelius Vanderbilt III, who died in 1942. In her day Mrs. Vanderbilt was one of the nation's most noted hostesses.

They call it "the season." The only reason I ever got to meet this woman is because I was a staff officer to Admiral Blandy, who was giving the party. I was glad to see her, because she was the only touch I ever had of that society.

Q: Well, they were generally pretty snobbish.

Captain Edwards: Yes, they were by themselves.

Q: How much coordination did you have with the type commanders?*

Captain Edwards: Very good. In my case, not so much with aviation because the aviation officer was a constructor. He was entirely involved with carriers. So I didn't have as much to do with the carriers as I did with the other ships. I worked through him. He had aviation problems, which I had nothing to do with. I only had ship problems.

Q: Were you in any sense a BuShips representative on the staff?

Captain Edwards: Yes, I was the BuShips representative.

---

*A type commander was a flag officer who had administrative control over the fleet ships of a given type, such as destroyers, cruisers, amphibious warfare ships, and so forth.

F. A. Edwards #5 - 352

Q: How much contact did you have with BuShips?

Captain Edwards: Well, letters, telephone calls, visits.

Q: Well, it was the other side of that coin you were describing earlier. During the war you were coordinating with the fleet people when you were in the bureau.

Captain Edwards: Yes, that's right. Obviously both sides of the coin have to be considered. I had no problems at all that I recall worth talking about. Again, it was a busy job. I was home only maybe one weekend out of a month or so.

Q: Did the flagship travel around quite a bit?

Captain Edwards: No. The ship didn't go too far, but we did travel by air. We'd go up to the Navy Department, for example, on planes. Blandy was a very active guy. He was always going somewhere, so we were on planes a lot of the time. In fact, sometimes I had more time in on planes as a passenger than the staff aviator did.

Q: Did you take part in any fleet exercises on board there?

Captain Edwards: No, Commander Second Fleet was the operational commander, and he picked his ships from the administrative type commanders to form a task force. I helped write some of their orders for exercises, but I personally did not participate.

Q: What kinds of exercises would these be?

Captain Edwards: Well, they had material problems, and they had to have fuel. I had nothing to do with the tactics part. I would write up the maintenance part, which might be a paragraph or page in the operation order.

Q: How much did you get involved in electronics matters?

Captain Edwards: Very little. I had an electronics man on my staff, and I let him carry the ball, unless it was something important that I should be involved. He'd tell me about it; otherwise, he'd take care of it.

Q: Did you see any effects from the Cold War on what you were doing?

Captain Edwards: I remember one night when Blandy got a dispatch from CNO about some Russian ship movements. I happened to be aboard, and he called me in and a couple of others and let us read this "eyes-only" dispatch. He asked me what my opinion was on what to do, and I told him. But what he did, I, of course, don't know. He was merely picking brains to find out what we thought.

Certain Russian ships had disappeared; CNO had lost track of them. And so Blandy put out a watered-down dispatch to the fleet. Later on they found these ships after we'd lost track of them. So that's the only operational emergency, I'll call it, that I had anything to do with.

Q: Was this revolt of the admirals a topic of discussion in the flag mess?

Captain Edwards: Oh, yes. It was a very bitter subject. It was direct interference by Louis Johnson, who was the SecDef then, with the organization and operations of the Defense Department.* He should have concerned himself with policy in general but not get into canceling ships, like the USS United States after her keel was laid.** He had her canceled without even consulting the bureaus or CNO

---

*Louis A. Johnson was Secretary of Defense in 1949-50. He was replaced by George Marshall soon after the outbreak of the Korean War because of a perception that his cost-cutting measures had weakened the nation's armed forces.
**In a real blow to postwar naval aviation, Johnson directed the end of construction of the super carrier United States (CVA-58) on 23 April 1949, five days after her keel-laying.

first. He was a Truman boy who was constantly messing around with fleet and air organizations. Of course, I was much below that sort of thing, but I knew it went on.

Q: Anything else to recall about that tour of duty?

Captain Edwards: While I was on that staff, BuShips made up a postwar destroyer design. They sent it out to various people, including myself, for comment. Well, I sent them a 40-page comment. I told them it was a pantograph job, just increasing the size of the previous destroyers without incorporating the necessary modernization. I said that they had to start over again. I don't know whether they liked that or not--probably not--but that was my reaction.

Q: I gather that design wasn't built.

Captain Edwards: It wasn't built, no. It was just a proposal to increase the size of the Gearing class by 10% or 15%. I felt we had to have something novel. So, I say, I went through the whole damn thing and wrote 40-some pages. Blandy signed it and sent it back to BuShips for comments and possible use.

Q: How did your next assignment come about?

Captain Edwards: When my time was up, I wanted Navy yard experience, so I went to BuShips and talked to people there. I was ordered to the New York Navy Yard then as the planning officer. That was in June of 1948.

New York at that time was probably the number-two Navy yard, in my opinion. Puget Sound was number one. So I was very glad to have the assignment. At that time Captain Whitgrove reported as the production officer.* Admiral Haeberle, who stood number one in his class, '17, naval constructor, was the shipyard commander.** I was his immediate assistant for planning and estimating. Whitgrove was his immediate assistant for production. I'd known Leland twice before, and we just got along wonderfully well. In fact, we usually had coffee together every morning.

Q: One thing you mentioned before the tape started was that you lived on board the battleship New Jersey for a while.

Captain Edwards: I went up there in June 1948. Our Navy yard quarters were not yet ready, and they weren't ready until fall. So I lived on board the New Jersey for perhaps

---
*Captain Leland D. Whitgrove, USN, Naval Academy class of 1922.
**Rear Admiral Frederick E. Haeberle, USN.

two months. Then I moved my family up to Quarters G, right next to the admiral's, so I was up on the front row there.

Q: Did the ship have services available, like light and water?

Captain Edwards: Oh, yes. I ate at the club. But for everything else I lived aboard the ship.

Q: Please tell me what was involved in your job of planning and estimating.

Captain Edwards: There were two main divisions. Later on, we had a third division. One of the main divisions was design, which involved over 200 draftsmen. They were doing all kinds of design work. At the same time we were finishing up the Oriskany, a carrier, and doing all kinds of alterations for various ships. And then planning and estimating was the other half of the main job. It had to write the job orders for work and handle the money to do these jobs. That's a big job. Then the third one came along later. That was for the Third Naval District. It was a sideshow, which I also ran.

Q: What did that involve?

Captain Edwards: Well, primarily arranging for overhauls and money. I say, that was a sideshow. The two main shows were the planning and estimating on one hand and design on the other hand. Design then was a big show, really, because they had done all kinds of work during the war. They had built the Missouri and Iowa and a couple of carriers.

Q: You mentioned before that you had attended the commissioning of the Missouri.*

Captain Edwards: Yes, she was commissioned in June '44, back when I was still in the Bureau of Ships. The Missouri's first chief engineer was Commander Maxwell, who had been my assistant in the North Carolina. He invited me to attend, so I stayed with him a couple of days.

I was in that job as planning officer of the New York Navy Yard when the liner United States was going to be constructed. The Navy Department gave permission for us to provide copies of the machinery plans of the Missouri to Gibbs & Cox for use on the United States, which they did. I turned over hundreds of the Missouri's machinery plans, since she had been built at that yard and they were available.

---

*USS Missouri (BB-63), the last battleship completed by the U.S. Navy, went into commission at the New York Navy Yard on 11 June 1944.

Q: Was it a fairly similar plant?

Captain Edwards: Yes, I'd say it was 95% similar.

Q: Both of those ships had great speed, phenomenal speed.

Captain Edwards: Well, the United States made almost 40 knots on her first ocean crossing.* In 1952, after the construction was complete, I went on her first sea trial, which was a junket. They had all kinds of important people. Somehow they found room for me. We were out for three or four days. They used the silverware and linens for the first time. We had the dining personnel from the United States Lines' other big liner.

Q: The America.

Captain Edwards: Yes. I knew the chief engineer, Kaiser, very well. He went out with me, and I visited him various times. He was the chief engineer of both of those ships—the America and the United States. The skipper during this junket was Harry V. Manning, who had rather a good name from the World War II period. He commanded one of our

---

*The highest speed recorded by the United States on her maiden voyage was 38.3 knots on 241,785 shaft horsepower. The designed shaft horsepower for the Missouri was 212,000.

merchant ships which was sunk by a submarine early in the war and caused a flap. He was very famous in the early 1950s; he was then a commodore.

Later on, my wife was going on a tour of Europe, over and back on the United States. I told her she wouldn't like it; it was too nice, too good, and too big. She said she'd make that decision for herself. I was pulling her leg, of course. It was then a state-of-the-art ship. She was beautiful, absolutely beautiful.

Q: William Francis Gibbs took a great personal interest in that ship.*

Captain Edwards: Yes, that was his baby. He used to go down and meet the ship between trips. It was his claim to fame.

Q: Crowning achievement.

Captain Edwards: It really was. But it's a shame; I saw her down in Norfolk here a couple of years ago. The paint is peeling off of her. Now they're talking about bringing her up to Baltimore. Some guy up there wants to make some money by taking care of her. It's a shame, absolutely a shame. The airplane put her in mothballs.

---

*Gibbs was one of the major partners in the Gibbs & Cox firm. His was the most prominent name connected with the design of the United States.

Even before that, the shipyard went into mothballs. The Navy was forced to give up the New York Naval Shipyard in the 1960s. There was a billion dollars' worth of heavy machinery and cranes, which was given away for $1.00. Just awful, sinful. Same way with the Boston yard, though to a smaller extent, because it was a smaller yard. It was given away--terrible.

We have people in charge who don't know or can't learn what the score is on maintenance of ships. Instead of having ships spread out to three or four yards, they want to put them all in one yard or two yards. And that way if a bomb fell, the whole works would go, and you'd also lose a lot of people--people you can't afford to lose. But we're doing the same damn thing over again that we did before World War II. It's just sinful.

They get these management consultants, you know. They're much brighter than we are--with no experience. So they decide what's to be done. The bureaus were done away with, which was a great mistake, I felt. In World War II the Bureau of Ships had nothing to hide. They had one ship that turned out bad. The bow of the heavy cruiser Pittsburgh fell off in a typhoon.* That's the only ship which we more or less needed to apologize for. Everything else, why, that was done very well, very commendably. But now they have these systems commands and that sort of

---

*On 4 June 1945 the bow of the USS Pittsburgh (CA-72) broke off during a typhoon near Japan.

thing; it's just a can of worms. If you went down there and wanted to find out something, you'd go from desk to desk to find what it's all about. In my day, they had these ship desks. If you had a destroyer, you went to the destroyer desk, and he would take you by the hand and take you around and give you the answers as necessary.

Q: Secretary McNamara was the culprit on closing that New York yard.*

Captain Edwards: It was sinful. I use that word repeatedly because it's true. A beautiful, valuable piece of property. It was farmed it out to little shipyards and whatnot.

Q: What do you remember specifically about the Oriskany job when you were there in the late Forties?

Captain Edwards: When we completed her, she had a lot of alterations that other ships of the class didn't have. So an awful lot of design work went on. She was, in effect, a sub-class because of so many major alterations.**

---
*Robert S. McNamara served as Secretary of Defense from 1961 to 1968.
**The Oriskany (CV-34) was launched in October 1945 and her construction suspended in August 1947. After construction was resumed, she was commissioned 25 September 1950. Principal alterations were a streamlined island structure, elimination of 5-inch gun mounts from the flight deck, ability to operate heavier aircraft, and 3-inch AA guns.

Q: Some of those things that were incorporated in her were later backfitted in other ships of the Essex class.

Captain Edwards: Yes, but I say, she in effect was a class by herself because of all these alterations.

That was a very interesting job socially, because that time was the highlight of Broadway. We saw practically every first-class Broadway show during those two years, '48 to '50. And we got Annie Oakleys, free tickets, through the Third Naval District headquarters, which provided them as a morale benefit for Navy people. I saw South Pacific there, for example. That was a wonderful show starring Mary Martin and Ezio Pinza. He really filled the house. When he sang, that house vibrated without any sound power or speaker, just his own voice. And Mary Martin, of course, was the leading gal.

Then we saw Henry Fonda in Mr. Roberts. He was wonderful. He'd been a reserve officer in World War II, so he was qualified to take that part. It hurt me when his daughter, Jane Fonda, became almost a traitor to this country. And then she married this billionaire down there, Turner, recently.* Oh, boy. The wrong people have the money.

---

*In late 1991 Jane Fonda, who had been an antiwar activist during the Vietnam War, married Ted Turner, head of a variety of broadcasting enterprises, including the Cable News Network.

We also had a lot of good social contacts there in this period. When I left the yard, they had a farewell dinner and gave me some things, including that picture there [on one wall of Edwards's office]. A professional artist made it.

Q: It has cartoons on it.

Captain Edwards: Yes. That was 1950, when I was detached and went back to the Bureau of Ships. As I mentioned, Admiral Haeberle was commander of the New York Naval Shipyard. Then he was transferred down to BuShips. When my time was up, I saw him, and he asked me to come down and be his assistant, or deputy, which I did.

Q: So you probably got there around the start of the Korean War, which began in June of 1950.

Captain Edwards: You're right. While I was still there in New York, my wife and I took a trip to Quebec, Canada. I was sitting on a bench there overlooking the river at the Chateau Frontenac Hotel when the radio came on blaring that the North Koreans had marched into South Korea. So I cut my leave short for a couple of days and soon went to Washington to fight the war there in a paperwork battle.

As I told you, one of the battles was engining these many landing craft that five years before had been put on hold.

Q: What was your new job in the Bureau of Ships?

Captain Edwards: I was the senior assistant to Rear Admiral Haeberle. In BuShips he was the officer in charge of the Ships Divisions. There were five divisions. One of them was Rickover's division, nuclear power. One was preliminary design. One was material. Altogether there were five divisions. Haeberle was later relieved as the head of the Ships Divisions by Wallace Sylvester of the class of '20.* So I had them both, and I was the straw boss for both of them--straw boss being a go-between for the divisions' heads and the boss.

Q: So you were sort of the executive officer.

Captain Edwards: That's right, and I had some very talented people working for me. One of my divisions was headed by Bobby Snyder, who was number two in the class of '27.** Another division was run by Bobby Watts, who was number one in 1928.*** Armand Morgan was number one in his

---

*Rear Admiral Evander Wallace Sylvester, USN, who stood third of 461 graduates in the Naval Academy class of 1920.
**Captain Philip W. Snyder, USN, who later became a rear admiral.
***Captain Charles R. Watts, USN.

class.* I was very fortunately placed with all this talent. I felt very pleased and honored. I was the "dumb colonel" to these people.** I stood only 119 in my class out of 412.

Q: What are your memories of your two bosses--Haeberle and Sylvester.

Captain Edwards: Haeberle stood number one in his class and became a naval constructor. He was very well equipped technically. He knew the score. But he was somewhat sensitive and a little bit difficult for some people to deal with. For some reason, fortunately, I was able to get along with him. When Haeberle later retired, he became the head of the naval architecture school up on Long Island, Webb Institute. In fact, when my wife and I went up there a couple of times we spent weekends with them. We got along just fine, but some people hated the hell out of him, and he hated the hell out of them. It just so happened we got along fine. After he left Webb Institute and completely retired he went to Coronado, California, to live. There again, we visited them out there, stayed overnight with them.

---
*Captain Armand M. Morgan, USN, stood first among 522 graduates in the class of 1924.
**Captain Edwards is here poking fun at himself. One old story has it that a group of brilliant planners and strategists kept a dumb colonel on the staff to read their expert writings. The rationale was that if the colonel could understand things, anyone could.

Sylvester was a constructor in the class of '20. As I said in prior remarks here, I got along with both of them fine. Sylvester was a more open fellow in a way. You could talk to him about things that you wouldn't bring up with Haeberle. But he was at first sort of aloof. It took me six months to warm up to him so I could unburden myself without feeling that I was imposing on him. And then he later became my good friend. In fact, he came out one weekend and spent the weekend with me here in Annapolis, and we went out boating together.

But I'd come in in the morning, and I had to commute, of course, every morning, and an hour or so each way. And I'd say, "Well, Wallace, I'm tired both physically and mentally." But he didn't get warmed up until perhaps 11:00 o'clock in the morning. Then in the afternoon he wasn't ready to go home when it was 4:30. That was just something he didn't worry about at all. So I'd leave there around, say, 6:00 o'clock at night, and I'd get home at maybe 7:00 o'clock at night. And I turned around, and at 7:00 o'clock the next morning, why, I was on my way back to the bureau. So it was a demanding situation.

Q: But I suspect the traffic then wasn't nearly as heavy as now.

Captain Edwards: I took the old route 214 because it was

what I called a byroad, and I knew all the turns. In fact, I bought a third-handed car, an old Studebaker, which I said knew the way. I put it in gear, and it knew the way. Also, I had a radio there which gave me checkpoints. When I hit a certain crossroads, I knew I was on time or behind time. So I'd get into the bureau at five or ten minutes before 8:00, day after day after day.

Q: Please tell me about your relationship with the bureau chief, Admiral Wallin.*

Captain Edwards: Wallin was a naval constructor, class of '17. I first met him many years ago. He was the Naval Academy roommate of the Augusta's supply officer, Lieutenant Commander Albert Schofield, a good friend of mine.** Then, as time went along, he came in as head of the bureau. He was a very phlegmatic, calm sort of fellow. Nothing seemed to really bother him, that is, externally. But I think he procrastinated in handling Rickover. In fact, I told him one day, one on one, "Chief, you better get rid of this guy, because he's going to take charge." But that didn't sink in soon enough, because after a while Rickover was running his own Navy, and Wallin was still trying to run the bureau.

―――――――

*Rear Admiral Homer N. Wallin, USN, Chief of the Bureau of Ships from 1951 to 1953.
**Lieutenant Commander Albert R. Schofield, SC, USN, was a shipmate of Edwards in the Augusta in the early 1930s.

Q: You said also you suspected that the reason he became chief of bureau is that he was involved in a couple of big salvage jobs.

Captain Edwards: He was at the right place at the right time. He was the principal salvage officer at Pearl Harbor. And then when the Missouri grounded down at Norfolk he was in charge of that salvage.* So that brought him to the attention of the CNO, and when it came time to appoint a new chief of bureau, Wallin got the job, which did not sit well with Haeberle, because Haeberle stood number one in his class, and his classmate Wallin wasn't even in the top ten.** He was not as brilliant a person as Haeberle, but he was not as temperamental as Haeberle. Haeberle was a temperamental fellow. In fact, I'd see him walk back and forth in his office sometimes, an hour at a time. What he was thinking about, I don't know. But I realized that he was not ready to handle any business at that particular moment. So I told these other officers who came down with their pet letters, "Skip it, Joe. Come back tomorrow."

---

*In January 1950 the battleship Missouri ran hard aground while heading to sea from Norfolk, Virginia. Admiral Wallin, then in command of the Norfolk Naval Shipyard, directed the refloating of the ship.
**Wallin stood number 23 of the 182 graduates in the class of 1917.

F. A. Edwards #5 - 370

Q: Do you think the Navy was well served by having Wallin as bureau chief?

Captain Edwards: I think he did a good job, yes. But my principal feeling about him was that he did not act properly and effectively with Rickover. He let him take charge. After the war Rickover headed the nuclear power division, which was one of the five divisions of the Ships Divisions. He was practically impossible to talk to or work with. He was running his own show and was not a team player, let me say. He was doing things without telling the chief of the bureau. He did not attend weekly meetings of heads of departments. He didn't wear a uniform, as we all had to wear, because he was working for the AEC as well.* His conversations were nasty. He wanted to start something if he could. I find myself at a loss for the exact words to pin on him, but he was the most disagreeable, non-cooperative naval officer that I ever tried to deal with. He was terrible.

Now, a lot of these younger people said, "Oh, he was wonderful." They didn't know the real Rickover--not like people of my time did. The great "Father of Nuclear Power" was a fake. Clay Blair, Jr., put that label on him.** He

---
*AEC--Atomic Energy Commission.
**Clay Blair, Jr., a correspondent for Time magazine, was quite a propagandist for Rickover and may well have helped him achieve flag rank through the favorable publicity he produced. After Rickover was promoted to rear admiral, Blair wrote a book titled The Atomic Submarine and Admiral Rickover (New York: Henry Holt Company, 1954).

was not even through the school when we in the Bureau of Ships decided during World War II to put the first nuclear plant into a submarine hull. I attended these conferences, because I had the destroyer and escort desk at that time. The first decision was to put it in a DE hull, because we had several hulls which were uncompleted due to the war dying down. Half a dozen people, of which I was one, finally decided to put it into a submarine hull, where there would be more natural dissipation of heat from the nuclear plant. That later became the Nautilus.* This plant was designed, I believe, by General Electric people. I've seen their names; I didn't know any of them. But the plant was all complete; they wanted a hull to put it in. Rickover was a fake. He was a brain picker. Very few people know that. I've told very few people, but I think it ought to be told to somebody who is in a position to spread the news that he was a fake.

Even though Rickover was only a division head, he was almost over the chief of the bureau, Wallin. I told the chief one time, "We're just country boys. That son of a bitch--you've got to watch him." One day I was in the car when Wallin was going up to testify to Congress; Rickover and the chief and myself were in the car. And Homer told him, "Now, don't talk about [a certain subject]." Well, as

---

*The world's first nuclear-powered ship, the USS Nautilus (SSN-571), was commissioned in 1954, shortly after Edwards retired from active duty.

soon as Rickover got on the stand, right away he talked about it. He ignored the chief. It was a nasty situation that he got away with because the right people were not given the chance to talk.

Rickover had what I'll call a guard outside of his office. I couldn't go in without an appointment. My boss couldn't go in his office; he had to see the guard first and explain who he was and so forth. It was all secret. We weren't let in on these secrets. He just got away with murder.

Now, as you know, about the time he died, the Congress found that he had accepted approximately $65,000 worth of gifts from the contractors whom he had been berating publicly. And he got away with that. Clay Blair may call him the "Father of Nuclear Power," but I think it was the world's greatest case of artificial insemination.

Q: You mentioned before the interview some consideration that you would be commander of the naval shipyard at Charleston.

Captain Edwards: Well, Haeberle told me before he left that I was on the books to be the commander of the Naval Shipyard Charleston. But after he left, that voice was stilled. It was not there. Some other people decided that a fellow named Dantzler, class of '24, deserved the job, and he got it.* Dantzler is long since dead, so I'm not

---
*Captain Tillman T. Dantzler, USN.

griping too much about it. He was a good guy and all that, but I felt I came first.

Q: Sometimes it's just a matter of who knows whom.

Captain Edwards: That's right, but I did not feel really hurt about it.

I also asked for the engineering experiment station over here across the river from the Naval Academy. The chief of the bureau by then was Leggett.* He told me I was too junior for it. Well, several months later he gave it to another classmate of mine who was junior to me. So, I mean, he was simply telling a political lie. That's all. It was just a white lie.

Q: Anything else about Leggett to remember?

Captain Edwards: Well, Leggett was a diesel boy and a good officer but I think more political than most engineers. He was on very good personal terms with an awful lot of rank topside, so he got to be chief of bureau, I think, later on because of that. We never had any trouble at all, but I just did not fully consider him as qualified as some other people did to be the chief of the bureau.

---
*Rear Admiral Wilson D. Leggett, Jr., USN, was bureau chief from 1953 to 1955.

Q: Did you get involved in the nuclear power issue at all yourself?

Captain Edwards: I took the short course--purely for my own education. But I had no desire to become a nuclear power man. Fortunately for me, I retired before it got into control. Just like I say about computers, fortunately I retired just before they got into control. I still use a filing cabinet.

Q: What else do you remember about that job?

Captain Edwards: Well, it was a very interesting job. I was very glad to have it, but it was a stress job. I never had any relaxation except maybe a half hour or so when Leland Whitgrove would come up from his office in the bureau. We'd sit down and have coffee together, and that was our recreation for the day.

Q: Finally you came up to 1954 and retirement. Did you feel some pangs of regret there?

Captain Edwards: I retired, of course, as a captain. The class of '22 was supposed to have three engineering numbers for selection to rear admiral, and my class, '23, should also have had three engineering numbers. When my class came up for selection in 1953, the Secretary of the Navy told the selection board that one of the selectees had to be an officer skilled in nuclear engineering. Well, the only one available at that time was Rickover.* Several others were going to school. Rickover had already been passed over when his class was up for selection. But because of the secretary's directive to the board when my class came up, Rickover was picked, because he was, of course, the only EDO who was skilled in nuclear engineering.

After the selection board was over, an admiral friend of mine on the board came to me and said, "I'm sorry, Speed [that was my nickname], but Hyman got your number." So '22 got four numbers, and my class got two numbers. So that's how Hyman got selected, by order of the Secretary of the Navy, and that's why I was passed over. I didn't know the secretary from a hole in the ground, and he didn't know me, but I was expendable. I was the senior nonnuclear engineer at that time. Rickover was the senior and the only nuclear engineer at that time. I worked with him--tried to work with him--three different times in my career. I failed miserably. He was a bastard of the lowest order. I won't go into that, but I can prove it with plenty of examples.

---

*Rickover's biography devotes an entire chapter to his initially being passed over and later being selected for rear admiral. For details see Norman Polmar and Thomas B. Allen, Rickover: Controversy and Genius: A Biography (New York: Simon and Schuster, 1982), pages 183-205.

I felt I was destroyed professionally by the Secretary of the Navy telling the selection board that they had to select Rickover, because they took my promotion number to do so. I felt pretty bitter about that, but, of course, as time went on, I said, "The hell with them." And now, 40 years later, I am saddened by the fact that my naval career was terminated in that manner.

Q: I can understand your bitterness.

Captain Edwards: I felt that the Navy was shortchanging itself, as far as I was concerned. Here I had spent a lifetime growing up in the job, and I had a lot of opinions, based on experience, which were thrown away, just out the window. And I felt I had probably ten years more in me as an engineer, but other people didn't think so. So I was retired as a captain on 1 July 1954.

Many of my class who made admiral are "tombstones," and a number of them are insistent about their rank.* If you ever called them captain, they right away would correct you, saying "I'm an admiral." It annoys me no end. So there was a certain feeling among our time, "After all, he's a tombstone." I know one classmate who was a captain

---

*"Tombstone" retirements were possible up to the year 1959. Those officers who had been awarded combat decorations in war received an honorary promotion of one grade upon retirement; they got the title but not increased pay.

for at least two or three years after he retired. Then he got some papers signed by a retired admiral, and they made the retired captain into a retired admiral. After that his wife was always saying, "The admiral this . . ." and "The admiral that . . ." Jesus Christ!

Q: Well, often it was a matter of circumstance, where people happened to be assigned.

Captain Edwards: That's right. Well, you went where you were ordered, and if you got promoted there, fine. If you weren't, fine. I had no problem about being a captain. But, I say, it annoyed me that these wives were always impressing you with the fact that their husbands were "admirals." They get the same retired pay that I do.

On a happier note--shortly after my retirement from the Navy, my wife and I experienced two very pleasant events. The first was when my wife sponsored the large minesweeper Salute at Luders Marine Construction Company, Stamford, Connecticut, and, second, when she was the guest of honor at the ship's commissioning at the New York Navy Yard.*

Q: You mentioned earlier that you had a civilian job after you retired.

---

*Mrs. Edwards christened the Salute (AM-470) when the ship was launched on 14 August 1954. The minesweeper was reclassified as MSO-470 on 7 February 1955 and commissioned 4 May 1955.

Captain Edwards: That's right. I didn't ask for a job, but J. J. Henry asked me to work for him, which I did. I also worked for two other companies part time. Between the three jobs I worked half as hard as I did in the Navy, and I got twice as much money.

Q: That's a pretty good deal.

Captain Edwards: I couldn't complain on that score. I worked for about five years for J. J. Henry and about the same time for a couple of other people, part time only.

Q: What sort of work did you do for Henry?

Captain Edwards: Among other things, I prepared three machinery operation manuals for the large aircraft carriers. Also, I prepared the specifications for a 10,000-ton cargo ship for the Maritime Administration. And then, by keeping abreast of what was going on in the contract field, I advised on conferences and what approaches to take. But it was entirely part time. I told Henry I wanted no job in his organization per se--just consultation. I didn't want to put somebody out of a job, and I didn't want to be beholden to him any time of day or night. I wanted to be semi-independent.

Q: Did you still live in Annapolis?

Captain Edwards: Yes. I told him I would not move, because I had lived there then for many years. I had no intention of moving. But I would travel, which I did. I went to New York or Philadelphia once a week, because his working office was in Philadelphia. His contract office was New York. He later on had one in Boston, with which I was not associated.

Q: Well, you showed me this manual you put together for the aircraft carrier <u>Saratoga</u>, CVA-60. It was just a massive thing. How did you go about doing that?

Captain Edwards: I took certain blueprints, which he furnished. And also I got the manuals written by the individual auxiliaries' manufacturers--like boiler manufacturers, turbine manufacturers, pump manufacturers, and so forth. From all these books, I extracted what I needed to make a full set of instructions--how to warm up, how to secure, how to operate at various speeds, and so forth. I did three of them. Each one took about 1,000 hours. And then before I retired, I did a similar thing on a smaller scale for destroyers, the 445 and 692 classes.

There was nobody to tell them what to do, so I prepared that operational manual for them. They printed maybe about 1,000 copies or so and distributed them to these destroyers. Same way for the carriers--maybe 500 copies for the use of the crews.

Q: You might almost use the term cookbook. It's the book you look into to find out how to do the job.

Captain Edwards: That's right. In fact, I gave a copy to one of the officers later on who was the head of the engineering department down at the academy. He'd been chief engineer of one of the large battleships. He said he wished the hell he'd had one for his ship. I did the dirty work, extracting all this information and getting it together, so each one wouldn't have to do it. He couldn't do it; he didn't have time to do it. He didn't have the access to do it.

Q: That was the value of having a company like Henry that could do that.

Captain Edwards: Henry's name went on it. I did 99% of the work. But we had some very good professional technical artists who drew these diagrams and sketches, which I reviewed and okayed.

Q: Why did you have 31 years of commissioned service instead of 30?

Captain Edwards: That was the law. Engineers were one year behind their general line compatriots. They had to retire in 30 years if they weren't selected by a certain time. But the engineers, the EDOs, had 31 years, because they were generally one year behind the selection of their general-line classmates.

Q: That's interesting. I hadn't heard that before.

Captain Edwards: That's true. There again, I felt I had probably ten more good years, but the Navy didn't think so, so it threw me out.

Q: Well, but you were still working essentially with the Navy, even if not for it directly.

Captain Edwards: That's right. But I felt the Navy shot itself in the foot by kicking out people like myself--not only me but others with similar backgrounds.

Q: What did you do after your time with Henry?

Captain Edwards: Well, I worked for Henry and two other companies. Then I quit altogether and started writing a book on battleship history, which is now kaput. It was impossible for a man in my position to finish that book and remain happily married. Because they were two different requirements. If I had been alone, I probably would have sat down and finished it up ten years ago. I'm not complaining, just explaining.

One of the other things I did during those years was keep an eye on the naval career of my son-in-law. He married Suzanne after he graduated from the Naval Academy. During the Vietnam War he was exec of an oiler for two trips out to Vietnam. His skipper was an aviator. The Navy ordered the prospective commanding officers of carriers first to command support ships. My son-in-law said his captain was a nice guy, but shipwise he didn't know his ass from a hole in the ground. He was not a ship's officer, but he was ordered there as skipper of an oiler. It was a system which looked good on paper but did not do justice to the Navy in practice.

Q: What was your son-in-law's name?

Captain Edwards: His name was Alecxih.* That is a

---

*Donald A. Alecxih graduated from the Naval Academy in the class of 1955. During the Vietnam War he was a lieutenant commander, the rank he held at retirement in 1975.

Slavic name, and his parents came from what is now Yugoslavia. His grandmother had property there. When the Communists took over, they simply said, "Get out." So she came to the United States, just after being forced out by the Communists. They were rather bitter about that.

Don was an excellent officer, in my opinion. Because he spoke a certain amount of Russian, he was ordered during the Cold War to a certain submarine which was making spying trips in the Siberian area. His job was to listen to the conversations going on between Russian ships. That was interesting duty.

Q: Certainly sounds like it.

Captain Edwards: Unfortunately, he is now dead. He had a double-bypass heart operation, and then during his recovery period he started jogging. He had a sudden collapse of an artery, and he died just like that in 1987. He was an excellent officer. He was tall, good-looking, blond guy.

Q: When did your first wife die?

Captain Edwards: In 1975. Bess had a total of four strokes over a period of ten years. I spent that entire time taking care of her. Finally, fortunately for her, and for me, she had a fourth stroke in 1975, and that was it.

Then I married my second wife 16 years ago. We have been very active. In back of you are 18 scrapbooks which are about all our cruises and tours. We made a dozen cruises, two extended train trips, and about 15 or 16 shore bus trips called TAUK tours. They're the top of all the shore tours. We had a great time. I don't regret it, but there wasn't enough time to live a full married life and complete the manuscript.

Q: For the record, we should put your present wife's name and background in this history.

Captain Edwards: I'm married now to Lydia Durel Whitgrove, the widow of my very good friend, Captain Leland D. Whitgrove, a naval constructor in the Naval Academy class of 1922.

She was born in Mexico of American parents. She was raised and educated there, where her father was a well-known mining engineer. She was fluent in and often taught Spanish. She had some 23 years in the Foreign Service, assigned as a staff officer to ambassadors in five Latin countries. She was widely traveled.

Q: Are there any other thoughts you want to put on the record?

Captain Edwards: I lived at Wild Rose Shores on the South River a total of 32 years. Then the place got too big for us, and we moved into Annapolis. We were in the President Point condominiums on Spa Creek for eight years. And during that time the Ginger Cove retirement home was being planned and built. We decided we wanted to move here when it was available, so we signed up ahead of time and got in line. We didn't move in until building 8000, where we are now, was finished. That was in February two years ago, 1990.

We do most of our shopping close by. On paper we have all the benefits of the commissary. But we go only once a month, and then it's just to get standard things, canned goods and that sort of thing because it's just too much trouble going there. For people who live close, the commissary is fine. But where we live now, five miles or so from there, it's a lot of trouble. And I'm no help now, so my wife goes there on shopping trips and uses one of these hand carts and a little knit bag for smaller things. We get one meal a day here as part of our rent. Then we have to eat our other meals on our own, and they are very light--perhaps a sandwich or a cup of coffee and maybe a cookie, something like that, for supper. That's all. Breakfast is cereal, orange juice, and coffee.

At Ginger Cove we have one of the two double units, which provide adequate living and storage spaces. We have a beautiful view of the adjacent woods and plantings. Two other classmates and several classmates' widows are here. We continue an active but limited social life. In view of the fact that I am not permitted to drive, we hire a chauffeur on occasion for shopping and essential activities. The nursing care is excellent. Food and services are very good. We feel lucky to be at Ginger Cove, because since we moved here I've had some severe physical problems, and I'd have been in real trouble out in town. I'd have been in a nursing home or whatnot. Here everything that can be done for me is being done. And I'm just very happy to be here.

Q: I'm happy to hear that it's worked out so well for you, and I am happy that you were able to take part in our oral history program. On behalf of myself and the Naval Institute, I certainly want to thank you for all your cooperation.

Captain Edwards: I had no intention of contributing to the oral history program--not because I didn't like it, but because I had nothing to contribute.

Q: Well, I disagree strongly. You had a great deal to contribute.

Captain Edwards: I was not a hero--more or less

intentionally, but I felt I contributed something to the Navy and the country which not everybody was aware of. I don't want kudos; I just want understanding--that's all.

Q: These recollections will be valuable for years to come because you remember things that most other people are not around to remember. Besides that, we've done a lot of line officers and not many engineers. So it's good to add your story in order to make a richer collection.

Captain Edwards: All these things I told you are true stories. I have many more, but there isn't time for them and there isn't room for them. I covered, I think, a very interesting period in the Navy's development, engineering-wise, at least. I started out in the coal burners and ended up with the 600-pound steam pressure geared turbines in the North Carolina class. I had, I considered, a good, well-rounded experience during those years--what the Navy was all about. I appreciate your interest in me and giving me this opportunity to unload my thoughts, good and bad.

Q: I thank you very much for doing so.

Index to the Oral History of
Captain Frederick A. Edwards, Sr., U.S. Navy (Retired)

Alcohol
Midshipmen drank from hidden flasks while watching the 1919 Army-Navy football game at the Polo Grounds in New York, 23, 36; various officers smuggled liquor aboard the battleship Nevada (BB-36) in Cuba in 1924 so they could transport it to California, 98-100; drunk sailors were rounded up by the shore patrol in Panama in the 1920s before being returned to their ships, 138-139; Edwards manufactured beer at his home in San Diego in the mid-1920s, 142-143; Edwards and shipmates drank so much champagne on liberty in Puerto Rico in 1931 that they had trouble functioning when they got back to their ship, the heavy cruiser Augusta (CA-31), 168-169; Captain Hugh Goodwin expected fellow staff officers to drink with him when he served as Atlantic Fleet chief of staff in the late 1940s, 339-340

Alecxih, Lieutenant Commander Donald A., USN (Ret.) (USNA, 1955)
Son-in-law of Edwards, he had varied duty, including being executive officer of an oiler and participating in intelligence operations, 382-383; died in 1987, 383

Alecxih, Suzanne
See Edwards, Suzanne

Antiair Warfare
The guns of the new battleship North Carolina (BB-55) proved most capable when tested in 1941, 280; the Bureau of Ordnance became interested in 20-millimeter and 40-millimeter guns before World War II, 296-297

Arizona, USS (BB-39)
Men from the destroyer Henshaw (DD-278) stole some metal stock that belonged to the Arizona when the two ships were moored near each other at the Puget Sound Navy Yard in the 1920s, 129

Armor
The heavy cruiser Augusta (CA-31) and other "treaty cruisers" commissioned around 1930 were lightly armored, 164-165

Army, U.S.
In the early 1920s received 16-inch guns for coast artillery pieces because the Navy did not complete the battleships for which they were intended, 78-79

Athletics
Edwards briefly played basketball and football at the Naval Academy around 1920, 21; Navy beat Army, 6-0, in football in the 1919 game at the Polo Grounds in New York, 22-23; train travel from Annapolis to the 1919 Army-Navy game in New York, 24-25; sports competition among fleet ships in the 1920s, 68, 143-144; Midshipman Fred Borries, Jr., needed academic help in order to stay eligible for football at the Naval Academy in the mid-1930s, 182-183; Borries was a non-reg midshipman but superb on the football field, 185-186; Midshipman Slade Cutter was another top-notch Naval Academy football player in the mid-1930s, 186-187

Atlantic Fleet
While in command of the Atlantic Fleet in 1913-14, Rear Admiral Charles Badger issued a facetious message prohibiting static in radio communications, 83-84; Admiral Marc Mitscher was sick and inactive while serving as fleet commander in chief in 1946-47, 334-338, 340-341; the staff moved into quarters ashore at Norfolk around 1947, 336; Admiral William H. P. Blandy was very energetic and able while serving as commander in chief in the late 1940s, 338-340; Captain Hugh Goodwin expected fellow staff officers to drink with him when he served as chief of staff in the late 1940s, 339-340; Edwards controlled repair money for fleet ships in the late 1940s, 343-345; various staff officers, 345-346; when captains and admirals returned to the East Coast from Sixth Fleet duty in the late 1940s, Admiral Blandy pumped them for information, 346-347; Admiral Blandy entertained Mrs. Grace Vanderbilt at a cocktail party in Newport in the late 1940s, 350-351; Commander Second Fleet was in operational command during fleet exercises, 352-353; search for Soviet ships that had been lost during surveillance in the late 1940s, 353-354

<u>Augusta</u>, USS (CA-31)
Characteristics of the ship when she went into commission in January 1931, 160-161; officers in engineering department, 160-161; description of engineering plant, including too-light brick work in the boilers, 162-163, 165, 167; the ship was lightly armored, 164-165; damage control capabilities were limited when the ship went into commission, 166-167; liberty stops in Puerto Rico and South Carolina soon after the ship began active service, 168-169; the crew had a great deal of confidence in Captain James O. Richardson, the first commanding officer, 170-173; Ensign Lloyd Mustin got

confined to the ship for a week in 1932 when he was late getting back aboard one day, 172-173; Vice Admiral Arthur L. Willard, embarked as Commanding Scouting Force, was fond of his creature comforts, 174-175; laundering of crew members' uniforms, 176; problems involved with blowing boiler tubes near Newport, Rhode Island in the early 1930s, 176-177; ceremonial aspects of being a flagship, 177-179; operations after reaching the Pacific, 179; high quality of enlisted men, 180-181

Aviators
Surface line officers sometimes resented naval aviators in the early 1930s, 170-171; an oiler in the Vietnam War was commanded by an aviator who was not suited for the duty, 382

Awards--Naval
Edwards was disappointed by receiving a commendation ribbon for his World War II service when reservists were receiving the more prestigious Legion of Merit, 331; in the 1950s many officers received "tombstone" promotions upon retirement because they had received combat decorations, 376-377

Badger, Rear Admiral Charles J., USN (USNA, 1873)
While in command of the Atlantic Fleet in 1913-14, Rear Admiral Charles Badger issued a facetious message prohibiting static in radio communications, 83-84

Badger, Captain Oscar C., USN (USNA, 1911)
Was overbearing, hypocritical, and demanding as commanding officer of the battleship _North Carolina_ (BB-55) in 1941-42, 292-296

Bahamas
The destroyer _Mahan_ (DD-364) assisted in the refloating of the light cruiser _Omaha_ (CL-4) after she went aground in the Bahamas in 1937, 217-218

Baldwin Locomotive Works
Edwards visited this plant in 1930 and discovered it wasn't making as many steam engines as before because of the Depression, 155-156

Baltimore, Maryland
Superstition in the early part of the 20th century had it that Naval Academy midshipmen had to lower the shades on their railroad cars while passing through Baltimore to keep the Naval Academy from losing in football, 24

Basketball
See Athletics

Bath Iron Works, Bath, Maine
  Top destroyer-building shipyard in the nation in World War II, 310-311

Bethlehem Ship Building Company, Squantum, Massachusetts
  Did a poor job of building destroyers in World War I, 145

Blacks
  Black enlisted men were involved in commotions on board the battleship New Mexico (BB-40) in the late 1930s, 231, 233; mess attendants and steward's mates in the battleship New Mexico (BB-40) in the late 1930s, 242-243

Blandy, Admiral William H. P., USN (USNA, 1913)
  Very energetic and able while serving as Commander in Chief Atlantic Fleet in the late 1940s, 338-340, 347-348, 350-351; when captains and admirals returned to the East Coast from Sixth Fleet duty in the late 1940s, Blandy pumped them for information, 346-347; passed over by President Harry Truman, who instead chose Admiral Louis Denfeld to be CNO in 1947, 348-349; gave orders during a search for Soviet ships that had been lost during surveillance in the late 1940s, 353-354

Bloch, Captain Claude C., USN (USNA, 1899)
  Demanded visiting ensigns observe Navy Regulations when touring the Naval Proving Ground in 1923, 77-78

Bluejackets' Manual, The
  Handbook that Edwards used in 1924 to train a squad of enlisted men on board the battleship Nevada (BB-36), 106-107

Board of Inspection and Survey
  As head of an InSurv team in 1936, Captain Joseph Evans facetiously suggested that the destroyer Mahan (DD-364) had so many engineering deficiencies that she should not get more than three days away from a Navy yard, 200-201; used its clout to help push for ship alterations in the late 1930s, 211-212

Borries, Midshipman Fred, Jr., USN (USNA, 1935)
  Needed academic help in order to stay eligible for football at the Naval Academy in the mid-1930s, 182-183; was a non-reg midshipman but superb on the football field, 185-186

Brazil
  The destroyer Mahan (DD-364) sold hundreds of bottles of Coca-Cola to local citizens while visiting Rio de Janeiro in 1936, 208-209; crew members from the ship had enjoyable liberty in Rio, 214-215; Edwards found it difficult to calculate the cost of oil when the Mahan refueled at Rio in 1936, 215-217

Broshek, Rear Admiral Joseph J., USN (USNA, 1908)
Headed the maintenance division of the Bureau of Ships during World War II, 301, 318

Brown, Vice Admiral Charles R., USN (USNA, 1921)
Non-regulation as a midshipman in the 1920s, he later distinguished himself as Commander Sixth Fleet in the 1950s, 40-41

Brown, Commander John J., USN (USNA, 1912)
As a Naval Academy duty officer in the early 1920s was energetic in putting midshipmen on report for various offenses, 19; was sometimes petty while serving as executive officer of the battleship New Mexico (BB-40) in the late 1930s, 231-233

Bruce, Captain Bryson, USN (USNA, 1907)
As head of the department of engineering at the Naval Academy in the mid-1930s, pumped midshipmen to find out their favorite instructors, 188

Bureau of Construction and Repair
Hesitant about authorizing ship alterations to the destroyer Mahan (DD-364) in the late 1930s, 211-213; new staterooms designed in the Bureau of C&R for the battleship New Mexico (BB-40) in the late 1930s were most uncomfortable, 244

Bureau of Engineering
Intervened in Edwards's case to get him selected for promotion shortly before World War II even though he had nearly all engineering duty, 297-300

Bureau of Ordnance
The bureau became interested in 20-millimeter and 40-millimeter guns before World War II, 296-297; involved in destroyer shipalts during World War II, 329

Bureau of Ships
Formed in 1940 by merger of two other bureaus, resulting in officers known as "con-engineers" because of the joining of their previous specialties, 260-262; supplied a vibration expert when the battleship North Carolina (BB-55) had problems with her propellers in 1941, 274; the destroyer and destroyer escort desk had a hectic workload in World War II, 300-301, 325-329; role in overseeing the maintenance and building of destroyers during World War II, 302-318; sites of headquarters in Washington during World War II, 307-308; consolidation of maintenance and construction of destroyers in World War II, 313-314; hierarchy in the bureau in World War II, 318-320; at the end of World War II, BuShips opted

to preserve a number of diesel engines that later proved useful for new construction, 332-333; Edwards controlled BuShips repair money for Atlantic Fleet ships in the late 1940s, 343-345; Edwards objected to a design formulated by BuShips in the late 1940s for an enlarged destroyer, 355; replaced by a systems command in the 1960s, 361-362; had a lot of talented officers in the early 1950s, 365-374

Burke, Captain Arleigh A., USN (USNA, 1923)
Played a prominent, active role as Atlantic Fleet chief of staff in 1946-47, because the fleet commander in chief, Admiral Marc Mitscher, was sick and inactive, 334-338; efforts to improve public speaking ability, 337-338

Caldwell, Commander Turner F., USN (USNA, 1905)
Not-too-demanding officer who commanded the destroyer Henshaw (DD-278) in the mid-1920s, 110

Caldwell, Vice Admiral Turner F., Jr., USN (USNA, 1935)
Navy flag officer who visited the destroyer Henshaw (DD-278) when she was commanded by his father in the mid-1920s, 110

Canada
Edwards and his family enjoyed visiting Vancouver, Canada, around 1940, 257

Cassin, USS (DD-372)
Destroyer that was rebuilt after being badly damaged by the Japanese attack on Pearl Harbor in 1941, 303-305

Charleston, South Carolina
While serving on shore patrol in Charleston in the early 1930s, Edwards found one of his sailors coming out of a house of prostitution, 169

Classified Information
Around 1940 people at the Puget Sound Navy Yard burned copies of superseded plans to avoid having them fall into the wrong hands, 258; shortly before World War II Edwards was involved in getting the goods on a group of potential saboteurs who had plans to damage hydro-electric facilities in the Pacific Northwest, 258-260; the existence of radar on board the new battleship North Carolina (BB-55) in 1941 was a well-kept secret until it was published in The New York Times, 268; Mrs. Oscar Badger showed up at the North Carolina's destination in Norfolk for Christmas in 1941, even though the ship's movement was classified, 294-295

Coaling Ship
Dirty, laborious process of taking coal aboard the battleship Michigan (BB-27) in the summer of 1920, 43-46;

the Michigan made a long voyage between coaling stops in 1920, 54

Cochrane, Vice Admiral Edward L., USN (USNA, 1914)
Did a capable job as Chief of the Bureau of Ships during World War II, 318-320; advised Edwards in 1946 about getting along with line officers on the Atlantic Fleet staff, 333-334

Colton, Commander Ernest B., USN (USNA, 1918)
Retired from the Navy in 1941 to take a job with the new Lake Washington shipyard, 248

Columbia University
Had nationally known scholars as instructors when Edwards studied mechanical engineering at the university in 1929-30, 152-154; graduation in 1930, 154-155

Comerford, Lieutenant Commander Francis J., USN (USNA, 1908)
Demanded first-salvo accuracy in a gunnery exercise by the battleship Nevada (BB-36) in 1924, 101

Commercial Ships
In the late 1940s, the New York Naval Shipyard supplied Gibbs & Cox with the plans for the engineering plant of the battleship Missouri (BB-63), to be used in the design of the United States, 358-359; Edwards went on the first sea trial of the United States in 1952, 359-360

Communications
Difficulty with short-range voice radio communications between battleships operating together in 1920, 53; Edwards provided training to the prospective radiomen of the USS West Virginia (BB-48) in 1923-24, 82-83; while in command of the Atlantic Fleet in 1913-14, Rear Admiral Charles Badger issued a facetious message prohibiting static in radio communications, 83-84

Cope, Lieutenant (junior grade) Harley F., USN (USNA, 1920)
Smuggled liquor aboard the battleship Nevada (BB-36) at Cuba in 1924 so he could transport it to California, 99

Craven, Captain Thomas T., USN (USNA, 1896)
As a U.S. naval commander in China had an amusing exchange of communications with a British admiral, 64

Cuba
Various officers smuggled liquor aboard the battleship Nevada (BB-36) in Guantanamo Bay in 1924 so they could transport it to California, 98-100

Cutter, Midshipman Slade D., USN (USNA, 1935)
Top-notch Naval Academy football player in the 1930s, gave the impression of being headed for a successful career, 186-187

Daisley, Ensign Gordon W., USN (USNA, 1923)
Served as senior man for a group of junior officers that toured the Naval Proving Ground, Dahlgren, Virginia, in 1923, 77-78

Damage Control
Capabilities were limited when the heavy cruiser Augusta (CA-31) went into commission in 1931, 166-167

Dancing
Naval Academy plebes took dancing lessons in 1919-20, 17-18; plebes rated the dates of upper classmen, 18-19

Dempsey, William Harrison "Jack"
Heavyweight boxing champion who was booed at the 1919 Army-Navy football game in New York because of his lack of participation in World War I, 22

Denfeld, Admiral Louis E., USN (USNA, 1912)
President Harry Truman passed over Admiral William Blandy when he chose Denfeld to be CNO in 1947, 348-349

Destroyers
Types of engineering plants in destroyer escorts built in World War II, 301-302; during the war the Bureau of Ships oversaw the repair and rebuilding of destroyers, 302-307; qualities of the Fletcher (DD-445) class that first went into service in 1942, 308-310; the Allen M. Sumner (DD-692) and Gearing (DD-710) classes were enlarged versions of the Fletcher class, 309-310; consolidation of construction and maintenance desks in BuShips during World War II, 313-314; shipalts to older destroyers in wartime, 327-329; at the end of World War II a Fletcher-class engineering plant was sent to the Naval Academy for training purposes, 331-332; Edwards objected to a design formulated by BuShips in the late 1940s for an enlarged destroyer, 355

See also Henshaw, USS (DD-278); Mahan, USS (DD-364)

Diesel Engines
Diesels were among the types of engineering plants in destroyer escorts built in World War II, 301-302; at the end of World War II, BuShips opted to preserve a number of diesel engines that later proved useful for new construction, 332-333

Disarmament
In 1924 the old battleship Illinois (BB-7) was demilitarized at the New York Navy Yard and several incomplete battleships were scrapped, 87-88

Disciplinary Matters
Duty officers put midshipmen on report for various offenses at the Naval Academy in the early 1920s, 19, 37, 40; few disciplinary problems in the destroyer Henshaw (DD-278) in the 1920s, 144

Downes, USS (DD-375)
Destroyer that was rebuilt after being badly damaged by the Japanese attack on Pearl Harbor in 1941, 303-305

Doyle, Chief Machinist Thomas H., USN
One of the few men who were in the commissioning crews of both the USS West Virginia (BB-48) in 1923 and the North Carolina (BB-55) in 1941, 287-288

Earle, Rear Admiral Ralph, USN (USNA, 1896)
Wrote an article concerning the Naval Academy for Boys' Life magazine around the time of World War I, later served as a college president following retirement from the Navy, 2-3; commanded the Naval Torpedo Station, Newport, Rhode Island, in the early 1920s, 74

Education
Methods of instruction at the Naval Academy in the early 1920s, 27-31; instruction in engineering at the Naval Academy in the mid-1930s, 28; Edwards studied mathematics and mechanics at the Naval Postgraduate School in 1928-29, 148-152; Edwards earned a master's degree at Columbia University, 1929-30, 152; Edwards was involved primarily with the class of 1935 while serving as an instructor in the mid-1930s, 181-194; Edwards sent his children to private schools in the early 1940s because he was not comfortable with the New York City public schools, 270, 323

Edwards, Bessie McKichan
Courtship and marriage to Frederick Edwards in August 1923, 72-73; packed up quickly to move when her husband was transferred to the USS Henshaw (DD-278) in 1924, 107; did Red Cross work during World War II, 324; sponsored the minesweeper Salute (AM-470) in the 1950s, 377; died in 1975 after a series of strokes, 383-384

Edwards, Captain Frederick A., Sr., USN (Ret.) (USNA, 1923)
Boyhood in Ohio at the beginning of the 20th century, 1-2; parents of, 1-3, 8-9, 23; in 1918-19 attended prep school in Annapolis, 3-7; farm work in Nebraska in 1919, 7-8; attended

the Naval Academy and graduated in 1923, 10-72; courtship and marriage to Elizabeth McKichan in August 1923, 72-73; joined other ensigns from the class of 1923 in making a training tour of various East Coast naval installations before reporting to his first ship, 74-81; served in the battleship West Virginia (BB-48) in 1923-24, 82-94; served in the battleship Nevada (BB-36) in 1924, 94-107; served in the destroyer Henshaw (DD-278) from 1924 to 1928, 107-147; preference for engineering duty over deck duty, 123-124; stationed at the Puget Sound Navy Yard, 1939-40, 147-148; student at Naval Postgraduate School, Annapolis, in 1928-29, 148-152; earned a master's degree at Columbia University, 1929-30, 152-155; three-month training course visiting various facilities, 155-156; served in the heavy cruiser Augusta (CA-31) from 1933 to 1935, 160-181; served as an instructor of engineering at the Naval Academy from 1933 to 1937, 181-194; birth of daughter Suzanne in 1933, 191; several times asked for new ships so he could be associated with state-of-the-art machinery, 194; served in the initial crew of the destroyer Mahan (DD-364), 1936-37, 195-218; served in the battleship New Mexico (BB-40) from 1937 to 1939, 219-244; served in the design section of the Puget Sound Navy Yard, 1939-40, 244-260; drove across country in December 1940 when he got orders to report to the North Carolina in New York, 262-263; served in 1941-42 in the battleship North Carolina (BB-55), 264-297; selected as an EDO in 1941, 297-300; had destroyer and destroyer escort desk in the Bureau of Ships in World War II, 300-333; headed planning and estimating for the New York Naval Shipyard from 1948 to 1950, 356-364; served in the Bureau of Ships, 1950-54, 364-374; post-retirement activities, 378-387

Edwards, Captain Frederick A., Jr., USN (Ret.) (USNA, 1950)
Born in San Diego Naval Hospital in 1926, 40, 111; suffered ear infection in the late 1920s, 190; attended military school in New Jersey during World War II, 270, 288, 323

Edwards, Lydia Whitgrove
Married Edwards in 1976, following the death of her first husband, Leland Whitgrove, 384

Edwards, Suzanne
Daughter born to Frederick and Elizabeth Edwards in Annapolis in 1933, 191; attended private school in New York in 1941-42, 270; went to private school in Washington, D.C., during World War II, 323; wife of naval officer Donald Alecxih, 382-383

Engineering Duty Officers
The Bureau of Ships was formed in 1940 by merger of two other bureaus, resulting in officers known variously as EDOs

and "con-engineers" because of the joining of their previous specialties, 260-262, 321; Edwards was selected as an EDO in 1941 after having been a commissioned officer for 18 years, 297-300; ran a year behind line contemporaries in terms of promotions, 381

Engineering Plants
Operation of coal-fired boilers in the battleship Michigan (BB-27) in 1920, 46-48, 50; triple-expansion engines in the Michigan, 51-52; the battleship West Virginia (BB-48) was outfitted with an electric-drive propulsion plant when commissioned in 1923, 93; description of the plant on board the destroyer Henshaw (DD-278) in the mid-1920s, 113-114; the Henshaw's performance in annual engineering competitions, 115-116; preventive maintenance of engineering equipment on board the Henshaw, 131-133; working conditions in the Henshaw's engineering plant, 133-134; Edwards heard of the possibility of gas-turbine ship propulsion in the late 1920s, 151-152; description of plant in the heavy cruiser Augusta (CA-31) in 1931, including too-light brick work in the boilers, 162-163, 165, 167; problems involved with blowing tubes in the heavy cruiser Augusta (CA-31) in the early 1930s, 176-177; the destroyer Mahan (DD-364), commissioned in 1936, had a number of engineering advances but a number of drawbacks as well, 195-201, Lieutenant Commander Hyman Rickover, assistant engineer officer of the battleship New Mexico (BB-40) in the mid-1930s, so intimidated enlisted men in his department that he left a legacy of fear, 222-225; fuel efficiency forms in the New Mexico, 226; the plant in the New Mexico got excellent results by using turbines and boilers installed when the ship was modernized in the early 1930s, 226-229; cleaning of the New Mexico's bottom to improve speed, 234-235; use of pressure-reducing valves in the New Mexico's auxiliaries, 239; plant in the AVP small seaplane tenders, 250; tests of the plant of the battleship North Carolina (BB-55) at the New York Navy Yard prior to the ship's commissioning in 1941, 266-270; the North Carolina had difficulties with propeller vibration when she first operated in 1941, 272-274, 284-285; process by which the North Carolina took on oil, 281-283; engine room watch conditions in the North Carolina early in World War II, 290; different types of propulsion plants in destroyer escorts built during World War II, 301-302; replacement of destroyer equipment damaged in battle in World War II, 306-307; at the end of World War II a Fletcher-class engineering plant was sent to the Naval Academy for training purposes, 331-332; at the end of World War II, BuShips opted to preserve a number of diesel engines that later proved useful for new construction, 332-333; in the late 1940s the New York Naval Shipyard supplied plans for the engineering plant of the USS Missouri (BB-63), to be

used in the design of the liner United States, 358-359; in the late 1950s Edwards prepared engineering plant operating manuals for the aircraft carrier Saratoga (CVA-60) and destroyers, 379-380

Enlisted Personnel
Hostility between ex-enlisted personnel and Naval Academy midshipmen during training cruises in the early 1920s, 60-61; the crew of the destroyer Henshaw (DD-278) was quite capable in the 1920s, 124-125; the Henshaw had a very good machinist's mate in the 1920s, 129-130; high quality of the enlisted men in the heavy cruiser Augusta (CA-31) in the early 1930s, 180-181; black enlisted men were involved in commotions on board the battleship New Mexico (BB-40) in the late 1930s, 231, 233; mess attendants and steward's mates in the battleship New Mexico (BB-40) in the late 1930s, 242-243; the battleship North Carolina (BB-55) was overmanned in 1941 to train personnel for new-construction ships, 283-284

Erly, Ensign Robert B., USN (USNA, 1937)
Quite energetic as a junior officer in the battleship New Mexico (BB-40) in the late 1930s, 241

Evans, Captain Joseph S., USN (USNA, 1907)
As head of an InSurv team in 1936, facetiously suggested that the destroyer Mahan (DD-364) had so many engineering deficiencies that she should not get more than three days away from a Navy yard, 200-201

Families of Servicemen
Edwards's son Frederick, Jr., was born in San Diego Naval Hospital in 1926, and Edwards had to pay the bill, 40, 111-112; pay for young married officer in the 1920s, 136; life for the Edwards family around San Diego in the mid-1920s, 142-143; Edwards's life with his family in Annapolis in the mid-1930s, 190-192; in the late 1930s the Pacific Northwest area was a pleasant place for families to live, 255-257; Edwards and his family enjoyed visiting Vancouver, Canada, around 1940, 257

Finnegan, L. L.
Civilian employee of the Puget Sound Navy Yard who began work there as a draftsman in 1917, became a marine engineer, and worked at the yard for more than 40 years, 253

Fire Control
Optical range finders were used for directing naval gunfire in the 1920s, 79-81, 101; the New York Navy Yard installed fire control equipment in the battleship West Virginia (BB-48) in 1923-24, 81-82, 86, 94; role of the plotting room during gunnery exercises involving the battleship Nevada

(BB-36) in 1924, 102-103; modernization of the battleship New Mexico (BB-40) in the early 1930s required that she depend on aircraft for spotting fall of shot for the guns, 230

Fletcher, Captain Frank Jack, USN (USNA, 1906)
Had a reputation as an austere man but good officer while commanding the battleship New Mexico (BB-40) in the late 1930s, 220-222

Fletcher (DD-445)-Class Destroyers
Fine ships that first went into service in 1942 and served well during World War II, 308-310; at the end of World War II a Fletcher-class engineering plant was sent to the Naval Academy for training purposes, 331-332

Florida, USS (BB-30)
Itinerary for Naval Academy training cruise in the summer of 1922, 42; first-class midshipmen stood bridge and engine room watches during the cruise, 61-63; description of engineering plant and gunnery setup, 65

Flusser, USS (DD-368)
Destroyer that got cracks around her machinery space hatches during the 1930s because of poor ship design, 198

Food
Wardroom meals on board the battleship North Carolina (BB-55) early in World War II, 290-291

Football
See Athletics

Frost, Lieutenant Daniel A., USN (Ret.) (USNA, 1921)
Shortly before World War II, while assigned to the 13th Naval District headquarters, was involved in getting the goods on a group of potential saboteurs who had plans to damage hydro-electric facilities in the Pacific Northwest, 258-260

Fuqua, Lieutenant Commander Samuel G., USN (USNA, 1923)
As a Naval Academy midshipman in the early 1920s, got the nickname "Ben" because he had one cross eye, 39; his wife and Edwards's wife had babies at the same time in 1926, 39-40

Gelm, Captain George E., USN (USNA, 1894)
Unfriendly while serving as commanding officer of the battleship Florida in 1922, 62

German Navy
The log of a U-boat indicated that she operated near the battleship North Carolina (BB-55) in 1941, before Germany and the United States were at war, 281; the North Carolina remained in the Atlantic in early 1942 as protection against the German battleship Tirpitz, 297

Gibbs & Cox
Marine Engineering firm that did a poor job of designing the destroyer Mahan (DD-364) and her sisters in the 1930s, 95-202; the firm seemed unwilling to learn from its mistakes, 213; received in the late 1940s plans for the engineering plant of the USS Missouri (BB-63), to be used in the design of the liner United States, 358-359

Goodwin, Captain Hugh H., USN (USNA, 1922)
Expected fellow staff officers to drink with him when he served as Atlantic Fleet chief of staff in the late 1940s, 339-340

Grand Coulee Dam
Around 1940 Edwards was involved in getting the goods on a group of potential saboteurs who had plans to damage this dam and other hydro-electric facilities in the Pacific Northwest, 258-260

Granite State
Former ship-of-the-line New Hampshire that served as a Naval Reserve training ship at New York City until the early 1920s, 25-26

Gunnery--Naval
The battleship Nevada (BB-36) was involved in frequent gunnery practices in 1924, 94, 101-104; the battleship Mississippi (BB-41) suffered a turret explosion during gunnery practice in June 1924, 103-105; gunnery exercises involving the destroyer Henshaw (DD-278) in the 1920s, 118-119; modernization of the battleship New Mexico (BB-40) in the early 1930s required that she depend on aircraft for spotting fall of shot for the guns, 230; initial tests for the guns of the new battleship North Carolina (BB-55) in 1941, 279-280

Guns
In 1923 the Naval Proving Ground, Dahlgren, Virginia, tested 16-inch guns that were converted to Army coast artillery pieces because the battleships for which they were intended were not built, 78-79; in 1924 the battleship Nevada (BB-36) required Navy yard repairs because of a cracked gun slide, 106; Edwards trained a squad of Nevada enlisted men in machine gun drill, 106-107; initial tests for the guns of

the new battleship North Carolina (BB-55) in 1941, 279-280; the Bureau of Ordnance became interested in 20-millimeter and 40-millimeter guns before World War II, 296-297

Habitability
Messing and berthing arrangements on board the battleship Michigan (BB-27) in 1920, 49-50, 54-56; working conditions in the engineering plant of the destroyer Henshaw (DD-278) in the mid-1920s, 133-134; description of officer stateroom in the Henshaw, 136; the destroyer Mahan (DD-364), commissioned in 1936, did not have fore-and-aft access inside the ship, 201-202; the engineering department of the battleship New Mexico (BB-40) installed new washroom facilities throughout the ship in the late 1930s, 225-226; engine room watch conditions in the battleship North Carolina (BB-55) early in World War II, 290

Haeberle, Rear Admiral Frederick E., USN (USNA, 1917)
Commanded the New York Naval Shipyard in the late 1940s, 356; asked Edwards to join him at the Bureau of Ships in 1950, 364; difficult for some people to deal with, 366-367, 369; said that Edwards was destined to command the shipyard at Charleston, 372

Haiti
President Stenio Vincent reviewed U.S. Navy ships during their visit to Haiti in 1938, 233

Hawaii
Naval academy midshipmen enjoyed liberty in the islands during midshipman cruises in the early 1920s, 59-60; operations in the islands by the destroyer Henshaw (DD-278) in the mid-1920s, 139-140; the battleship New Mexico (BB-40) was listed at Pearl Harbor in the late 1930s to scrape the bottom, 235

Hazing
Treatment of junior midshipmen at the Naval Academy around 1920, 11-16, 25

Heavy Seas
Riding characteristics of the destroyer Henshaw (DD-278) in rough weather in the 1920s, 119-121, 140-141; handling characteristics of the destroyer Mahan (DD-364), which was commissioned in 1936, 206

Henry, J. J.
Marine engineering firm that employed Edwards as a consultant in the late 1950s, 378-380

Henshaw, USS (DD-278)
Demands on officers of the deck during formation steaming during the mid-1920s, 107-108; because of the grounding of the destroyer Young (DD-312) at Point Honda in September 1923, the Henshaw was reactivated and restored to the fleet, 108-109; Lieutenant (junior grade) Virgil Korns a capable engineer officer of the ship in the mid-1920s, 109; Commander Turner Caldwell was a not-too-demanding skipper, 110; Lieutenant Commander Ralph Wentworth was an excellent skipper in the mid-1920s 111-112; description of engineering plant, 113-114; participated with other destroyers in annual engineering competitions in the 1920s, 115-116; both ship's spaces and the enlisted men looked sharp for inspections in the 1920s, 116, 121-122; participated with other destroyers in gunnery exercises in the 1920s, 118-119; riding characteristics in rough seas, 119-121; role as plane guard for aircraft carriers, 122; search for missing planes from the Dole flight, 122-123; capable enlisted crew, 124-125; procedures for refueling at sea in the 1920s, 125-127; maintenance and upkeep of equipment in the mid-1920s, 127-128, 131-133; refueling in port, 127-128; the Puget Sound Navy Yard did periodic overhauls to the ship, 128-129, 146-147; men from the Henshaw stole some metal stock that belonged to the Arizona (BB-39) when the two ships were moored near each other, 129; record keeping for engineering and commissary, 130-131; working conditions in the engineering plant, 133-134; description of officer stateroom, 136; liberty for the crew in Panama, 137-139; Pacific operations in 1925, 139-140; treatment of the ship to kill rats on board, 141-142; life for the Edwards family around San Diego, 142-143; the Henshaw had not been well built during World War I, 145

Higgins, Rear Admiral Ronald D., USNR (Ret.) (USNA, 1923)
Served as a midshipman officer in the early 1920s, then managed to be promoted to rear admiral on retirement, even though he was out of the Navy for many years, 63

Hill, Commander Tom B., USN (USNA, 1922)
Made a quip about the presence of radar on board the new battleship North Carolina (BB-55) in 1941, 268; comments about Captain Oscar Badger, 293-294; quip to Andy Shepard of the North Carolina upon his departure in 1941, 296

Hinckley, Commander Robert M., Jr., USN (USNA, 1935)
Needed academic help to graduate from the Naval Academy in the 1930s, then served as a ship commanding officer during World War II, 183-184

Honda, Point
See Point Honda

Huschke, Lieutenant Commander Paul W. F., USN (USNA, 1917)
German-born U.S. naval officer who was the first chief engineer when the heavy cruiser Augusta (CA-31) went into commission in 1931, 160-161

Hustvedt, Captain Olaf M., USN (USNA, 1909)
Was an excellent manager while serving as first commanding officer of the battleship North Carolina (BB-55) in 1941, 276-277

Idaho, USS (BB-42)
Following modernization in the early 1930s, did not have as efficient an engineering plant as did her sister New Mexico (BB-40), 226-228

Illinois, USS (BB-7)
Old battleship that was demilitarized at the New York Navy Yard in 1924 and converted to a Naval Reserve training ship, 87

Indianapolis, USS (CA-35)
Heavy cruiser that carried President Franklin D. Roosevelt and his party on a cruise to the Caribbean and South America in late 1936, 207, 214

Inspection and Survey, Board of
See Board of Inspection and Survey

Inspections
Emphasis on cleanliness in fleet battleships in the 1920s, 66; Edwards had to train a squad of men on board the battleship Nevada (BB-36) to prepare for an admiral's inspection, 106-107; both ship's spaces and the enlisted men of the destroyer Henshaw (DD-278) looked sharp for inspections in the 1920s, 116, 121-122; men of the heavy cruiser Augusta (CA-31) looked sharp at inspections in the early 1930s, 175-176

Intelligence
Around 1940 people at the Puget Sound Navy Yard burned copies of superseded plans to avoid having them fall into the wrong hands, 258; shortly before World War II Edwards was involved in getting the goods on a group of potential saboteurs who had plans to damage hydro-electric facilities in the Pacific Northwest, 258-260

Jacobs, Captain Walter F., USN (USNA, 1906)
As commanding officer of the battleship New Mexico (BB-40) in the late 1930s was friendly but not a top-notch officer, 221-222

Jacobs, Mrs. Winnie
As wife of the skipper of the battleship <u>New Mexico</u> (BB-40) in the late 1930s, she organized the wives of other officers, 222

King, Admiral Ernest J., USN (USNA, 1901)
Ordered unpopular gray uniforms for officers in World War II, 330

Kniskern, Rear Admiral Leslie A., USN (USNA, 1922)
Served as a junior officer in the battleship <u>Nevada</u> (BB-36) in 1924 and later became a flag officer as an engineering specialist, 100, 102-103

Korns, Lieutenant (Junior grade) Virgil E., USN (USNA, 1920)
Served as a capable chief engineer in the destroyer <u>Henshaw</u> (DD-278) in the mid-1920s, 109

Lake Washington Shipyard
Seattle shipyard that took employees from the Puget Sound Navy Yard when it began constructing AVP small seaplane tenders around 1940, 248

Landers, Midshipman Wilbur Nelson, USN (USNA, 1925)
Midshipman who was a college graduate before beginning his studies at the Naval Academy, 31

Leave and Liberty
Activities for midshipmen on liberty in the Caribbean in the early 1920s, 56-58; liberty in Hawaii in 1920, 59-60; liberty activities for ships' crews in Panama in the mid-1920s included drinking and visiting prostitutes, 137-139; Edwards and his shipmates drank so much champagne on liberty in Puerto Rico in 1931 that they had trouble functioning when they got back to their ship, the heavy cruiser <u>Augusta</u> (CA-31), 168-169; while serving on shore patrol in Charleston in the early 1930s, Edwards found one of his sailors coming out of a house of prostitution, 169; crew members from the destroyer <u>Mahan</u> (DD-364) had enjoyable liberty in Rio de Janeiro in 1936, 214-215

Leggett, Rear Admiral Wilson D., Jr., USN, 1921)
As chief of the Bureau of Ships in the early 1950s, seemed more political than most engineers, 373

Logistics
Positioning of parts for repair and maintenance of destroyers in World War II, 302-307, 316-318

Luby, Captain John McL., USN (USNA, 1894)
　　Experienced near-collision with the Pennsylvania (BB-38) while commanding the battleship Nevada (BB-36) in 1924, 96

Lucky Bag
　　Members of the Naval Academy class of 1923 autographed each others' copies of the yearbook shortly before graduation, 69-70

Mahan, USS (DD-364)
　　This destroyer, commissioned in 1936, had a number of engineering advances but a number of drawbacks as well, 195-201; the ship did not have fore-and-aft access inside the ship, 201-202; as the ship's first commanding officer, Commander John B. W. Waller was often very difficult for his subordinate officers to live with, 202-205, 215-216; tactical characteristics, 205-206; handling qualities in rough seas, 206; outfitted to take President Franklin D. Roosevelt on board if necessary, 207-208; shakedown cruise to the Caribbean and South America in 1936, 207-211, 214-215; sold hundreds of bottles of Coca-Cola to local citizens while visiting Brazil in 1936, 208-209; ship's service sales to crew, 208-210; refueling at sea and in port, 210-211, 215-217; assisted in the refloating of the light cruiser Omaha (CL-4) after she went aground in the Bahamas in 1937, 217-218

Maintenance
　　Upkeep of the USS Henshaw (DD-278) and other ships at the San Diego destroyer base in the mid-1920s, 127-128; preventive maintenance of equipment on board the Henshaw, 131-133; positioning of parts for repair and maintenance of destroyers in World War II, 302-307, 316-318; Edwards controlled BuShips repair money for Atlantic Fleet ships in the late 1940s, 343-345

Manpower
　　The battleship North Carolina (BB-55) was overmanned in 1941 to train personnel for new-construction ships, 283-284

Mare Island Navy Yard, Vallejo, California
　　Rebuilt the destroyers Cassin (DD-372) and Downes (DD-375) after they had been badly damaged during the Japanese attack on Pearl Harbor in 1941, 303-305

Maxwell, Lieutenant Commander William S., USN
　　Former Russian who served as chief engineer of the battleships North Carolina (BB-55) and Missouri (BB-63) during World War II, 286-287, 358

McCully, Rear Admiral Newton A., USN (USNA, 1887)
As Commander Control Force Atlantic Fleet in 1922, daily went out for a swim from his flagship Florida (BB-30), 64

Medical Problems
The flu epidemic of 1918 affected the Naval Academy and the nearby prep school in Annapolis, 6-7; men of the Omaha (CL-4)-class light cruisers developed tuberculosis in the 1920s, 134; a member of an InSurv team had a heart attack on board the destroyer Mahan (DD-364) in 1936 because of fireroom heat, 201; Admiral Marc Mitscher was sick and inactive while serving as Commander in Chief Atlantic Fleet in 1946-47, 334-338, 340-341

Medusa, USS (AR-1)
The Puget Sound Navy Yard constructed the ship over a period of time in the 1920s to keep the work force occupied, 145-146

Michigan, USS (BB-27)
Itinerary for Naval Academy training cruise in the summer of 1920, 41; laborious process of coaling ship in 1920, 43-46; messing and berthing arrangements in 1920, 49-50, 54-56; triple-expansion engines, 51-52; operation of turrets in 1920, 52-53; difficulty with short-range voice communications between battleships operating together in 1920, 53; long voyage without coaling ship, 54; hostility between ex-enlisted personnel and Naval Academy midshipmen in 1920, 60-61

Mills, Vice Admiral Earle W., USN (USNA, 1918)
As a result of getting acquainted during the trials of the destroyer Mahan (DD-364) in 1936, helped Edwards be assigned as first chief engineer of the battleship North Carolina (BB-55) in 1941, 265; was informed in 1941 of Edwards's desire for engineering duty only, 299; able assistant chief of BuShips during World War II, 318-320, 333-334

Minorities
Black enlisted men were involved in commotions on board the battleship New Mexico (BB-40) in the late 1930s, 231, 233; mess attendants and steward's mates in the battleship New Mexico (BB-40) in the late 1930s, 242-243

Mississippi, USS (BB-41)
Suffered a turret explosion during gunnery practice in June 1924, 103-105; following modernization in the early 1930s, did not have as efficient an engineering plant as did her sister New Mexico (BB-40), 226-228

Missouri, USS (BB-63)
　　After she was built at the New York Naval Shipyard, the plans for her engineering plant were supplied to Gibbs & Cox for the design of the liner United States, 358-359; ran aground in 1950, 369

Mitscher, Admiral Marc A., USN (USNA, 1910)
　　Was sick and inactive while serving as Commander in Chief Atlantic Fleet in 1946-47, 334-338, 340-341; death of in February 1947, 338

Movies
　　The destroyer Mahan (DD-364) was given a supply of new movies in late 1936 because of the possibility that she would have President Franklin D. Roosevelt on board, 207-208

Murdaugh, Commander Albert C., USN (USNA, 1923)
　　Angry over being ordered as chief engineer of the battleship North Carolina (BB-55) in 1942, 286

Mustin, Ensign Lloyd M., USN (USNA, 1932)
　　Spent a week confined to the heavy cruiser Augusta (CA-31) in 1932 because he was late getting back aboard one day, 172-173

Naval Academy, U.S., Annapolis, Maryland
　　An article concerning the academy appeared in Boys' Life magazine around the time of World War I, 2-3; Edwards attended Bobby Werntz's prep school in Annapolis in 1918-19, 2-7; flu epidemic of 1918, 6-7; plebe indoctrination in 1918-19, 10-16, 25; midshipman uniforms, 16-17; dancing lessons for midshipmen, 17-18; plebes rated upper classmen's dance dates, 18-19; duty officers put midshipmen on report for various offenses in the early 1920s, 19, 37, 40; Naval Reserve officers were trained at the academy during World War I, 20; Army-Navy football game of 1919, 22-25; methods of instruction during the early 1920s, 27-31; instruction in engineering in the mid-1930s, 28; Rear Admiral Henry B. Wilson as superintendent in the early 1920s, 31-33; visit by Assistant Secretary of the Navy Franklin D. Roosevelt in 1919, 33-34; social life for midshipmen, 35-36; classmate associations in the class of 1923, 37-38, 69-70; summer training cruises on board battleships, 1920-22, 41-66; Edwards objects to large classes and women at the Naval Academy in the 1990s, 66-67; leadership positions for upper classmen in the early 1920s, 68; the class of 1923 did well in terms of flag selections, 69; graduation of the class of 1923, 69-70; Edwards was involved primarily with the class of 1935 while serving as an instructor in the mid-1930s, 181-183, 187-190; Midshipman Fred Borries, Jr., needed academic help in order to stay eligible for football in the

mid-1930s, 182-183; Borries was a non-reg midshipman but superb on the football field, 185-186; Midshipman Slade Cutter was another top-notch football player in the mid-1930s, 186-187; limited contacts between faculty and civilians in Annapolis in 1930s, 192-193; at the end of World War II a _Fletcher_-class engineering plant was sent to the Naval Academy for training purposes, 331-332

Naval Postgraduate School, Annapolis, Maryland
   Edwards studied mathematics and mechanics at the school in 1928-29, 148-151

Naval Proving Ground, Dahlgren, Virginia
   Visited by just-commissioned ensigns in 1923 as part of familiarization tour before reporting to their first ship, 77-78; tested 16-inch guns that were converted to Army coast artillery pieces because the battleships for which they were intended were not built, 78-79

Naval Reserve, U.S.
   Reserve officers were trained at the Naval Academy during World War I, 20; the _Granite State_, a former ship-of-the-line, served as a Naval Reserve training ship at New York City until the early 1920s, 25-26; regular and reserve officers got along splendidly in the battleship _North Carolina_ (BB-55) early in World War II, 65; the old battleship _Illinois_ (BB-7) was demilitarized at the New York Navy Yard in 1924 and converted to a Naval Reserve training ship, 87; Edwards was disappointed by receiving a commendation ribbon for his World War II service when reservists were receiving the more prestigious Legion of Merit, 331

Naval Torpedo Station, Newport Rhode, Island
   Visited by just-commissioned ensigns in 1923 as part of familiarization tour before reporting to their first ship, 74-75

Naval War College, Newport, Rhode Island
   Edwards lectured at the college as fleet staff officer in the late 1940s, 77

Navy Regulations
   Captain Claude Bloch demanded that visiting ensigns observe Navy Regulations concerning calls on seniors when touring the Naval Proving Ground in 1923, 77-78

Nevada, USS (BB-36)
   Involved in gunnery practices in 1924, 94, 101-103; operations in formation, 95; near-collision with the battleship _Pennsylvania_ at San Pedro in 1924, 95-96;

relationship among junior officers, 97-98; various officers smuggled liquor aboard in Cuba for transportation to California, 98-100; in 1924 the ship required Navy yard repairs because of a cracked gun slide, 106; Edwards trained a squad of <u>Nevada</u> enlisted men in machine gun drill, 106-107

<u>New Mexico</u>, USS (BB-40)
Was a happy ship in the late 1930s because of the quality of the people on board, 219, 231, 239; commanded by Frank Jack Fletcher and Walter Jacobs in the late 1930s, 220-222; the assistant engineer officer, Lieutenant Commander Hyman Rickover, so intimidated enlisted men in his department that he left a legacy of fear, 222-225; ; the engineering department installed new washroom facilities throughout the ship in the late 1930s, 225-226; the engineering plant got excellent results by using turbines and boilers installed when the ship was modernized in the early 1930s, 226-229; modernization required that she depend on aircraft for spotting fall of shot for the guns, 230; Commander J. J. Brown was sometimes petty while serving as executive officer in the late 1930s, 231-233; involved in fleet review for the President of Haiti in 1938, 233; dry-docking in Panama, 233-234; bottom cleaning in Hawaii, 235; landing force, 236; shore patrol, 236-237; use of pressure-reducing valves for auxiliaries, 239; junior officers, 240-242; black mess attendants and steward's mates, 242-243; Edwards made copies of the ship's plans for the <u>New Mexico</u> when he was stationed at the Puget Sound Navy Yard in 1939, 245

Newport, Rhode Island
Summer home of the wealthy people of New York, 75-76; home of many Navy people in the years before World War I, 112; problems resulting from blowing boiler tubes by the heavy cruiser <u>Augusta</u> (CA-31) in the early 1930s, 176-177; Admiral William Blandy entertained Mrs. Grace Vanderbilt at a cocktail party in Newport in the late 1940s, 350-351

<u>See also</u> Naval Torpedo Station, Naval War College

New York City
The Polo Grounds was the site of the 1919 Army-Navy football game, 22-23; the <u>Granite State</u>, a former ship-of-the-line, served as a Naval Reserve training ship at New York until the early 1920s, 25-26; crime plagued the area around the New York Navy Yard in the 1920s 91-92; Edwards sent his children to private schools in the early 1940s because he was not comfortable with the New York public schools, 270; New Yorkers were not particularly patriotic prior to the beginning of World War II, 271; Navy people went to popular Broadway shows during the late 1940s, 363

New York Navy Yard/Naval Shipyard
Retired Admiral Henry B. Wilson frequently had lunch at the shipyard officers club in the late 1940s, 32; installed fire control equipment in the battleship *West Virginia* (BB-48) in 1923-24, 81-82, 86, 94; demilitarized the battleship *Illinois* (BB-7) and scrapped incomplete battleships in 1924, 87; Rear Admiral Charles P. Plunkett was colorful commandant in the early 1920s, 90-91; crime plagued the area around the Navy yard in the 1920s 91-92; completion of construction and machinery testing of the battleship *North Carolina* (BB-55) in 1941, 264-270; the yard added a lot of new civilian employees after the attack on Pearl Harbor in 1941, 271-272; instituted modifications to the carrier *Oriskany* prior to her completion in 1950, 357, 362-363; supplied plans in the late 1940s for the engineering plant of the USS *Missouri* (BB-63), to be used in the construction of the liner *United States*, 358-359; the yard went out of Navy service in the 1960s, 361-362

News Media
Radio personality Walter Winchell and newspaperman Hanson Baldwin spent time on board the new battleship *North Carolina* (BB-55) in 1941, 278-279

Nichols, Commander William R., USN (USNA, 1918)
Served as design superintendent at the Puget Sound Navy Yard in the late 1930s, 245, 253-254

Norfolk Naval Base
The Atlantic Fleet staff moved into quarters ashore at Norfolk around 1947, 336

Norfolk Navy Yard
Site of fitting out and commissioning of the battleship *West Virginia* (BB-48) in 1923, 81-82, 88-89; scrapped the incomplete battleship *North Carolina* (BB-52) in 1923, 87-88

North Carolina, USS (BB-55)
Regular and reserve officers got along splendidly in the crew early in World War II, 65; completion of construction and machinery testing at the New York Navy Yard in 1941, 264-270; had difficulties with propeller vibration when she first operated in 1941, 272-274, 284-285; the ship was known as "The Showboat" when she was new, in part because show people visited, 275; commissioning ceremony in April 1941, 275-276; Captain Olaf Hustvedt was excellent as first commanding officer, 276-277; radio personality Walter Winchell and newspaperman Hanson Baldwin spent time on board the ship in 1941, 277-278; underway trials for the ship and her systems in 1941, 279-280; process by which the ship took on oil, 281-283; the ship was overmanned in 1941 to train

personnel for new-construction ships, 283-284; task force operations early in World War II, 288-290; engine room watch conditions in the ship early in World War II, 290; wardroom meals, 290-291; Commander Andrew Shepard as executive officer, 292; Captain Oscar C. Badger was overbearing, hypocritical, and demanding as commanding officer in 1941-42, 292-296; remained in the Atlantic in early 1942 as protection against the German Tirpitz, 297

O'Hare, Ensign Edward H., USN (USNA, 1937)
Future aviation ace was not impressive as a junior officer in the battleship New Mexico (BB-40) in the late 1930s, 240-242

Omaha, USS (CL-4)
The destroyer Mahan (DD-364) assisted in the refloating of this light cruiser after she went aground in the Bahamas in 1937, 217-218

Oriskany, USS (CV-34)
Completed by the New York Naval Shipyard in 1950 after alterations changed her considerably from her original design, 362-363

Panama
Edwards found bargains, including Panama hats, while shopping in the canal zone in the early 1920s, 57-58; the destroyer Henshaw (DD-278) once hit a submerged obstruction while going through Gatun Lake in the 1920s, 114; fresh-water washdowns in Gatun Lake, 115; women were readily available for sailors on liberty in the mid-1920s, 137-138; drunk sailors were rounded up by the shore patrol in Panama in the 1920s before being returned to their ships, 138-139; dry-docking of the battleship New Mexico (BB-40) in the late 1930s, 233-234

Pay and Allowances
Pay for junior officer in the 1920s, 136; the cut in Navy pay in the early 1930s was offset for Edwards by his promotion to lieutenant, 159; Edwards was sufficiently well off as a lieutenant commander in the late 1930s to be able to afford a live-in servant, 256

Pennsylvania, USS (BB-38)
Near-collision with the battleship Nevada (BB-36) at San Pedro, California, in 1924, 95-96

Plunkett, Rear Admiral Charles P., USN (USNA, 1884)
Colorful commandant of the New York Navy Yard in the early 1920s, 90-91

Point Honda
  Because of the grounding of the destroyer Young (DD-312) here in September 1923, the USS Henshaw (DD-278) was reactivated and restored to the fleet, 108-109

Polo Grounds
  New York ball park that was the site of the 1919 Army-Navy football game, 22-23

Postgraduate School
  See Naval Postgraduate School

Power, Lieutenant Commander Harry D., USN (USNA, 1920)
  As chief engineer of the battleship New Mexico (BB-40) in the late 1930s, was a fine officer who served as front man for the department, 219-220

Pratt, Rear Admiral William V., USN (USNA, 1889)
  As Commander Battleship Division Four, made a masterful speech at the funeral of men killed in a turret explosion on board the battleship Mississippi (BB-41) in June 1924, 104

Promotion of Officers
  Commodore Ralph Wentworth deserved to be an admiral, but he got stuck serving ashore in World War II, 113; the cut in Navy pay in the early 1930s was offset for Edwards by his promotion to lieutenant, 159; the Bureau of Engineering intervened in Edwards's case to get him selected for promotion shortly before World War II, even though he had nearly all engineering duty, 297-300; the Bureau of Personnel did block promotions of officers during World War II, 323-324; Hyman G. Rickover's selection for rear admiral in 1953 was politically directed by the Secretary of the Navy, 374-376; in the 1950s many officers received "tombstone" promotions upon retirement because they had received combat decorations, 376-377

Propulsion Plants
  See Engineering Plants

Prostitution
  Women were readily available for sailors on liberty in Panama in the mid-1920s, 137-138

Puerto Rico
  Edwards and his shipmates drank so much champagne on liberty in Ponce in 1931 that they had trouble functioning when they got back to their ship, the heavy cruiser Augusta (CA-31), 168-169

Puget Sound Navy Yard, Bremerton, Washington
Did periodic overhauls to the destroyer Henshaw (DD-278) in the mid-1920s, 128-129, 146-147; constructed the repair ship Medusa (AR-1) over a period of time in the 1920s to keep the work force occupied, 145-146; Edwards conferred with ships' officers about their desires when he was stationed at the yard in 1939-40, 147-148; capability around 1940 for reproducing large quantities of ships' plans, 245-247; the yard did design work on small seaplane tenders and yard tugboats in the late 1930s, 246-247, 249-252; accomplished alterations to destroyers in the late 1930s, 252, civilian employees at the yard as World War II approached, 253-254; the Pacific Northwest area was a pleasant one in which to live and work, 255-257; around 1940 people at the yard burned copies of superseded plans to avoid having them fall into the wrong hands, 258; shortly before World War II Edwards was involved in getting the goods on a group of potential saboteurs who had plans to damage hydro-electric facilities in the Pacific Northwest, 258-260

Radar
The existence of radar on board the new battleship North Carolina (BB-55) in 1941 was a well-kept secret until it was published in The New York Times, 268

Radio
Difficulty with short-range voice communications between battleships operating together in 1920, 53; Edwards provided training to the prospective radiomen of the USS West Virginia (BB-48) in 1923-24, 82-83; while in command of the Atlantic Fleet in 1913-14, Rear Admiral Charles Badger issued a facetious message prohibiting static in radio communications, 83-84

Railroads
Train travel from Annapolis to the 1919 Army-Navy football game in New York City, 24-25

Range Finders
Optical range finders were used for directing naval gunfire in the 1920s, 79-81, 101-102

Refueling
Dirty, laborious process of taking coal aboard the battleship Michigan (BB-27) in the summer of 1920, 43-46; the destroyer Henshaw (DD-278) took on oil in the 1920s, 125-128; at sea and in port for the destroyer Mahan (DD-364) in the mid-1930s, 210-211, 215-217; process by which the battleship North Carolina (BB-55) took on oil, 281-283

Retirement
In the 1950s many officers received "tombstone" promotions upon retirement because they had received combat decorations, 376-377; Edwards's post-retirement activities, 378-387

Richardson, Admiral James O., USN (USNA, 1902)
The crew of the heavy cruiser Augusta (CA-31) had a great deal of confidence in Richardson when he was serving as commanding officer in the early 1930s, 170-173

Rickover, Rear Admiral Hyman G., USN (USNA, 1922)
As assistant engineer officer in the battleship New Mexico (BB-40) in the mid-1930s so intimidated enlisted men in his department that he left a legacy of fear, 222-225; tried to go around Edwards in dealing with destroyer matters in BuShips during World War II, 317; difficult to deal with while serving in BuShips in the early 1950s, 368, 370-372; selection for rear admiral in 1953 was politically directed by the Secretary of the Navy, 374-376

Roosevelt, Franklin D.
As Assistant Secretary of the Navy, visited the Naval Academy in 1919 and spoke to the midshipmen, 33-34; description of the furnishings of his home in Hyde Park, New York, 34-35; the heavy cruiser Indianapolis (CA-35) carried President Roosevelt and his party on a cruise to the Caribbean and South America in late 1936, 207, 214; the destroyer Mahan (DD-364) was prepared to accommodate Roosevelt if necessary, 207-208

Root, Ralph
Very capable as senior mathematics instructor in the Postgraduate School at Annapolis in the late 1920s, 149

St. Kitts
Island in the West Indies that Edwards found disappointing for liberty in the early 1920s, 56

Salvage
The destroyer Mahan (DD-364) assisted in the refloating of the light cruiser Omaha (CL-4) after she went aground in the Bahamas in 1937, 217-218

San Francisco, California
Eye-opening sights of transvestites greeted shore patrol officers in the city in the late 1930s, 236-237

Saratoga, USS (CVA-60)
Aircraft carrier for which Edwards prepared an engineering manual in the late 1950s, 379

Scouting Force
  While serving as Commander Scouting Force in 1931, Vice Admiral A. L. Willard demanded the perquisites of rank on board his flagship, the heavy cruiser Augusta (CA-31), 174-175

Seaplane Tenders
  The Puget Sound Navy Yard did the design work for the AVP-type tenders in the late 1930s, 246-247, 249-252; the Lake Washington Shipyard took some of the Navy yard's employees to use their expertise in building the AVPs, 248

Seasickness
  Riding characteristics of the destroyer Henshaw (DD-278) in rough weather in the 1920s, 119-121

Security
  Around 1940 people at the Puget Sound Navy Yard burned copies of superseded plans to avoid having them fall into the wrong hands, 258; shortly before World War II Edwards was involved in getting the goods on a group of potential saboteurs who had plans to damage hydro-electric facilities in the Pacific Northwest, 258-260; the existence of radar on board the new battleship North Carolina (BB-55) in 1941 was a well-kept secret until it was published in The New York Times, 268

Senn, Captain Thomas J., USN (USNA, 1891)
  Served as first commanding officer of the battleship West Virginia (BB-48) when she was commissioned in 1923, 89-90

Shepard, Commander Andrew G., USN (USNA, 1917)
  Helped line up USO shows for the new battleship North Carolina (BB-55) in 1941, 275; displayed sense of humor as executive officer of the North Carolina, 292; involved with 20-millimeter and 40-millimeter guns while in Bureau of Ordnance before World War II, 296-297

Shipbuilding
  The Bethlehem Ship Building Company, Squantum, Massachusetts, did a poor job of constructing destroyers during World War I, 145; the Puget Sound Navy Yard constructed the repair ship Medusa (AR-1) over a period of time in the 1920s to keep the work force occupied, 145-146; the destroyers Cassin (DD-372) and Downes (DD-372) were rebuilt after being badly damaged at Pearl Harbor in 1941, 303-305; Bath Iron Works was the top destroyer-building yard in the nation in World War II, 310-311; use of welding and riveting in World War II, 312-313; at the end of World War II, BuShips opted to preserve a number of diesel engines

that later proved useful for new construction, 332-333; the carrier <u>Oriskany</u> (CV-34) was completed by the New York Naval Shipyard in 1950 after alterations changed her considerably from her original design, 362-363

Ship Design
Design of the heavy cruiser <u>Augusta</u> (CA-31) and others of her lightly armored type that went into service around 1930, 164-165; the destroyer <u>Mahan</u> (DD-364), commissioned in 1936, had a number of engineering advances but a number of drawbacks as well, 195-201; the <u>Mahan</u> did not have fore-and-aft access inside the ship, 201-202; new staterooms designed in the Bureau of C&R for the battleship <u>New Mexico</u> (BB-40) in the late 1930s were most uncomfortable, 244; the Puget Sound Navy Yard did design work on small seaplane tenders and yard tugboats in the late 1930s, 246-247, 249-252; the sinking of the destroyer <u>Reuben James</u> (DD-245) in 1941 provided lessons for officer distribution in subsequent classes 314-315; Edwards objected to a design formulated by BuShips in the late 1940s for an enlarged destroyer, 355; the New York Naval Shipyard supplied plans in the late 1940s for the engineering plant of the USS <u>Missouri</u> (BB-63), to be used in the construction of the liner <u>United States</u>, 358-359

Shore Patrol
Patrols were needed in the area around the New York Navy Yard in the 1920s because of the amount of crime, 91-92; role in Panama in the 1920s included rounding up drunken sailors but not interfering with prostitution, 138-139; while serving on shore patrol in Charleston in the early 1930s, Edwards found one of his sailors coming out of a house of prostitution, 169; eye-opening sights of San Francisco greeted shore patrol officers in the late 1930s, 236-237

<u>Sinclair</u>, USS (DD-275)
Got a good score by using dubious practices during a gunnery exercise in the 1920s, 118

Sixth Fleet, U.S.
When captains and admirals returned to the East Coast from Sixth Fleet duty in the late 1940s, Admiral Blandy, CinCLantFlt, pumped them for information, 346-347

Skinner Ensign Charles R., USN (USNA, 1920)
Track man who led Naval Academy plebes in the mile run in the summer of 1919, 11

Smuggling
Various officers smuggled liquor aboard the battleship <u>Nevada</u> (BB-36) in Guantanamo Bay in 1924 so they could transport it to California, 98-100

South Carolina, USS (BB-26)
Itinerary for Naval Academy training cruise in the summer of 1921, 41-42

Stark, Admiral Harold R., USN (USNA, 1903)
Served as first executive officer of the battleship West Virginia (BB-48) when she was commissioned in 1923, 89, 288

Strite, Lieutenant Robert, USNR (USNA, 1921)
One of the few men who were in the commissioning crews of both the USS West Virginia (BB-48) in 1923 and the North Carolina (BB-55) in 1941, 287-288

Sullivan, Lieutenant Commander John R., USN (USNA, 1918)
As first lieutenant of the battleship New Mexico (BB-40) in the mid-1930s, squabbled with the ship's assistant engineer, Lieutenant Commander Hyman Rickover, 223

Suzano, Lieutenant Commander Pedro, Brazilian Navy
Brazilian naval officer who was a cooperative host to crew members from the destroyer Mahan (DD-364) visiting Brazil in 1936, later his country's minister of marine in the 1960s, 214-215

Sylvester, Rear Admiral Evander Wallace, USN (USNA, 1920)
Capable officer who ran the ships divisions of the Bureau of Ships in the early 1950s, 365, 367

Thirteenth Naval District
Shortly before World War II, Lieutenant Daniel Frost of the district office was involved in getting the goods on a group of potential saboteurs who had plans to damage hydroelectric facilities in the Pacific Northwest, 258-260

Thomson, Earl W.
Professor known as "Slipstick Willie" taught at the Naval Academy for many years, 29-30

Torpedoes
Recently commissioned ensigns had a familiarization tour at the Naval Torpedo Station in Newport in 1923 because battleships still carried torpedoes then, 75; description of the torpedo room in the new battleship West Virginia (BB-48) in 1923, 84-86

Training
Naval Reserve officers were trained at the Naval Academy during World War I, 20; Naval Academy midshipman summer training cruises on board battleships, 1920-22, 41-66; ensigns from the Naval Academy class of 1923 went on a

training tour of various naval facilities before reporting for duty to the battleship West Virginia (BB-48); Edwards provided training to the West Virginia's prospective radiomen in 1923-24, 82-83; in 1924 Edwards trained a squad of Nevada enlisted men in machine gun drill, 106-107; after completing postgraduate school in 1930, Edwards had a three-month course visiting various engineering facilities, 155-156; various equipment manufacturers trained prospective crew members of the battleship North Carolina (BB-55) in 1941, 269; the North Carolina was overmanned in 1941 to train personnel for new-construction ships, 283-284; at the end of World War II a Fletcher-class engineering plant was sent to the Naval Academy for training purposes, 331-332

Trinidad
Island that served as one of the stops on the shakedown cruise of the destroyer Mahan (DD-364) in 1936, 207

Truman, President Harry S
Passed over Admiral William Blandy when he chose Admiral Louis Denfeld to be CNO in 1947, 348-349

Turrets
Operation of on board the battleship Michigan (BB-27) in the summer of 1920, 52-53; the battleship Mississippi (BB-41) suffered a turret explosion during gunnery practice in June 1924, 103-105; in 1924 the battleship Nevada (BB-36) required Navy yard repairs because of a cracked gun slide, 106

USO
See United Service Organization

Uniforms--Naval
Types worn by Naval Academy midshipmen in the early 1920s, 16-17, 22-23; cleaning and marking of on midshipman training cruises in the 1920s, 46; members of the Naval Academy class of 1923 purchased full sets of uniforms, including old-fashioned formal outfits, upon graduation, 71-72; when Edwards got his master's degree from Columbia University in 1930, some naval officers had gotten too big for their uniforms, 154-155; laundering of on board the heavy cruiser Augusta (CA-31) in the early 1930s, 176; Admiral Ernest J. King ordered unpopular gray uniforms for officers in World War II, 330

United Service Organization
Provided entertainment for the new battleship North Carolina in 1941, 275

United States, SS (Passenger Liner)
In the late 1940s, the New York Naval Shipyard supplied Gibbs & Cox with the plans for the engineering plant of the battleship Missouri (BB-63), to be used in the design of the United States, 358-359; Edwards went on the liner's first sea trial in 1952, 359-360

Vanderbilt, Grace
Widow of Cornelius Vanderbilt III, she was entertained by Admiral William Blandy at a cocktail party in Newport in the late 1940s, 350-351

Venereal Disease
Fleet sailors were given lectures and prophylactic treatments in the late 1930s, 237

Vincent, Stenio
President of Haiti who reviewed U.S. Navy ships in 1938, 233

Waller, Commander John B. W., USN (USNA, 1914)
As first commanding officer of the destroyer Mahan (DD-364) in 1936, he was often very difficult for his subordinate officers to live with, 202-205, 215-216

Wallin, Rear Admiral Homer N., USN (USNA, 1917)
Low-key officer who served as Chief of the Bureau of Ships in the early 1950s, 368-371

Washington, D.C.
Different sites that served as headquarters for the Bureau of Ships in World War II, 307-308

Washington (D.C.) Navy Yard
Site of the Navy Optical School visiting by junior officers for indoctrination in the early 1920s, 79-81

Washington, USS (BB-56)
Had difficulties with propeller vibration when she first went into commission in 1941, 273; task force operations early in World War II, 288-290

Weather
The 1919 Army-Navy football game at the Polo Grounds in New York was played in a steady rain 22-23; rain was a problem for people sleeping topside in the USS Michigan in 1920, 55; riding characteristics of the destroyer Henshaw (DD-278) in heavy seas in the 1920s, 119-121, 140-141

Wentworth, Commodore Ralph S., USN (USNA, 1912)
Officer and gentleman who commanded the destroyer Henshaw (DD-278) in the mid-1920s, 111; asked Edwards to be his exec

when he took command of the destroyer Hull (DD-350) in 1935, 112-113; deserved to be an admiral but served ashore during World War II, 113; mistakenly thought his career was ended when he hit an underwater obstruction in the Panama Canal while commanding the Henshaw, 115

Werntz, Robert L. (USNA, 1884)
Operated a Naval Academy preparatory school in Annapolis that Edwards attended in 1918-19, 3-7

West Virginia, USS (BB-48)
After graduation from the Naval Academy in 1923, some 15-20 ensigns destined for the ship went on a familiarization tour of ordnance facilities for several months, 74-75; West Virginia was the last U.S. battleship to be built with torpedo tubes, 75; commissioned and fitted out at the Norfolk Navy Yard in 1923, 81-82, 88-89; the New York Navy Yard installed fire control equipment in the ship in 1923-24, 81-82, 86, 94; nearly collided with a tugboat and barge off New York City in December 1923, 82; description of the ship's torpedo room, 84-86; Captain Thomas J. Senn was the first commanding officer, 89-90; electric-drive engineering plant, 93; a few men were in the commissioning crews of both the West Virginia in 1923 and the North Carolina (BB-55) in 1941, 287-288

Whitgrove, Captain Leland D., USN (USNA, 1922)
Served as production officer at the New York Naval Shipyard in the late 1940s, 356; served with Edwards in BuShips in the early 1950s, 374; his widow married Edwards in 1976, 384

Willard, Vice Admiral Arthur L., USN (USNA, 1891)
While serving as Commander Scouting Force in 1931, demanded the perquisites of rank on board his flagship, the heavy cruiser Augusta (CA-31), 174-175

Wilson, Admiral Henry B., USN (Ret.) (USNA, 1881)
Officer who was popular as superintendent of the Naval Academy in the early 1920s, 31-33; as a retired officer in the late 1940s frequently had lunch at the New York Naval Shipyard, 32

Winchell, Walter
Popular radio commentator who spent time on board the new battleship North Carolina (BB-55) in 1941, 278-279

Women
Edwards objects to the presence of women at the Naval Academy in the 1990s, 67; women performed well while working for Edwards during World War II, 67-68; WAVES did a creditable job in a clerical role in the Bureau of Ships during World War II, 326

World War I
   Naval Reserve officers were trained at the Naval Academy during the war, 20

Young, USS (DD-312)
   Because of the grounding of the Young at Point Honda in September 1923, the USS Henshaw (DD-278) was reactivated and restored to the fleet, 108-109

www.ingramcontent.com/pod-product-compliance
Lightning Source LLC
Chambersburg PA
CBHW082148070526
44585CB00020B/2137